English, Later British, Line

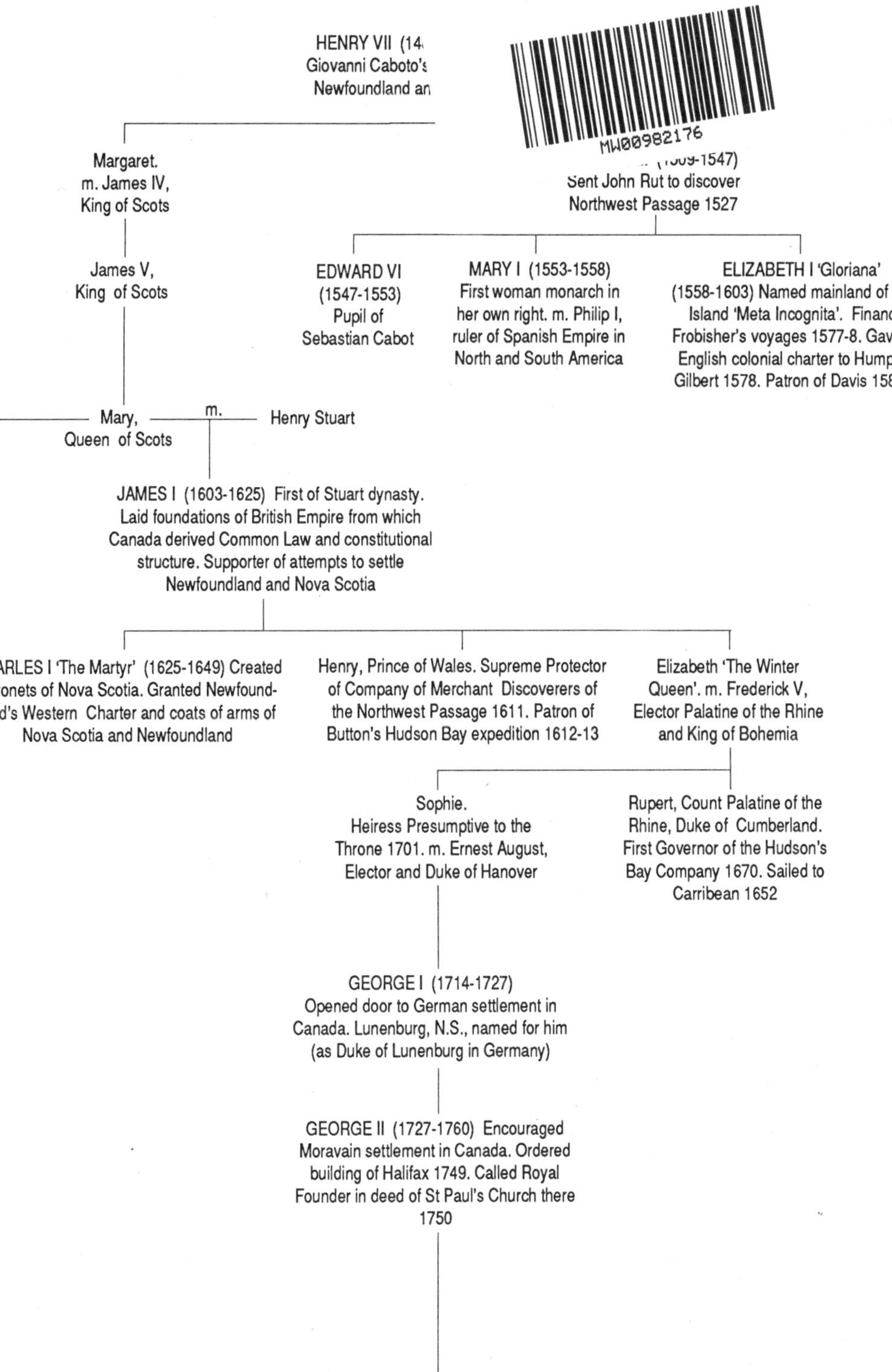

HENRY VII (14
Giovanni Caboto's
Newfoundland an
MW00982176
(1509-1547)
Sent John Rut to discover
Northwest Passage 1527
Margaret.
m. James IV,
King of Scots
James V,
King of Scots
EDWARD VI
(1547-1553)
Pupil of
Sebastian Cabot
MARY I (1553-1558)
First woman monarch in
her own right. m. Philip I,
ruler of Spanish Empire in
North and South America
ELIZABETH I 'Gloriana'
(1558-1603) Named mainland of Baffin
Island 'Meta Incognita'. Financed
Frobisher's voyages 1577-8. Gave first
English colonial charter to Humphrey
Gilbert 1578. Patron of Davis 1585-87
Mary,
Queen of Scots
m.
Henry Stuart
JAMES I (1603-1625) First of Stuart dynasty.
Laid foundations of British Empire from which
Canada derived Common Law and constitutional
structure. Supporter of attempts to settle
Newfoundland and Nova Scotia
HARLES I 'The Martyr' (1625-1649) Created
Baronets of Nova Scotia. Granted Newfound-
and's Western Charter and coats of arms of
Nova Scotia and Newfoundland
Henry, Prince of Wales. Supreme Protector
of Company of Merchant Discoverers of
the Northwest Passage 1611. Patron of
Button's Hudson Bay expedition 1612-13
Elizabeth 'The Winter
Queen'. m. Frederick V,
Elector Palatine of the Rhine
and King of Bohemia
Sophie.
Heiress Presumptive to the
Throne 1701. m. Ernest August,
Elector and Duke of Hanover
Rupert, Count Palatine of the
Rhine, Duke of Cumberland.
First Governor of the Hudson's
Bay Company 1670. Sailed to
Carribean 1652
GEORGE I (1714-1727)
Opened door to German settlement in
Canada. Lunenburg, N.S., named for him
(as Duke of Lunenburg in Germany)
GEORGE II (1727-1760) Encouraged
Moravain settlement in Canada. Ordered
building of Halifax 1749. Called Royal
Founder in deed of St Paul's Church there
1750

continued on back cover

ROYAL OBSERVATIONS

Canadians & Royalty

by

Arthur Bousfield and Garry Toffoli

Cartoons by Vince Wicks

Dedicated to

Hereward Senior
Professor of History
McGill University

His knowledge and love of monarchy
and Canada's British and French heritage
have inspired the authors
and many other Canadian monarchists.

ROYAL OBSERVATIONS

Canadians & Royalty

by

Arthur Bousfield and Garry Toffoli

Cartoons by Vince Wicks

Toronto and Oxford

Dundurn Press

1991

Selection and introduction, copyright © Arthur Bousfield and Garry Toffoli, 1991.
Cartoons on cover and in text, copyright © Vince Wicks, 1990.

All rights reserved. No part of this publication may be reproduced, stored in a retrieval system, or transmitted in any form or by any means, electronic, mechanical, photocopying, recording, or otherwise (except brief passages for purposes of review) without the prior permission of Dundurn Press Limited.

Cover Design: Karen Dahlstrom

Text Design and Production: Green Graphics

Printing and Binding: Gagné Printing Ltd., Louiseville, Quebec, Canada

The writing of this manuscript and the publication of this book were made possible by support from several sources. The publisher wishes to acknowledge the generous assistance and ongoing support of **The Canada Council**, **The Book Publishing Industry Development Programme** of the **Department of Communications**, and **The Ontario Arts Council**.

Care has been taken to trace the ownership of copyright material used in the text. The author and publisher welcome any information enabling them to rectify any reference or credit in subsequent editions.

J. Kirk Howard, Publisher

Canadian Cataloguing in Publication Data

Bousfield, Arthur 1943-
Royal Observations
Includes index
ISBN 1-55002-076-5

1. Royal visitors - Canada - Anecdotes. 2. Visits of state - Canada - Anecdotes.
I. Toffoli, Garry, 1953- . II. Title

FC223. R6B6 1991 971 C90-095726-3
F1029.9.B6 1991

Dundurn Press Limited
2181 Queen Street East, Suite 301
Toronto, Canada
M4E 1E5

Dundurn Distribution Limited
73 Lime Walk
Headington, Oxford
England
OX3 7AD

ROYAL OBSERVATIONS

Canadians & Royalty

INTRODUCTION

Royal Observations is a book of stories, quotations and incidents. It does not aspire to be a comprehensive history of Canada or of the Monarchy of Canada. That is still to be written. It is rather a collection of snapshots of Canadian history, but the authors hope no less useful or interesting because of it. Two patterns emerge in the book. First is that members of the Royal Family were present or involved in virtually all the major events that have shaped Canada. Secondly Canadians have much more in common, regardless of their language, ethnicity or residence, than they perhaps acknowledge today. Much, if not most, of that common experience revolves around the Monarchy, which is the most important shared institution within Canada.

It will be noticed too that these quotations and anecdotes include many of our lighter moments. Though Canadians possess a living tradition of humorous writing from Leacock to Harron, Canadians as a whole are not thought of in the world as a people with an ability to laugh at themselves or with a well developed sense of humour. The emphasis Monarchy places on individuals and family with their natural eccentricities and foibles has created a store of royal folk humour and in that way the Crown has done Canadians a favour by making life less sombre. The serious, the poignant and the formal have not been neglected however for such emotions are also part of Canada's story.

But why publish another book of anecdotes on the Monarchy after the appearance of Lady Longford's definitive *Oxford Book of Royal Anecdotes*? The question may be a natural one for readers but is easily answered. Like many books written on the shared Monarchy of the Commonwealth, Lady Longford's acclaimed work focuses on the United Kingdom, drawing on the rich drama, poetry and history of the Crown almost exclusively in that important context. By now however it is evident that each Commonwealth Monarchy has its own history. This is an authentic development and not one necessarily hostile to or exclusive of the shared experience. But just as a separate biography can be written of Elizabeth II as Queen of Canada, Queen of Jamaica, Queen of New Zealand, Queen of Australia, Queen of The Bahamas, and so forth, so each realm of the Queen has its own accumulation of incident and popular tradition surrounding the Monarchy.

With the United Kingdom experience to draw on, Lady Longford neither needed nor chose to draw extensively on Commonwealth history. Nevertheless the Commonwealth experience is barely less rich than the United Kingdom one, and this is especially so in the case of Canada which has a longer history than some of the other realms and one that was royal from the beginning in both French and British communities. It is a glimpse of the Canadian heritage of the Crown that *Royal Observations* attempts to present.

Except where they appear in an appendix to books such as W.L. Morton's *The Kingdom of Canada* or Jacques Monet's *The Canadian Crown*, Canada's Kings and Queens have been unfairly neglected in recent histories. This neglect is unfair because not only did those royal figures initiate, pay for and promote much of the discovery and European settlement of Canada, but after 1786 they or members of their families were often personally present and involved in its affairs. They made an important contribution to stimulating the development of a sense of Canadianism. They also provided the focus and framework that allowed Canadian society to regard itself as a family rather that a corporation of individual shareholders on the republican model. An important characteristic of a family is the memory its members have of individuals through stories and anecdotes. In *Royal Observations* the attempt has been made to offer a few such recorded sayings — official and unofficial — and anecdotes that show the country's Kings and Queens in their role as the Canadian Royal Family.

The book is divided by thematic chapters for the sake of simplicity but the chapters are not mutually exclusive. Many stories could easily fit into more than one chapter and the editors have allocated the stories to the most relevant chapters. The genealogical charts on the front and back inside covers may help readers in placing many of the persons referred to in the text.

The material in *Royal Observations* includes not only observations by the Royal Family and their official representatives about Canada and Canadians but observations about them by their fellow countrymen. Observing is a two-way activity. While not able to cover every event or community in Canada, if *Royal Observations* leaves readers with a better understanding of their country it will have achieved its aim.

1

"CAN YOU COME BACK IN ABOUT TEN MINUTES?"

MOTHER OF CONFEDERATION

Queen Victoria is undoubtedly a prominent figure in Canadian folklore. Cities, such as Victoria and Regina, innumerable Queen's and Victoria counties and similarly named streets, parks, neighbourhoods, hotels and buildings all owe their names to her. No self-respecting community failed to erect a statue of the great monarch, at various stages of her life. Partially this was because Victoria was the Sovereign for much of Canada's formative years and also because, despite many changes, Canada remains a Victorian country because of its historical birth, much as the United States remains an eighteenth century country in its outlook.

But Victoria's association with Canada was far from merely symbolic. Her father Prince Edward, Duke of Kent was the most Canadian member of the Royal Family in his day, having lived in British North America almost continuously from 1791 to 1800 (a third of his life to that point) as a young man. Although her father died while she was still a small child, Princess Victoria was visited regularly by her father's friends from Canada and kept relatively well informed of Canadian affairs.

As Queen, Victoria paid even closer attention to her North American domain with understanding references in her diary to events such as the 1837 Rebellion (she insisted that while legitimate punishment be meted out there was to be no vengeance against rebels, one of whom, George Etienne Cartier, she, in later years, made a baronet). Although she never came to Canada she arranged for most of her children to come, and encouraged such developments as Confederation. And of course she chose the capital city – Ottawa.

The Queen's role in promoting Canadian unity truly made her the "Mother of Confederation" and at her death Victoria Day, that uniquely Canadian holiday, was created as a memorial day to perpetuate the celebration of her birthday. It is now also the official birthday of her successor Queen Elizabeth II.

When Queen Victoria died the *Mail and Empire* noted that the private mourning of people expressed "How near the Queen was to the hearts of her people, and how the thought of her had become part of the routine of life". Although Canada never saw its Sovereign in person Canadians felt a personal bond to her that has left us a legacy of incident and story, real and apocryphal, reverent and irreverent, of the kind that can only flow from deep, intimate bonds.

Two Canadian authors are received by young Princess Victoria

Un recueil des gravures de scènes canadiennes, [des *British Dominions in North America* et du *Topographical Dictionary of Lower Canada*] dans une reliure élégante, velours et or, fut présenté à la duchesse de Kent. Mon père eût l'honneur de lui présenter les gravures en personne, au palais de Kensington. En cette occasion j'accompagnai mon père. On nous reçut avec beaucoup de grâce et de bienveillance. Après une conversation prolongée, au cours de laquelle mon père parla des nombreuses faveurs et de la protection dont il était redevable à feu le duc de Kent, Son Altesse Royale nous demande si nous n'avions été présentés à la princesse Victoria. Mon père ayant répondu que nous n'avions pas encore eu cet honneur, Son Altesse se leva du sofa où elle était assise, sonna la dame de service et lui demanda de prier la princesse de venir.

La future reine d'Angleterre entra quelques instants plus tard. Nous vîmes une belle jeune fille de quatorze ans dont le maintien indiquait une heureuse combinaison de dignité, de candeur et de grâce. Et c'est ainsi que nous eûmes, par la faveur spéciale de son auguste mère, le remarquable honneur d'une audience particulière de celle qui devait être une des plus grandes souveraines du monde.

Je n'oublierai jamais la bonté et la condescendance que la duchesse de Kent témoigna à mon père, et à moi-même incidemment, pendant cette audience que Son Altesse daigna prolonger pendant près d'une demi-heure.

Ecrivant aujourd'hui dans la trente-cinquième année du règne glorieux et prospère de la reine Victoria, une reine qui vit dans le coeur de ses sujets et qui commande l'admiration de toutes les Cours étrangères, c'est avec un sentiment de satisfaction et de sincère loyauté que je me rappelle cette audience à Kensington Palace en l'année 1832.

> *"Robert Bouchette ardent Patriote et fervent Royaliste", extracts from the Mémoires of Robert Shore Milnes Bouchette, edited by Elinor Senior, Monarchy Canada.*

♛ ♛ ♛

On the Rebellions of 1837. A despatch to the Lieutenant-governor of Upper Canada expressed

the Queen's confidence that, on the part of her loyal and faithful subjects in the Province, no vindictive feeling will mingle with their zealous and strenuous endeavours to put down insurrection and revolt.

♛ ♛ ♛

Queen Victoria's amnesty to the rebels of 1837 in Upper Canada.

VICTORIA, by the Grace of God, of the United Kingdom of Great Britain and Ireland, Queen, Defender of the Faith, &c. &c. &c.

To all to whom these Presents shall come -

GREETING:

Whereas in cases arising out of the late unhappy revolt, and in the course of the administration of justice against persons implicated therein, it has been our anxious desire to extend our Royal mercy and forgiveness to our deluded and misguided Subjects, to the utmost limits compatible with the public peace, and the security of our loyal and faithful people: And whereas, in furtherance of our desire to extend our Royal clemency as above declared, we have heretofore granted our pardon to numerous offenders who have been convicted, and have also forborne to prosecute others who had rendered themselves, by their misconduct, liable to punishment; and we being resolved still further to extend our Royal clemency, and to make a final declaration of our will and pleasure with respect to all such of our Subjects as are, or have been in any way implicated in the said revolt, we have this day issued our several Royal Proclamations, in pursuance of an Act of our Provincial Parliament of our said Province of Upper Canada, passed in the first year of our reign, entitled, "An Act for the more speedy attainder of persons indicted for High Treason, who have fled from this Province, or who remain concealed therein to escape from justice" - calling upon and requiring such of our Subjects as have been indicted for the crime of High Treason, and who have withdrawn themselves from the Province, for the causes in the said Act mentioned, to surrender themselves to justice, that their several cases may undergo legal investigation and final adjudication.

And we do now make known and declare to all our Subjects who have not been indicted for any Treason, Misprision of Treason, or Treasonable offence, or who are not now in custody, charged, or liable to be charged with Treason, invasion, or hostile incursion into this Province, or who being charged with either of the said offences, have made their escape from any of our Gaols, or other place of confinement, that they may return to their homes, and that no prosecution for or on account of any offence by them done or committed, and in any way relating to, or connected with the said revolt, shall be instituted or continued, but that all such prosecutions shall terminate and be for ever void, hereby freely offering to all those our Subjects who may have been implicated in the said revolt, (excepting as aforesaid) our gracious amnesty, pardon and forbearance, for and on account of such offences, (excepting as aforesaid) and our Royal assurance, that, relying on their future loyalty and good conduct, they shall be received under our protection, absolved and released from all punishment or prosecution, as hereinbefore declared.

IN TESTIMONY WHEREOF, we have caused these our Letters to be made Patent, and the Great Seal of our said Province to be hereunto affixed. - Witness our trusty and well-beloved SIR GEORGE ARTHUR, K.C.H., Lieutenant-General of our said Province, and Major-General Commanding our Forces therein, at Toronto, this twenty-second day of October, in the year of our Lord one thousand eight hundred and thirty-eight, and in the second year of our Reign.

Upper Canada Gazette, 25 October 1838.

There is also a legend of the Queen's involvement in the project [of building a Roman Catholic Cathedral in St John's]. The story is so elaborate that it almost has the ring of truth. On the whole, the tale would appear to be a myth, but it cannot be completely dismissed. The Queen Victoria legend is based on a unconfirmed story handed down by the Dempsey family of St John's, who were close friends of Bishop Fleming. This family has it as a tradition that it was their personal financial assistance that enabled the Bishop to go to England. Mrs Dempsey is supposed to have suggested that Dr Fleming approach Queen Victoria directly. She had information that the eighteen-year-old

Queen rode her carriage through Rotten Row, in Hyde Park, each morning. If he were to stand there in clerical purple and offer her a salutation, she would likely stop.

According to the story this is just what he did. Her Majesty called for the carriage to stop and asked the identity of the reverend gentleman. When advised he was the Roman Catholic Bishop of her Colony of Newfoundland she invited him into her carriage. In the course of an interview at Buckingham Palace, Dr Fleming acquainted the Queen with the numerous problems he faced in acquiring land for his cathedral. The young Victoria promised to take measures to overcome the difficulties. Shortly after this interview, the Bishop is supposed to have received word that the grant of land had finally been made. Though it is not mentioned in the Prelate's very incomplete papers, there seems to be some far-fetched corroboration for the story in his statement that the new cathedral would be a lasting memorial to the benevolence of Queen Victoria. In a sermon preached by Bishop Howley, on her death in 1901, he spoke of the procuring of the land as "due to the gracious gift of Queen Victoria", and stated that the signing of the deed of grant was one of the first acts of the young Queen, who had only come to the throne the previous year.

This peculiar story does not end there. Her Majesty is supposed to have opened a coffer containing gold and offered some to Dr Fleming who, somewhat embarrassed, took but a few sovereigns. More were pressed upon him. As he was about to depart, Victoria is said to have requested a return favour from the Bishop. She asked that the new cathedral in St John's be named for St John the Baptist. The Bishop willingly agreed and, as he was leaving the palace, the Queen, seeing the day was damp and cold, took off her stole, folded it lengthwise and wrapped it around the neck of the inadequately protected clergyman. This supposed shawl of the Queen is still in the possession of descendants of the Dempsey family in St John's. It is purple, with an elaborate ornamental silk design of the Thistle, Rose, and Shamrock.

Paul O'Neill, A Seaport Legacy - The Story of St John's, Newfoundland.

♛ ♛ ♛

News of the Royal Family often took a long time to reach Canadians in the days when navigation provided the only means of communication. Thus Toronto celebrated Queen Victoria's wedding in April, 1840, although it actually took place on 10 February that year.

Thursday 2nd April — weather very fine indeed. Great Ball at Government House last night in honour of the Queen's marriage. General holiday by Proclamation. An ox was roasted whole and people sat down to dinner in the market place with the 32nd & 93rd Regiment bands playing all the time. In the evening there was a general illumination. Mary and I walked about the town until 11 o'clock.

Mary Larratt Smith, Young Mr Smith in Upper Canada.

♛ ♛ ♛

[The Pitcher Plant] the provincial flower of Newfoundland is found in bogs and marshes, blooming in May and June. The flower derives its popular name from its tubular leaves which fold lengthwise to form a deep vase at their base where pools of rain-water collect. More than 100 years ago, Queen Victoria chose the Pitcher Plant to be engraved on the newly minted Newfoundland penny. On 22 June 1954, the Newfoundland Cabinet designated the unusual plant as the official flower of the province.

The Arms, Flags and Emblems of Canada.

♛ ♛ ♛

While on this subject [Yankee braggadocio and impudence] I may as well relate a laughable circumstance which took place in the public stage-coach. Mr H.I. V - , a rising lawyer in the county of Peterborough, was travelling between Cobourg and Toronto, having for one of his companions a thin, sallow-looking importation from the United States. Among other topics the conversation turned upon the marriage of our young Queen, when the names of several royal and noble personages were mentioned by the different passengers. The Yankee listened with great attention to the various opinions expressed, when, addressing himself to the lawyer, he said -

"I guess now, Mister, you all make a mighty fuss about that Miss Kent, why our Mat's [Matthew Van Buren, President of the United States] son John went over the herring-pond the hul way to see her; but I guess he din't like her well enough to take her."

"Why, you impudent scoundrel, is that the way you speak of our lovely young queen! I will teach you to use more becoming language toward the Sovereign Lady of the realms."

So saying the loyal young lawyer seized the fool by the collar, and ejected him from the coach in the most summary manner possible, and at the greatest risk of breaking the long neck of the ill-behaved Yankee, who would scarcely venture to lampoon Her Majesty in the presence of English gentlemen again. I guess he had had enough of it.

Samuel Strickland, Twenty-Seven Years In Canada West Or The Experience Of An Early Settler.

♛ ♛ ♛

On 25 April 1849 a Montreal mob burned the Parliament Buildings of the Province of Canada.

The members hurried out by a back way, unnecessarily fearful of their safety from the crowd, while [Sir Allan] MacNab, always a bibliophile, got up a cry to save the legislature's magnificent library. William Badgley joined him in this desperate task. If contemporary reports are to be believed, it must have been now that MacNab and some other members passed the portrait of Queen Victoria through a window to safe hands outside.

Donald R. Beer, Sir Allan Napier MacNab.

♛ ♛ ♛

Queen Victoria was a beacon of liberty to those beyond Canada's borders, as these two verses from the song "Away to Canada" sung to the tune of "O Susanna," indicate.

I'm on my way to Canada, that cold and dreary land,
The dire effects of slavery I can no longer stand.
My soul is mixed within me so, to think that I'm a slave,
I'm now resolved to strike the blow for freedom or the grave.
O Righteous Father, wilt Thou not pity me,
And aid me on to Canada, where coloured men are free?

I heard old Queen Victoria say if we would all forsake
Our native land of slavery and come across the lake,
That she was standing on the shore with arms extended wide
To give us all a peaceful home beyond the rolling tide.
Farewell, old master, this is enough for me.
I'm going straight to Canada, where coloured men are free.

From a Negro paper called The Voice of the Fugitive published in Sandwich [now Windsor], 1 January 1851.

♛ ♛ ♛

Queen Victoria took a personal interest in choosing the new capital city and in naming new towns. In 1857 she chose the capital of the Province of Canada [Ontario and Quebec],

In the judgement of Her Majesty the City of Ottawa combines more advantages than any other place in Canada for the permanent seat of the future Government of the Province, and is selected by Her Majesty accordingly .

Queen Victoria to the Colonial Secretary.

♛ ♛ ♛

The Queen also selected another well-known Canadian name.

The Queen has received Sir Edward Bulwer Lytton's letter. If the name of New Caledonia is objected to as being already borne . . . it may be better to give the colony west of the Rocky Mountains another name. New Vancouver, New Columbia and New Georgia . . . do not appear on all maps. The only name which is given the whole territory in every map the Queen has consulted is "Columbia", but as there exists a Columbia in South America and the citizens of the United States called their country also Columbia, at least in poetry, "British Columbia" might be, in the Queen's opinion, the best name.

Queen Victoria to the Colonial Secretary,
24 July 1858.

♛ ♛ ♛

On Confederation. A remark by the Queen when receiving a Nova Scotian delegation in London.

I take the deepest interest in it [the movement towards Confederation], for I believe it will make them [the provinces of British North America] great and prosperous.

W.A. Harkin, Political Reminiscences of
The Right Honourable Sir Charles Tupper.

♛ ♛ ♛

An exchange with Sir John A. Macdonald. On 27 February 1867, the eve of Confederation, Queen Victoria received some of the Fathers of Confederation in separate private audiences. She also held courts for their wives and daughters. At the audience for Macdonald, for which Princess Louise, soon herself to live in Canada, was present, the following exchange occurred.

Queen Victoria: I am very glad to see you on this mission. I hope all things are going well with you.
Macdonald: I am happy to inform Your Majesty that all things have been prosperous with us, and by the aid of Lord Carnarvon, our measure has made great progress and there have been no delays.
Queen Victoria: It is a very important measure and you have all exhibited so much loyalty.
Macdonald: We have desired in this measure [Canadian Confederation] to declare in the most solemn and emphatic manner our resolve to be under the sovereignty of Your Majesty and your family forever.

Affectionately Yours: The Letters of
Sir John A. Macdonald and His Family.

The Queen's proclamation of Confederation.

We do ordain, declare, and command that on and after the First day of July, One Thousand Eight Hundred and Sixty-seven, the Provinces of Canada, Nova Scotia, and New Brunswick, shall form and be One Dominion, under the name of Canada.

...ours the Queen whose virtues transmute the sacred principle of loyalty into personal affection.

George M. Grant, the concluding line of his Ocean To Ocean, Sandford Fleming's Expedition Through Canada In 1872.

But the Queen took a personal interest as well in those who were serving her in the new nation

In May 1879, because of his military activities, he [Sir Casimir Gzowski] received an honour that has been bestowed on very few Canadians – that of being appointed Honorary Aide-de-Camp to Her Majesty Queen Victoria. This meant that he took annual trips to London where he was present at many Court ceremonies at Windsor Castle frequently meeting Her Majesty. The story goes that she was much taken with the handsome and interesting Polish gentleman from the Colonies, even at times taking him driving with her through the streets of London.

Ludwik Kos-Rabcewicz-Zubkowski and William Edward Greening, Sir Casimir Stanislaus Gzowski: A Biography.

[Sir George Etienne] Cartier gave me an account of his staying at Windsor with the Queen, and how he *would* go to the Anglican service much to Sir H. Bulwer's annoyance, who wanted to make Cartier an excuse for not going at all! He says the English ladies are both "pretty and handsome". He said the Queen dined with her household to do him honour, a thing she never does on Sundays. She asked a great deal about Canada.

Frances Elizabeth Owen Monck, My Canadian Leaves.

But enough. However, be it announced that Her Majesty Queen Victoria invited Angus MacAskill to Windsor Castle. He soon called upon her. She gave him a cordial reception. She chatted pleasantly with him for a few hours.

She was highly *interested* in his great size, and complimented him very warmly. She presented him with two rings of gold.

MacAskill regretted that there were no means of showing his power of lifting, but he thought of a plan to leave a token of his strength on the sly. He walked back and forth before the Queen, secretly pressing the carpet with his heels. When he left, the carpet, though thick and strong, was cut here and there in the bread cutter fashion, by the heels of the giant.

The Queen said afterwards that he was the tallest, the stoutest and the strongest man that ever entered the palace.

MacAskill was well pleased with his visit. Yet he was not intoxicated by the honour, but preserved his wonted composure. 'Tis true, her kindness increased and enlivened his love for her, yet there were others he loved best, loyal as he was. Chief among those were his parents and his brother and sister.

Still our hero was a model of loyalty, but, in ordinary matters, with him "the man was the gold and all that".

James D. Gillis, The Cape Breton Giant:
A Truthful Memoir.

♛ ♛ ♛

Here I may recount a touching incident which evinces the gracious kindness and thoughtfulness of our late beloved Queen Victoria. My husband and I were dining at the Austrian Embassy [in Berlin], and next to me at table was a gentleman attached to the household of the Empress Frederick (then Crown Princess). He turned to me and said, "The Princess knew that I should meet you this evening, and she told me to give you this". He handed me a telegram, which I found to be from our late Queen to Her Royal Highness, and which ran as follows: "Am anxious to recommend Madame Albani to you. She is my Canadian subject, an excellent person, known to me, a splendid artiste, and I take much interest in her.

THE QUEEN"

I could hardly speak for pleasure, for I had no idea the Queen was aware of my being in Berlin or having intended to go there, but I managed to say, "Pray tell the Princess that I shall keep and treasure this".

Emma Lajeunesse, Madame Albani,
My Forty Years Of Song.

♛ ♛ ♛

Queen Victoria it seems was in the mind of virtually every nineteenth century Canadian. On 13 July 1885 Louis Riel handed the following poem of his own composition to Superintendent Burton Deane, the NWMP [RCMP] officer responsible for him during his imprisonment, trial and execution.

Béni soit Dieu qui glorifie
Le Règne de Victoria:
C'est un Dieu que je me confie
Puisque c'est lui qui me créa.

Dieu veuille que le Règne voie
L'éclat des plus beaux cheveux blancs;
Et qu'elle avance dans la joie
Du plus gracieux de ses ans.

Fasse Jésus-Christ qu'elle atteigne
Ce grand age qui n'est pas vieux,
On la grâce des années règne
Plus, en remontrant vers les cieux.

Plaise a Jésus-Christ qu'elle vive
Pour le moins encore vingt-ans:
Que Sa Majesté soit active
En bonne santé, tout le temps.

Qu'elle aime, mais sans préfèrence,
Le Peuple Canadien Français:
Que toute la Nouvelle France
Trouve auprès d'elle un libre accès.

Sous son admirable couronne
Sous son règne majestueux
Puissant race Anglo-Saxonne
Rendez les Irlandais heureux.

Que Jésus le Fils de Dieu même
Fasse étinceler sur les mers
Et les terres, le diadème.
De la Reine, dans l'Univers.

Captain R. Burton Deane, Mounted Police Life in Canada, A Record of Thirty-one Years' Service.

♛ ♛ ♛

Telegram to Marquess of Lansdowne, Governor General of Canada, 5 May 1886

Opening of the [Indian and Colonial] Exhibition went off splendidly; delighted to see so many of my Canadian subjects.

Victoria R. and I.

♛ ♛ ♛

The prominent Torontonian and Canadian soldier, G.T. Denison was among those in London for the Queen's Golden Jubilee.

I went to England at the end of May, 1887, for the Jubilee. I was fortunate enough to meet the Duke of Connaught [Queen Victoria's third son and future Governor General] at dinner at Lord Salisbury's. After dinner His Royal Highness came over and spoke to me, and asked me if I had a seat in the Abbey for the celebration. I said I had not, and never expected to get one. He said of course I ought to have one. Whether he took any action or not I cannot say, but I do know that I received two tickets a couple of days after, and my wife and I saw the brilliant scene from capital seats over the west door.

George Taylor Denison, Soldiering In Canada.

♛ ♛ ♛

Sir Wilfrid Laurier at Queen Victoria's Diamond Jubilee.

The weeks in Britain were crowded and memorable. A lavish and kindly hospitality filled the visitor's days and nights. "I am not sure whether the British Empire needs a new constitution", Mr Laurier wrote to a Canadian friend, "but I am certain that every jubilee guest will need one".

Oscar Douglas Skelton, Life And Letters Of Sir Wilfrid Laurier.

♛ ♛ ♛

Queen Victoria died 22 January 1901 and the entire nation mourned her.

The city yesterday wore a distinct air of depression. This was not created merely by the display of mourning emblems, although these were profuse... The sorrow brooding over the community was reflected even in the faces and demeanour and the subdued conversation of the people on the streets. The Queen's death seemed to weigh on the minds of everyone and impose a sombre restraint. The private and personal concern was more touching than any public or ceremonial expression of grief. It showed, as no ceremony could, how near the Queen was to the hearts of her people, and how the thought of her had become part of the routine of life.

Countless flags hang at half-mast, and most of the stores and offices exhibit tokens of mourning. Goods in black generally fill the windows . . . The front of Eaton's is draped in its whole length, and over each of the main entrances on Queen and Yonge streets is a statue of the Queen in a setting of Union Jacks. The fine facade of R. Simpson and Company's store is also hung with black festoons . . . The whole front of the Albany Club is draped in black.

Mail and Empire, Toronto.

♛ ♛ ♛

I was born on May 28th 1898 and the first specific memory I have is of Queen Victoria's death. That was because of the atmosphere in the drawing-room of our home in Sault Ste. Marie. My parents were upset and therefore I was upset. The "mother" Queen had died and the boys were coming home from the Boer War without the Queen. And that distress was conveyed to me and has stayed in my mind.

Loveday Cadenhead, Toronto.

♛ ♛ ♛

Prime Minister John Diefenbaker on his father's reaction to Queen Victoria's death.

It was natural for Father, who was deeply devoted to the Monarchy throughout his life and defended it strongly against all comers, to take the family to see the Duke and Duchess of Cornwall and York, when they visited Toronto in 1901. It was a great day. Mother, however did not share Father's devotion to the Crown, having inherited the memories of the slaughter of the clans at Culloden. Bonnie Prince Charlie was to her a living, not an historical figure. She had a feeling toward the English that was not one of complete adulation, and she could not take the same pride as Father in being a part of an Empire on which the sun never set. When Queen Victoria died, Father regarded it as one of the most calamitous events of all time. Would the world ever be the same? I can see him now. When he came home to tell us the news, he broke down and cried.

John G. Diefenbaker, One Canada.

♛ ♛ ♛

Memorial services in many cities of Canada were timed to coincide with the Queen's burial at Windsor.

It was a day when all the city went to church. In the morning the great bronze bell in the civic tower tolled out its dirge . . . In the afternoon the occasion became the more solemn when the city's garrison, nigh two thousand men paraded with bands playing the Dead March, and when the roll of muffled drums smote upon the heart . . .

Thus in this city were the inevitable sad rites in behalf of the best beloved Sovereign that the world has known celebrated. And over the city there was the consciousness that not by it alone was the tribute of sorrow being paid, but that half a world was also in gloom.

Mail and Empire, Toronto.

2

OH LOOK THE QUEEN MUM IS WAVING... SHE REMEMBERS ME.

STUMPING THE DOMINION

A reality of Canadian life is that in sharing our Sovereign with some sixteen other countries, the reigning Monarch and the Royal Family are not constantly present in the country. There are of course the compensating benefits, such as a less parochial view of the world and the sense of belonging to an international as well as a national family, gained from the arrangement. And the international prestige held by the Canadian head of state is far greater by virtue of her transcending status than it could ever be for a head of state (monarch or president) who was exclusively Canadian.

As a result of the Royal Family's residence outside the country though, it is through royal tours that Canadians and the Crown interact in the most personal way. Such tours are not new, the first was in 1786, almost a century before Confederation, and while they have changed to meet the demands of new generations and exploit the potential of new technology, they retain common threads. The Royal Family have never regarded these tours as visits to a foreign land where they were guests, but as excursions in their own country, which of course they are. "I am going home to Canada tomorrow", the Queen remarked in California in 1983 as casually and naturally as any other Canadian might have.

Royal tours have allowed the Royal Family to gain a deeper

understanding of the country, as they have seen more of it than most native-born residents ever see. But the tours have also profoundly affected the Royal Family. "This has made us", King George VI said of the 1939 tour of Canada which gave him and the Queen the self-confidence that they could indeed fill the vacuum left by his brother's abdication. It was also on that 1939 tour that the royal walkabout was created as the King and Queen unexpectedly plunged into a crowd of veterans after unveiling the War Memorial in Ottawa.

Royal tours are rich with anecdote created as the Royal Family and their Canadians met, made each other laugh, shared happy and sad moments, discussed the significance of Canada and Canadian values and made real the role of monarchy in giving a human face to government. No selection of anecdotes of tours can ever be complete, because as it is being compiled a new tour, with new stories, is already in the planning stages.

WILLIAM IV

King William IV was the first member of the Royal Family to come to Canada, as a young Prince William in 1786 while serving with the Royal Navy. Prince William's first glimpse of Canada - Newfoundland - was not a favourable one, as he reported in a letter to his father King George III written from the Pegasus at St John's, 21 September 1786.

The face of the country is truly deplorable: the season as far backward as the beginning of April: a small brushwood for the first five hundred yards in shore & then a most dreadful inhospitable & barren country intersected by fresh water ponds, lakes & bogs: I am informed that the woods are very large thirty miles from the sea, and are of prodigious size & extent. Few people have ever visited the inland parts of the island so that they are scarce known; it is not even determined whether they are inhabited; on the northern coast the Esquimaux Indians cross over from Labrador & settle in the island & are there employed as servants to dress the fish. During the fishing season the number of people are prodigious that come out to attend the different branches concerned in the cod fishery; not five out of a hundred remain in the winter, but return to Europe: the servants whose business is to cure the fish & go along shore in the shallops, are almost to a man Irish, & full as savage as any Indian that has had no education.

The Later Correspondence of George III.

♛ ♛ ♛

During the last fortnight of our stay at Placentia I read Divine Service in the Court House for an example to the Magistrates to perform that duty every Sunday till the arrival of the missionary from England. I twice lead prayers & my congregation consisted of all the Protestants & many of the Catholicks.

Prince William to his father, 21 September 1786,
The Later Correspondence of George III.

♛ ♛ ♛

When Prince William fell in love, which he did all too frequently, it was with young girls. The sister-in-law of Solicitor-General [of Nova Scotia] Richard John Uniacke, the young and beautiful Anne Delesdernier, first engaged his attentions. One night Uniacke's coachman caught the gallant prince on a ladder outside Anne's room, attempting to watch her undress; the coachman gave Prince William a sound whipping as he was descending the ladder. Prince William was so smitten with Anne that he planned an elopement; Uniacke found out in time and sent Anne into the country . . . At one riotous drinking session in a room on Water Street, built on piles and overhanging the water, the Prince and his friends were nearly drowned when the piles gave way and the room collapsed into the harbour. Prince William found Halifax "a very gay and lively place full of women and those of the most obliging kind".

Brian C. Cuthbertson, The Loyalist Governor:
Biography of Sir John Wentworth.

♛ ♛ ♛

The next day, Monday the 5th November, he had fixed to land as a prince of the blood to receive the address from the Governor and Council [of Nova Scotia], to dine with them, and to go to a ball given by the town. I went to breakfast with him at eight, found the cutter waiting for me at the dockyard and a royal midshipman attending. His Royal Highness was on the quarter-deck when I went on board. We immediately went below to breakfast, and which consisted of tea, coffee, and all sorts of cold meat, cold game, etc. etc. His Highness breakfasted almost entirely on cold turkey. His purser made breakfast, and his first lieutenant and two of the midshipmen (who take it in turn) breakfasted. They did not stay two minutes after.

And then his Royal Highness, with the greatest condescension possible, showed me first of all the different clothing of his barge's crew for the different climates. He made the coxwain put on each of the dresses and cap. Then he showed me his orderly books, and the books belonging to the lieutenants and midshipmen. Then he explained the whole business of the ship and the different stations in every possible situation for every man and officer in the ship, all under different heads, in the most exact manner; a copy of which all the officers have (in a book). He then showed me the ship's books kept by the purser of all the men's accounts, necessaries and clothing, forms of the different returns, etc. etc.

I went home to get the regiment ready to receive his Royal Highness.

At two o'clock the garrison marched down and lined the streets from the wharf to the Government House. A captain's guard with colours was formed on the right to receive him, and a detachment of artillery with three field pieces fired a royal salute on his landing. His Royal Highness left the Commodore's ship about a quarter after two in his own barge (which was steered by an officer). His barge's crew most elegantly dressed, and the handsomest caps I ever saw. Black velvet, and all except the coxwain's with a silver ornament in front and the King's arms most elegantly cast. The coxwain's was of gold, and his Royal Highness told me it cost fifty guineas. As he was steered by an officer, what is termed the strokesman wore the coxwain's cap. The Commodore's ship lay about half a mile from the wharf where he landed, and as he passed the ships, followed by the Commodore and captains of the fleet in their barges, his Royal Highness and the Commodore each having the standard of England hoisted in their barge, he was saluted by each of them separately, having their yards manned, etc. When he came within a hundred yards of the wharf his barge dropped astern, and the Commodore's and captains' pushed on and landed to receive him immediately on his stepping out of his barge (the Governor, Council, House of Assembly, etc., and all the great people being there to receive him). He was saluted by the field pieces on the wharf and proceeded through the line of troops to the Government House, the soldiers with presented arms, the officers and colours saluting him as he passed, and all the bands playing 'God save the King'.

When he entered Government House he was saluted by the twenty-four pounders on the Citadel Hill. On his being arrived in the levée room, the different branches of the legislature being there assembled and all the officers allowed to be present, the Governor presented the address, to which his Royal Highness read his answer, and read it with more energy and emphasis than anything I ever heard. At the same time he had the most majestic and manly appearance I ever beheld.

General William Dyott, Dyott's Diary 1781–1845.

♔ ♔ ♔

He was received in Quebec [in 1787] with all the pomp and ceremony due the son of our sovereign ... As was the custom, a grand ball was given at the Château Saint-Louis. Dinner was at four o'clock, and the ball commenced between six and seven. The young prince danced with a few of the more important ladies, be they beautiful, ugly, or merely plain, then kicked up his heels a little and chose his own partners from among the prettiest girls in the room. Lady Dorchester was greatly displeased with this departure from the etiquette laid down for him, and could be heard to exclaim from time to time, "That young man has no regard for the proprieties!"

The young sailor was having such a good time that it wasn't until somewhere between eleven o'clock and midnight that a peculiar circumstance struck him. He then asked my uncle, Charles de Lanaudière, aide-de-camp to Lord Dorchester, whether it was usual in Quebec for ladies and gentlemen to stand during their meals.

"It is out of respect for Your Royal Highness that everyone remains standing in your presence", replied the aide-de-camp.

"Then", said the prince, "tell them my Royal Highness permits them to dispense with this etiquette".

After consulting Lord and Lady Dorchester, the aide-de-camp proclaimed that His Royal Highness, the Duke of Clarence, would allow the ladies to be seated. Not a few of the said ladies, particularly the old ones, were badly in need of this dispensation.

A Man of Sentiment, The Memoirs of Philippe-Joseph Aubert de Gaspé 1786-1871.

♔ ♔ ♔

As for the Province of Canada it vastly surpasses all the accounts I can give to your Majesty of its magnitude, beauty & fertility: the Province in extent is larger than all Europe: the views in summer are magnificent, & where in England the eye commands a view of ten miles, in Canada for many leagues the corn & the sky appear to meet. The ground is rich & if the industrious Englishman tilled it instead of the lazy Canadian, it would be inestimable. The country about Quebec is vastly inferior in beauty & richness to that about Mon[t]real. My time was too short this year to go higher up than Mon[t]real, but next summer I shall most certainly proceed as far as possible.

Prince William to his father, from H.M.S. Pegasus at Quebec, 9 October 1787, The Later Correspondence of George III.

EDWARD VII

Prince Albert Edward, Prince of Wales, later King Edward VII, whose tour of British North America in 1860 helped bring about Confederation. He said to both houses of the Nova Scotia Legislature, 30 July 1860.

Most heartily do I sympathise in the pride with which you regard the laurels won by sons of Nova Scotia, and the affection with which you honour the memory of those who have fallen [in the Crimean War] in the service of my country and yours.

♛ ♛ ♛

To the Catholic Bishops of Canada, Quebec City, 26 August 1860.

I accept with the greatest satisfaction the welcome which you offer me in your own name as the Catholic Bishops of the Province of Canada, and on behalf of your clergy, and I assure you that I feel deeply the expression of your loyalty and affection for the Queen.

I rejoice to think that obedience to the laws and submission to authority, which form the bond of all society and the condition of all civilisation, are supported and enforced by your teaching and example.

♛ ♛ ♛

On 29 August 1860 the Prince of Wales opened Montreal's Crystal Palace.

I am not ignorant of the high position obtained by Canada in the Great Exhibition of 1851, which was opened under the happy auspices of the Queen and the Prince Consort; and carrying out the design of the memorable undertaking, this smaller, but to Canada most interesting, collection of the products of your land, and of works of art and industry, has my entire sympathy, and claims my best wishes for its success. I hope and believe it will realise all the objects for which it has been designed.

♛ ♛ ♛

From Montreal [the Prince of Wales] went to Ottawa, where he laid the cornerstone of the Federal Parliament building and rode a timber shoot down the Ottawa River; then on, past Kingston, to Toronto and across Lake Ontario to the Niagara Falls, where he saw Charles Blondin, the French acrobat, walk across the Falls on a tightrope, pushing a man in front of him in a wheelbarrow. Blondin offered to put the Prince into the wheelbarrow for the return journey across the tightrope to the United States. The Prince accepted the offer, but was naturally prevented from going. So Blondin went back by himself, this time on stilts, leaving the Prince to travel on to Hamilton.

Christopher Hibbert, Edward VII.

♛ ♛ ♛

The Prince of Wales on laying the cornerstone of the Parliament Buildings, Ottawa, 1 September 1860.

In this city, at your request, I am about to lay the first stone of a building in which, before long, the deliberations of the Parliament of Canada will be held; and from which will emanate the laws which are to govern the great and free people of these Provinces . . . I do not doubt, that, with its increase of population and influence, this city will prove itself worthy of the country of which it is now the Capital, and will justify the selection which your Sovereign made, at the request of her Canadian subjects.

It has been most gratifying to me to witness the demonstrations which have met me on every occasion during my progress through this magnificent country, and which evince the feelings towards your Queen entertained alike by all races, all creeds, and all parties.

♛ ♛ ♛

At Toronto, 7 September 1860.

My only regret is, that the Queen has been unable, herself, to receive the manifestations of the generous loyalty with which you have met her representative – a loyalty tempered and yet strengthened by the intelligent independence of the Canadian character.

♛ ♛ ♛

There are always unexpected and light-hearted moments to any royal tour.

[In 1860] The Prince spent several days in the Niagara Peninsula: he saw the Falls and much of the surrounding country. On one occasion, the Royal party made an unannounced visit to an orchard. The Prince picked a peach, and after taking a bite exclaimed: "How I wish my mother could taste such delicious peaches". The owner of the orchard, ignorant of the speaker's identity, called down through the branches, "Why didn't you bring the old woman along with you?"

C.W. Jeffreys and A.J. Casson,
The Visits Of Royalty To Canada.

♛ ♛ ♛

The Prince of Wales at a Canadian Ball.

Never has the Prince seemed more manly nor in better spirits. He talked away to his partner . . . He whispered soft nothings to the ladies as he passed them in the dance, directed them how to go right, & shook his finger at those who mixed the figures . . . In short was the life of the party. During the evening though he and the Duke of Newcastle enquired for a pretty American lady Miss B. of Natchez, whom they met at Niagara

Falls and with whom the Prince wished to dance. His Royal Highness looks as if he might have a very susceptible nature, and has already yielded to several twinges in the region of his midriff.

New York Herald, 19 September 1860

♛ ♛ ♛

Artemus Ward [pseudonym of the American wit Charles Farrar Browne] recounts his audience with the Prince of Wales at Sarnia in 1860.

At larst I've had an intervu with the Prince, tho' it cum purty nere costin' me my valerable life. I cawt a glimpse of him as he sat on the pizaro of the hotel in Sarnia, and elbode my way through a crowd of men, children, sojers, and Injins that was hangin' round the tavern. I was drawin' near to the Prince when a red faced man in millingtary close grabd holt of me and axed me where I was going all so bold.

"To see Albert Edard, Prince of Whales", sez I, "who be you?"

He said he was Kurnel of the Seventy-fust Regiment, her Majesty's troops. I toled him that I hoped the Seventy-Onesters were in good health, and was passing by when he ceased holt of me agin, and said in a tone of indignant cirprise:

"Impossible! It can't be! What sir! did I understan' you to say you was actooaly goin' into the presents of his Royal Iness?"

"That's what's the matter with me", I replied.

"But sir, its onprecedented. Its orful sir. Nothing like it hain't happened sins the Gunpowder Plot of Guy Forks! Ow-doshus man, who air you?"

"Sir", sez I, drawin' myself up and puttin' on a defiant air, "I'm a 'merican sittuzin, my name is Ward, I'm a husband, an' the father of twins, which, I am happy to state look like me. By perfeshun I'm a exhibiter of wax work and sich".

"Good gracious!" yelled the Kurnel, "the idea of an exhibiter of wax figures goin' into the presents of Royalty! The British Lyon may well roar with rage at the thawt!"

Sez I, "Speakin' of the British Lyon, Kurnel, I'd like to make a bargin with you fur that beast for a few weeks tu add to my show". I did'nt mean nothin' by this. I was only gettin' orf a goak, but you orter to hev see the old Kurnel jump up and howl. He actooally foamed at the mowth.

"This can't be real", he showted. "No-no, It's a orrid dream. Sir, you air not a human bein' - you hev no existens - yure a myth!"

"Wall", sez I, "old hoss, yule find me a ruther onkomfortable Myth ef you punch my inards in that way ag'in", I began to get a leetle riled, for when he called me a Myth he puncht me purty hard. The Kurnel now commencet showting for the Seventy-onesters. I at fust thought I'd stay and becum a Martar to British Outraje, as sich a course mite git my name up and be a good advertisement for my show, but it occurred to me if some of the Seventy-onesters should happen to insert a bayonet into my stummick, it mite be onpleasunt, and I was on the pint of runin' orf, when the Prince hisself kum up and axed me what the matter was. Sez I, "Albert Edard, is that yu?" and he smilt and sez it was. Sez I, "Albert Edard, hears my keerd. I cum to pay my respeks to the futhur king of Ingland. The Kurnel of the Seventy-onesters hear is ruther smawl pertaters, but of course you ain't to blame for that. He put on as many airs as tho' he was the Bully Boy with the glass eye".

"Never mind", sez Albert Edard, "I'm glad to see you Mr Ward, at all events", and he tuk my hand so pleasant-like, and larfed sweet that I fell in love with him at once. He handed me a segar and we sot down on the Pizaro, and commenct smokin' rite cheerful".

"Wall", sez I, "Albert Edard how's the old folks?"

"Her Majesty and the Prince are all well", he sed.

"Duz the old man take his Lager Bier reg'lar?" I inquired.

The Prince larfed, and intermatid that the old man did'nt let many kegs of that beveridge spile in the cellar in the course of a yere. We sot and talked there sum time about matters and things, and bimeby I axed him how he liked bein' Prince as fur as he hed got.

"To speak plain, Mister Ward", he sed, "I don't much like it. I'm sick of all this bowing & scarping & crawling & hurrain over a boy like me. I would rather go threw the country quietly & enjoy myself in my own way, with the other boys, and not to be med a show of to be garpen at by everybody. When the people cheer me I feel pleased, fur I know they meen it, but if these one-hos offishuls cood know how I see threw all their moves and understan exackly what they air after, and knowd how I larft at em in private, they'd stop kissin my hands & fawnin over me as they now do. But you know, Mister Ward, I can't help bein' a Prince, and I must do all I kin to fit myself fur the persishun I must sumetime ockepy."

"That's troo", sez I "sickness and the doctors will carry the Queen orf one of these dase, sure's yer born".

The time haven arove fur me to take my departer, I riz up and sed, "Albert Edard, I must go, but previs to doin so I will observe that you soot me. Yure a good feller Albert Edard, & tho Ime agin Princes as a general thing, I must say I like the cut of yure Gib. When you git to be King try and be as good a man as yure muther's bin. Be just and Jenerous, espeshully to showmen, who have allers bin aboozed sins the days of Noah, who was the fust man to go into the Meenagery bizness, & ef the daily papers of his time are to be bleeved Noah's colleckshun of livin' wild beests beet enny thing ever seen sins, tho I make bold to dowt ef his snaiks was ahead of mine. Albert Edard, adoo!" I tuk his hand, which he shook warmly, and given him a perpeteooal free pars to my show, and also parses to take home for the Queen & Old Albert, I put on my hat & walkt away.

"Mrs Ward", I solilerquised, as I walkt along, "Mrs Ward, ef you could see your husband now, jest as he prowdly emerjis from the presents of the future King of Ingland, youd be sorry you called him a Beest just becawz he come home tired I night and wanted to go to bed without taking orf his boots. Youd be sorry for trying to deprive your husband of the priceless Boon of liberty Betsy Jane".

Quoted in Robert Cellem, Visit Of His Royal Highness The Prince Of Wales To The British North American Provinces And United States In The Year 1860.

PRINCE LOUIS OF BATTENBERG

Prince Louis' first encounter with Canada was when he was serving on the Atlantic Station of the Royal Navy and before he officially became a member of the Royal Family. This story is from his own account of his early life.

In August, 1872, Lord Dufferin, the Governor General, and his beautiful and charming young wife, came to Halifax on a visit. Every kind of entertainment was got up in their honour, of which our ball in the "R.A." was the most brilliant. I was a member of the Ball Committee of three; the elaborate programme in blue and gold was my special charge. On the morning of the ball I went to the printer to fetch them, and was told that the only man who could do such a delicate job had broken his neck the night before. He had only begun to set it up. I took off my coat and set to work (I used to do a good deal of printing for my amusement as a boy.) About an hour before the guests were expected I arrived on board with the precious programmes. Amongst the distinguished strangers invited were Mr David Macpherson, a Canadian Senator from Toronto, and his lovely daughter Isabel (later Lady Kirkpatrick), with whom I made great friends. They invited me to their beautiful country place, Chestnut Park, near Toronto. As soon as the C.-in-C.'s inspection was over I took a month's leave and started off on September 11th by steamer to Portland (Maine), and thence to Detroit, Chicago, St Louis, Cincinnati, Toledo, Cleveland, Buffalo, Toronto once more, and back to Halifax via St John, N.B. Both times I spent a week-end with the Macphersons, which was delightful. The father, a widower who had a large shipping business in the city, went to his office forenoon and afternoon. There were saddle horses and pony traps in the stables, and a grand piano for duets, on which Miss Isabel and I, being the only other occupants of the house, played. Frequently dinner parties, followed by small dances, took place. Altogether I had a splendid time, and tears were shed on both sides on my final departure.

Mark Kerr, Prince Louis of Battenberg, Admiral Of The Fleet.

GEORGE V

The arrival of the Duke and Duchess of Cornwall and York (George V and Queen Mary) in Toronto in 1901 was a spectacular occasion.

. . . the royal procession formed and proceeded by way of St George, Bloor, Jarvis, Carlton, Yonge, King and Bay streets to the city hall amid cheering crowds, the memory of whose enthusiasm even now stirs the blood of him who witnessed it. It is said that 250,000 people took part in that marvellous demonstration . . . On the royal party approaching the city hall, the bands of the Grenadiers and the 13th Battalion played the opening bars of the Wagner number specially prepared for the occasion. The effect of the chorus composed of 1,000 adult voices was most impressive, and at the culminating words 'Prince of England, hail' outstretched hands greeted the royal guests in earnest of Toronto's welcome. The Duchess having accepted a bouquet of orchids from Miss Evelyn Cox, the Mayor proceeded to read the civic address. Unfortunately at the same moment the musical chorus burst forth anew, completely drowning Mr Howland's voice.

Sir Joseph Pope, The Tour of Their Royal Highnesses.

♛ ♛ ♛

Instead of a dramatic performance, since the Court was still in official mourning for Queen Victoria, a concert in Massey Music Hall was the featured entertainment for the evening of the great day [of the visit of the Duke and Duchess of York to Toronto, 10 October 1901], the opening of a three-day music festival . . . The royal party was late in arriving, and the guest singer, Madame Calvé, who had delayed her opening song as long as she could, was caught in the middle of it when "God Save The King" drowned her out and the audience turned its back on her to stare at the Duke and Duchess. "Probably no singer ever fought against greater odds than Madame Calvé", commented the *Mail and Empire* next day. "In her several numbers she had to sing first against a brass band out on the street, then against a chorus of fish-horns, then against a cavalcade of fire-engines and hose reels, and finally against a band of pipers. When the pibroch sounded it was too much for the risibilities of her listeners".

Mollie Gillen, The Masseys: Founding Family.

♛ ♛ ♛

On [the 1901] tour the Yorks came to realise how widespread Grandmamma's [Victoria's] influence had been, and learned to attach a new importance to the private lives and examples of those called on – as Princess May defined it – "to assume the power and symbolism of her great office". The impression went deep and remained indelible in her mind. She would never again be quite the same person, at least in her outward behaviour, and she no longer could abide a lapse from any of her family in what she considered "the proper Royal attitude".

Anne Edward, Matriarch: Queen Mary and the House of Windsor.

♛ ♛ ♛

...the Duke and Duchess of York visited the country [around Lethbridge and McLeod]. We then gathered up, from all surrounding districts, a force of about 250 officers and men, formed them into a camp at Calgary, and had the honour of being there reviewed by the Heir to the British Crown. After the review, the royal party went to a hill adjoining the city, where a large number of Blackfeet and other Indians were encamped. Mounted braves in all the extravagances of their native costume lined the road of approach on either side for about a mile, and at the summit their chiefs and head men, under the aegis of the Indian Department, were permitted to see and speak to their future King. This ceremony being completed, their Royal Highnesses and suite took luncheon at the barracks as guests of the officers of the Mounted Police. The mess-room of "E" Division was a capacious and handy room for the purpose, and the walls were decorated with a large number of well-preserved animals' heads, which had been lent to us for the purpose by owners scattered over a great extent of territory.

His Royal Highness was observed to take particular notice of these heads with the eye of a sportsman. The officers had all been presented to their Royal Highnesses before luncheon, and after that function a smart travelling escort, under command of the late Inspector Montague Baker, conducted the royal visitors to their train.

We had already entrained an escort for duty on the Pacific Coast, and of this, as being by many years senior superintendent of the Force, it was my birthright to go in command, but I had got mixed up with a criminal prosecution in Montana, which was to be tried in Great Falls within a few days, and, as it was necessary that I should attend the trial, I was perforce compelled to abandon the trip to the coast.

Soon after the occurrences just described, his Royal Highness was graciously pleased to ordain that the Force should be known as the Royal North-West Mounted Police.

Captain R. Burton Deane, Mounted Police Life in Canada, A Record of Thirty-one Years' Service.

♛ ♛ ♛

The 1901 tour of the Duke and Duchess of Cornwall and York inspired Stephen Leacock to reflect in his inimitable way on royal tours in Canada in a lecture delivered in the United Kingdom.

A loyal British subject like myself in dealing with the government of England should necessarily begin with a discussion of the Monarchy. I have never had the pleasure of meeting the King except once on the G.T.R. platform in Orillia, Ontario, when he was the Duke of York and I was one of the welcoming delegates of the town council. No doubt he would recall it in a minute.

But in England the King is surrounded by formality and circumstance. On many mornings I waited round the gates of Buckingham Palace but found it quite impossible to meet the King in the quiet sociable way in which one met him in Orillia. The English, it seems, love to make the kingship a subject of great pomp and official etiquette. In Canada it is quite different. Perhaps we understand kings and princes better than the English do. At any rate we treat them in a far more human heart-to-heart fashion than is the English custom, and they respond to it at once. I remember when King George – he was, as I say, Duke of York then – came up to Orillia, Ontario, how we all met him in a delegation on the platform. Bob Curran – Bob was Mayor of the town that year – went up to him and shook hands with him and invited him to come right on up to Orillia House where he had a room reserved for him. Charlie Janes and Mel Tudhope and the other boys who were on the town council gathered round the royal Prince and shook hands and told him he simply must stay over. George Rapley, the bank manager, said that if he wanted a cheque cashed or anything of that sort to come right into the Royal Bank and he would do it for him. The Prince had two aides-de-camp with him and a secretary, but Bob Curran said to bring them uptown too and it would be all right. We had planned to have an oyster supper for the Prince at Jim Smith's hotel and then take him either to the YMCA Pool Room or else to the tea social in the basement of the Presbyterian Church.

Unluckily the Prince couldn't stay. It turned out that he had to get right back into his train and go on to Peterborough, Ontario, where they were to have a brass band to meet him, which naturally he didn't want to miss.

But the point is that it was a real welcome. And you could see that the Prince appreciated it. There was a warmth and a meaning to it that the Prince understood at once. It was a pity that he couldn't have stayed over and had time to see the carriage factory and the new sewerage plant. We all told the Prince that he must come back and he said that if he could he most certainly would. When the Prince's train pulled out of the station and we all went back uptown together (it was before prohibition came to Ontario) you could feel that the institution of royalty was quite solid in Orillia for a generation.

But you don't get that sort of thing in England. There's a formality and coldness in all their dealings with royalty that would never go down with us. They like to have the King come and open Parliament dressed in royal robes, and with a clattering troop of soldiers riding in front of him. As for taking him over to the YMCA to play pin pool, they never think of it. They have seen so much of the mere *outside* of his kingship that they don't understand the *heart* of it as we do in Canada.

Stephen Leacock, My Discovery of England.

PRINCE LOUIS OF BATTENBERG

The 1905 visit of Prince Louis of Battenberg in the Maritimes.

About this time Prince Louis was delighted with a letter he received from an Irish-American in Chicago, who said he was 'hoping for an opportunity to plaster your Royal Puss with rotten eggs'. It was given a special page to itself in Prince Louis's newspaper cutting book.

Mark Kerr, Prince Louis of Battenberg,
Admiral of The Fleet.

In Halifax, 1905.

For tact Prince Louis was unbeatable, but it was at a dinner in Canada that I heard him make his only slip during the many years I knew him. A dinner party given by a high dignitary of the Church in a Canadian town was attended by about forty people, only two of whom were ladies. In contrast to all the other functions it was extremely dull. After trying to converse on different subjects with his host and his neighbour on the other side, and getting no response, Prince Louis almost gave up hope, but as a last resource he said to his right-hand neighbour: "Who is that plain-looking lady a little way down the table on the other side, and sitting next to Mr – ?" His neighbour stiffly replied: "That is my mother!" on which Prince Louis hastily remarked: "Oh, I don't mean that one, I mean the one on the other side of him". To which came the chilling response, "That is my sister!"

Mark Kerr, Prince Louis of Battenberg,
Admiral of the Fleet.

GEORGE VI

King George VI's first trip to Canada was as Midshipman Prince Albert on board HMS Cumberland in 1913.

Amongst his friends in the Greynviles was a cadet whose likeness to him was so great that once at Dartmouth the other's father had mistaken thePrince for his own son. These two entered into a pact of secrecy, the outcome of which was that on certain occasions during the rest of the cruise when Prince Albert was due to make an appearance (but not to speak) at some minor public function and had something better to do, such as playing lawn-tennis, his friend would take his place as a "stand-in" and smile charmingly at the crowds. This substitution was carried out more than once and always without detection.

John W. Wheeler-Bennett, King George VI.

♛ ♛ ♛

"We shot the rapids to Montreal. We struck a rock while shooting the Long Sault Rapids but no harm was done. The Lachine Rapids were the most exciting." It was a wonderful day and one which Prince Albert enjoyed a good deal more than the social functions which followed at Quebec. He was still profoundly shy in the company of those whom he did not know and at the various balls which were given for the cadets nothing would tempt him on to the dance floor. He preferred to get away into a corner from which he resisted all efforts to dislodge him. Again and again pretty Canadians girls were introduced and, though he was never boorish, it was observed that the conversation soon flagged. On one occasion, however, his reserve melted. Lieutenant-Commander Spencer-Cooper, gripping his trousers with both hands, confided to him that the ultimate catastrophe had happened – the two back braces buttons had come off. The Prince was delighted. All his shyness left him, and partner after partner was informed, with a giggle, of the predicament which had afflicted the Lieutenant-Commander. He was quite sorry when that ball ended.

John W. Wheeler-Bennett, King George VI.

PRINCE ARTHUR OF CONNAUGHT

In 1918 Prince Arthur of Connaught, son of the Duke [and grandson of Queen Victoria] toured Canada.

Canada's inland lakes can provide a thrill or two for the traveller which the seafarer least expects to experience after leaving the Pacific and Atlantic oceans . . . Yesterday afternoon His Royal Highness Prince Arthur of Connaught, son of Canada's former Governor General, was given a taste of a Lake Ontario squall. It was not on the schedule, and it will stand out as one of the unusual events of the Prince's visit. His Royal Highness and party left Beamsville in two motor launches of the R.A.F. at 3.15 in the afternoon, expecting to be off Toronto Bay at 5.45. Instead they ran into a severe electric storm half an hour out from Beamsville, and they were an hour and twenty minutes late reaching this city . . .

Shortly before 4 o'clock lightning flashed and the thunder rolled, and the lake became quite choppy, with heavy seas rolling. Waves broke over the sides, and engine trouble developed. Finally the first launch had to tow the second launch until the engine could be repaired. Meanwhile both launches were blown a considerable distance out into the lake. It had been intended that they should enter the bay through the western gap, but when driven out into the lake it was found necessary to make Toronto through the eastern channel.

From 6.30 until 7 o'clock his Honour the Lieutenant-Governor, Sir John Hendrie, Dr Alexander Fraser, A.D.C., and a guard of honour of 200 men from the C.O.T.C., under Major Needler, waited at the Harbour Commission's office on the lakefront for the royal party. Capt. Lou Scholes, Director of Athletics for this Military District, left the Commission's office at 5.30 o'clock in a Harbour Commission launch, with a party of newspapermen, to meet the visitors. They found big seas running when they entered the lake through the western gap, and returned to the dock. Two more trips were made to the gap, and when they returned the last time at 7.15, they found His Royal Highness had arrived ten minutes earlier by way of the eastern gap, and had left for Government House.

The Globe, 14 August 1918.

EDWARD VIII

The Prince of Wales was critical of the arrangements for his 1919 tour of Canada.

From Newfoundland and the Maritime Provinces, the *Renown* steamed up the St Lawrence River to Quebec. My party had meanwhile been joined by two Canadians officials who had drawn up my itinerary. One of these was a genial artillery officer, Major-General Sir Henry Burstall, whom I had met during the war. The other was an elderly civil servant, Sir Joseph Pope, who, because he had helped to arrange my father's Canadian tour eighteen years before, had been entrusted with the preparation of mine. The Governor General of Canada, the Duke of Devonshire, an old friend of my father's, had recommended Sir Joseph to me with the assurance that everything could be left in his "safe and experienced hands". When on our first meeting I went over the schedule prepared for me, it was plain that Sir Joseph had faithfully followed the 1901 model. State drives in horse-drawn landaus with mounted escort, mounted military parades, civic lunches, official dinners, sight-seeing detours to notable landmarks – it all had a decidedly Victorian flavour ...

However, the crowds that I encountered in Quebec, and subsequently throughout Canada, proved so volatile and vigorous as to constitute at times an almost terrifying phenomenon. Uncontrolled, almost ferocious in their determination to satisfy their curiosity about me, they again and again broke through and swamped the police lines. They snatched at my handkerchief; they tried to tear the buttons off my coat. Yet, while all this provided welcome proof that the Royal Family still possessed a sure claim upon the affections of overseas British communities, I came to fear not only for my own safety but for that of the Canadians themselves.

Old Sir Joseph Pope, from whose "safe and experienced hands" the crowds were literally snatching me, apologised for their behaviour, saying, "I simply cannot understand what has come over the Canadian people, Sir. This utter lack of control – it is not at all what I would have expected". That part I had not minded at all; in fact, I rather enjoyed it. But I was convinced that these mounted State progresses Sir Joseph had organised along Buckingham Palace lines were an open invitation to disaster. They were all very well in London, where the Royal Mews maintained an ample supply of trained horses, and the escorts of the Household Cavalry through long usage had brought to unrivalled precision the technique of mounted ceremonial. The saddle and carriage horses provided in Canada were unaccustomed to this kind of work, and there was constant danger of their becoming frightened by the crowds, and trampling people under foot. Yet despite several close calls, I could not persuade Sir Joseph or General Burstall of the wisdom of dispensing with this obsolescent and cumbersome form of transportation, It required a spectacular incident at Toronto to break down their resistance.

The Great War Veterans Association of Canada had arranged for me to inaugurate "Warrior's Day" at the Canadian National Exhibition. A tremendous parade, at which some 27,000 veterans would be massed at the Exhibition Grounds, was to be the climax of the occasion. My part required that I mount a horse, pass down the ranks, and then ride solemnly to a platform at the side of the field where I would dismount, then walk up the steps and make a speech.

When General Burstall had finished outlining the program, I said, "But, General, do you think it's a good idea for us to ride on this occasion? You know the veterans. They are not going to keep their ranks once I appear. God knows what this horse will do. Frankly, I am all for using a motor".

But the General persuaded me to put aside my apprehensions with the argument that the local military organisers would be disappointed if I did not ride. "The horse, Sir," he said, reassuringly, "has been specially trained". So, at the appointed hours, followed by the General and other officers, I rode out upon the field, still uneasy in my own mind.

What I feared would happen did happen. The moment I appeared the veterans broke ranks and, cheering and yelling, surged around me. At first my mount showed commendable control. Then, as the human mass engulfed us both, I felt its body quiver. Fortunately, even if its instinct had been to rear up and bolt, the crowd held it as in a vise. The next thing I knew I was being lifted off the horse's back by strong hands and passed like a football over the heads of the veterans. Dishevelled, shaken, and breathless, I eventually found myself on the platform, clutching the crumpled notes of my speech. The roar of cheering had changed to laughter. I wish Papa could have seen this, I thought to myself. I cast a glance back for the horse. It had vanished.

That evening when Sir Henry came to apologise for the contretemps of the afternoon, I looked at him reproachfully and said, "I trust, General, that we have seen the last of horses at these public shows".

"I was afraid you were going to say that, Sir", he answered sadly. "I shall send out the necessary orders."

If it was the last of the horses, it was also, for reasons that by now must be self-evident, the last of Sir Joseph Pope. All his meticulous preparations had collapsed. As the crowds took charge, he had subsided into the background, protesting again and again that "this will never do". Inquiry revealed that he had quietly got off the train with his baggage at an intermediate stop, without even a farewell message.

H.R.H. The Duke of Windsor, A King's Story.

♛ ♛ ♛

The Prince traversed the country by train.

I progressed westward in a magnificent special train provided by the Canadian Pacific Railway. My quarters were in the rear car, which had an observation platform. This last adjunct, while providing me with a continuous view of the varied Canadian landscape, had, however, the drawback of making me vulnerable to demands for ad lib speeches from the crowds gathered at every whistle stop.

Hoping to please, I would always oblige. As I hurried to the back observation platform, Martin Burrell would usually prime me with such pertinent facts as were likely to appeal to local pride. These I would hopefully weave into the standard three-minute speech I had by then evolved. But on more than one occasion disconcerting bursts of laughter instead of the customary applause informed me that I had made the lamentable blunder of confusing my audience with a rival community some distance down the track. Yet, these experiences were all to the good, and taught me to think on my feet. As I became more sure of myself, I began to enjoy these informal meetings. Getting off the train to stretch my legs, I would start up conversations with the people of Canada – farmers, section hands, miners, small-town editors, newly arrived immigrants from Europe. It was the first time that a British Prince had ever stumped a Dominion in quite that way, and the impressions of Canada I formed in this manner proved far more instructive than anything I learned on the formal "red carpet".

H.R.H. The Duke of WIndsor, A King's Story.

♛ ♛ ♛

Edward VIII's 1919 Canadian tour as Prince of Wales followed the unrest of the Winnipeg General Strike but he insisted on leading the Labour Day Parade in Ottawa that year. In Calgary he touched on the country's problems.

Serious difficulties and controversies must often arise, but nothing can set Canada back, except the failure of different classes and communities to look at the wider interests of the Dominion as well as their own immediate needs. I realise that scattered communities, necessarily preoccupied with the absorbing task of "making good", often find it difficult to keep the wider view. Yet I feel sure that it will be kept steadily before the eyes of all the people of the West, whose very success in making the country what it is proves their staying-power and capacity.

♛ ♛ ♛

The Prince had one good story to tell his father, King George V, about his 1919 tour of Canada.

When I arrived home my father, who had never been to the United States, asked me innumerable questions about various American phenomena – the height of New York's skyscrapers, the number of automobiles on the streets, the state of President Wilson's health, and the size of his staff employed at the White House. But most of all he was curious about life in America under prohibition. An abstemious man himself, he considered it an outrage for the government of any country to attempt to regulate the conduct of its citizens in such a manner. And of all the information that I brought back I think what delighted him most was the following doggerel picked up in a Canadian border town:

> Four and twenty Yankees, feeling very dry,
> Went across the border to get a drink of rye.
> When the rye was opened, the Yanks began to sing,
> "God bless America, but God save the King!"

H.R.H. The Duke of Windsor, A King's Story.

♛ ♛ ♛

The future Edward VIII insisted that he came to Canada as a Canadian – he wrote back to his father, "I'm rubbing it in, that although not actually Canadian-born, I'm Canadian-born in spirit, and come over here as such, and not as a stranger - and that goes down well".

Trevor Hall, Royal Canada.

♛ ♛ ♛

After an official banquet at the King Edward Hotel during the first of their two August 1927 stays in Toronto, the Prince of Wales and his brother Prince George slipped away to a private party at D.L. McCarthy's house on Elm Avenue.

Miss Murdoch, lovely in a smart gown of white sequins with beaded fringe was the favoured partner of the Prince of Wales, who indulged in his favourite Charleston. But, according to the young people at the party, it was a Charleston of his own – and, strange to say, an exceedingly graceful one.

Monarchist League of Canada Archives, unheaded and undated newspaper clipping.

♛ ♛ ♛

On his 1927 Canadian tour with his brother Prince George, the future Duke of Kent, the two Princes were accompanied by the United Kingdom Prime Minister, Stanley Baldwin.

I was momentarily disconcerted upon landing at Quebec to find that I was expected to ride in an open landau again. It was almost as if the ghost of old Sir Joseph Pope had made a reappearance. "Those damn horses again", I muttered to [Prince] George. "I thought I had talked these Canadians out of this eight years ago." My own misgivings certainly had not abated with the passage of time; and, when upon clambering in with the Governor the carriage started off with so violent a jerk as to almost snap our necks, I became alarmed.

"A fine pair of horses", exclaimed the Governor, mistaking my anxious glance for one of approval. He was in high spirits as we raced through the streets; so were the horses. By the time we had reached the suburbs the landau began swaying and lurching from side to side, and it was evident that the horses had bolted. Only after the Governor had cautioned and instructed the straining, sweating coachman in French did he managed to steady the frantic animals and get them under control.

Delivered shaken but intact at the Governor's residence, I was recovering from this harrowing experience when his daughter arrived with my brother. They had watched from the carriage behind as we had rocketed out of sight. This charming lady, apologising for what had happened, then divulged that her father's hobby was driving horses; that the speed with which he drove was the terror of the Province; and that with the idea of paying me a compliment he had brought out his liveliest pair. "I begged my father", she said, "not to do it. I knew this would happen. But he would not listen." Mr Baldwin had of course decided upon a safer if less spectacular form of transportation – Mr

Mackenzie King's automobile. Watching them drive up, I thought to myself wistfully that there are occasions when not so much is expected of Prime Ministers.

H.R.H. The Duke of Windsor, A King's Story.

GEORGE VI

[see Chapter 3, The People's King]

ELIZABETH II

[see Chapter 4, Elizabeth II of Canada]

QUEEN ELIZABETH THE QUEEN MOTHER

The dinner for Queen Elizabeth the Queen Mother [in 1954] was given a Scottish flavour by the presence of the Pipe Major and two other pipers from the Black Watch of Montreal, of which she is Colonel-in-Chief. A little incident in connection with this is worth recording. With Her Majesty's permission, I proposed her health, after the toast to the Queen, and the military band, without instruction, played "God Save the Queen' again. At that moment, however, the pipers had been told to come into the ballroom playing their pipes while they approached the head table to get their "quaichs" from me. They proceeded according to orders – nothing human would have stopped them! I turned to Her Majesty and said, "I'm afraid, Ma'am, there has been a slip in the staff work". She smiled at me and, like a good Scotswoman, observed that the pipes were winning – and they were!

Vincent Massey, What's Past Is Prologue:
The Memoirs of the Right Honourable
Vincent Massey.

PRINCESS MARY, THE PRINCESS ROYAL, COUNTESS OF HAREWOOD

The Princess Royal came later, both to the Citadel and to Government House. An incident took place that showed the impression she had made on Quebec. The Prime Minister of the province, when he heard that she was not going to his town, Three Rivers, said that if this was so Three Rivers would go to her. He got to work on the telephone and the result was that during the short stop of her train in that station thousands of people came to greet her.

Vincent Massey, What's Past Is Prologue:
The Memoirs of the Right Honourable
Vincent Massey.

PRINCE WILLIAM OF GLOUCESTER

In 1964 Prince William of Gloucester, grandson of King George V, paid a private visit to Canada with a friend Tom Troubridge who left an account of it.

Our first stop in Canada was Quebec City where General Vanier, the Governor-General of Canada, had arranged for us to stay in his official residence in the Citadel. This large grey fortress, which sits above the city, was still very much an army barracks. On arrival, we found our way barred by an implacable French-Canadian sentry whom no amount of reasoning in our schoolboy French would convince that [Prince] William was who he was, and, even if he were, that we were invited to stay in the Governor-General's house in the middle of the compound. Salvation eventually arrived in the form of Mr Haut O'Brien, who was in charge of the Residence, and who looked after us marvellously while we were in Quebec. The guards of the citadel had obviously been well briefed after our ignominious arrival, as now, whenever we left the Citadel, William was treated to a crashing present arms. This performance caused considerable surprise to the usual gaggle of tourists hanging around the gate who looked in amazement at the two scruffy youths in jeans and Breton berets slinking out between the lines of saluting soldiery.

Giles St Aubyn, William of Gloucester: Pioneer Prince.

QUEEN ELIZABETH THE QUEEN MOTHER

One lovely June day many years ago I was driving south on Bayview Avenue in Metro Toronto, just south of Highway 401, with my three-year-old son, Andrew. We had noticed policemen at each corner of Fifeshire and then at intervals. The traffic lights at York Mills were red for me, so I leaned across toward the open window to ask the officer what was happening.

"The Queen Mother is coming", he replied. (I had forgotten she was due to arrive that afternoon to stay, of course, with her old friend Mr E.P. Taylor, whose house was just down the road.) Now, it happened, that just after the officer spoke those words, a street cleaner travelling north approached us.

A few weeks later, again driving young Andrew in the back seat with his friend Judy, with great excitement Andrew exclaimed, "Look Judy, there's the Queen Mother". "Where Andrew?" asked Judy. "There, Judy, there", said Andrew with impatience, pointing to - you guessed it - a street cleaner.

"Andrew, that's a street cleaner. That's not the Queen Mother." "It is, Judy. It is so. The policeman said so." It took a very long time to convince young Andrew otherwise.

Carolyn Walk, Willowdale

♛ ♛ ♛

I was a Naval Aide-de-Camp to Vincent Massey for almost two years during the 1950s. Since 1974 I have served Lieutenant Governors of Nova Scotia in the same category ... except that it is a part time duty. I have been fortunate in meeting many members of the Royal family over the years as a result....

In 1979 The Queen Mother came to Halifax to open the Nova Scotia Tattoo and the Gathering of the Clans. She stayed at Government House, as did her Private Secretary, Sir Martin Gilliat. I was in the front hall as they arrived. As I was introduced to Sir Martin he commented "Ah yes, we have met before." I mumbled something about "I think not", rather hoping he did not hear.

That night at a small dinner before the Tattoo he made a point of coming up to me and repeating that we had met, he thought. I allowed as how I had only met The Queen Mother once before, 22 years ago, when ... I got no further. Sir Martin brightened and said "You were with the Governor General, and you came to Montreal in the viceregal train. We had stopped in Montreal for fuel, en route to Australia, and we went on board the train for tea".

He was absolutely right! I regret I did not remember him. He told me that the only reason he remembered was that he had just joined Her Majesty's staff and this was his first trip, and he was petrified. Not too petrified to recall, and recognise, a young officer, twenty years later in a different city. The Queen Mother is well served with a staff like that.

Ian F. McKee, Halifax

♛ ♛ ♛

A recollection of the Queen Mother's stay in Saskatchewan.

In 1985 we in Saskatchewan had the privilege in having her come to see us. My wife and I recall meeting her at the airport and driving with her to the Legislative Building. We saw her inspect the guard of honour, saw her have her walkabout amongst the guides, the scouts and brownies, the beavers, and the war brides, and the veterans. Then she had to enter the Legislative Building for the official welcome. And I am sure all of you know the steep flight of stairs that goes up to the Chamber. I suggested to her that perhaps she might prefer to take the lift. She would have no part of that. "Come on, let's go!" she said. And so we climbed the stairs to the Chamber level, and I am sure that when we got to the top I was breathing much harder than the Queen Mother. And she was only eighty-five at that time. After the official welcome, we got into the horse-drawn landau to proceed to the Hotel Saskatchewan for lunch. As you all know, the Queen Mother is a keen judge of horseflesh. As we were proceeding across Malcolm Street Bridge, she said "There's something wrong. These horses can't get into a proper gait. They can't gallop, they can't canter, they can't trot, they can't walk, and unless something is done about it they'll all go and have a sleep". So I said to her, "Yes, Ma'am", but what do you suggest. She said "Signal to the lead car and have them speed it up a bit". Of course the messenger said "His Honour wants you to speed it up". The horses fell into a proper and appropriate gait and the Queen Mother was quite happy.

Address by Hon. Frederick Johnson, former Lieutenant-Governor of Saskatchewan, at a service of thanksgiving for the 90th birthday of Queen Elizabeth The Queen Mother, St Mary's Church, Regina, 9 September 1990.

PRINCE OF WALES (CHARLES)

Prince Charles is the third Prince of Wales to travel in Canada.

The ordeal of pursuit through such arduous terrain [in the Northwest Territories in 1970] led the press corps to compose a song for the prince, complaining about the difficulties of keeping up with him "across the ice floes". Next day Prince Charles, his equerry, his private secretary, and his detective performed a ditty he had written himself, appropriately enough to the Welsh hymn tune "Immortal Invisible":

Impossible, unapproachable, God only knows
The light's always dreadful and he won't damn well pose,
Most maddening, most curious, he simply can't fail,
It's always the same with the old Prince of Wales.

Insistent, persistent, the press never end,
One day they will drive me right round the bend,
Recording, rephrasing every word that I say:
It's got to be news at the end of the day.

Disgraceful, most dangerous to share the same plane,
Denies me the chance to scratch and complain.
Oh where may I ask you is the Monarchy going
When princes and pressmen are in the same Boeing?

Anthony Holden, Prince Charles.

♛ ♛ ♛

After the Prince [of Wales arrived in Winnipeg in April 1979 for his first visit to his regiment the Royal Winnipeg Rifles], I went with him in the limo from the base to the Fort Garry Hotel. This was not a well-announced visit, but there were still a few groups of school children along the way – their teachers had brought them out. At one corner we stopped at a red light, and the Prince put the window down and chatted with the teacher and the kids, told them how delighted he was to see them, and they asked him a few questions. You know how kids are, they ask the darndest questions, but he answered just the same. One asked him where his crown was. I guess they expected to see one of those Imperial Margarine crowns on him. And he said, Oh, it's in the trunk. Along the way, we had a nice conversation. He said he hoped we didn't have any outlandish regimental surprises in store for him. I said, no, why? Well, he said, I'm the Colonel in Chief of the Gurkha Rifles and when I went over there and visited the troops, they seemed to think I would enjoy eating some roasted snake. I don't know why they should think I'd enjoy that. It was obvious they didn't. But, he said, that's the sort of thing they expect of people like me. And I said, we don't have anything like that in store for you.

The Prince is just an absolute delight to be with. In no time flat you almost forget that he's the Prince of Wales. He's the kind of guy you wouldn't think twice about inviting out for a round of golf, to do a little shooting, or to have a couple of beers. He's definitely the best.

Lieut-Col. W.R. Spence in Larry Krotz,
Royal Visits, a Manitoba album.

PRINCESS MARGARET

Princess Margaret was here for the 1974 celebrations of Winnipeg's centennial. I was by then Judge of Citizenship Court, and thought I'd like to hold a citizenship court ceremony and have the Princess present the certificates. I checked it with the government, and they checked with the Princess, and we got word that she would be very pleased to attend the ceremony.

We rented the Manitoba Theatre Centre for this. After I had conducted the ceremony, the swearing in, Princess Margaret presented the certificates and had a little chat with everybody. And she really seemed to enjoy doing that. By design, I had selected a representative group of people from various countries. We called them in beforehand to prepare them, and they all came out in their best clothes. Some of the men had been in the armies in Europe, and they stood at attention during the ceremony. I remember one poor woman, she had been in a concentration camp in the war. She was standing there trembling, and the Princess held her by the hand. These people still run into me occasionally, and they still talk about how Princess Margaret, the sister of the

Queen, presented their citizenship certificates. Some even wrote that on the bottom of their certificates and had them framed.

Lieut-Col. W.R. Spence in Larry Krotz, Royal Visits, a Manitoba album.

LADY MOUNTBATTEN

In 1985 Lady Mountbatten, daughter of Earl Mountbatten of Burma, one of the giants of twentieth century history, came to Canada to attend a variety of official functions. It was something of a "state visit". She arrived at the school of which I was Headmaster, Appleby College, to open the newly-constructed Arts Building. Preceding the opening ceremonies and ribbon cutting, an inspection of the Cadet Corps guard was organised somewhat at the last moment. The Cadets were quickly drilled, briefed, polished and mustered on parade.

Despite the feverish pace of last-minute preparation, the youngsters presented themselves remarkably well, resplendent in their scarlet tunics and gleaming brass. The ranks were perfectly dressed and not a body twitched. Lady Mountbatten, accompanied by the Pooh-Bahs of the Cadet Corps and me, wended her way between the ranks, observing everything, missing nothing and by her manner, putting one and all at ease. The solemnity of the occasion was lost to none. At last the inspecting party arrived at the centre of the rear rank and there Lady Mountbatten paused to chat with one of the lads. She happened upon the shortest and youngest Cadet present, and as fate would have it, in real life the scruffiest, sloppiest, least organised but perhaps nicest kid at the school. True to form, the boy's boots were an absolute disaster. Everyone's truly shone, but not his.

"Hummm", eventually concluded Lady Mountbatten, "and did you polish your boots this morning?"

"No, Ma'am", meekly confessed the blushing youngster.

"Pity", mused the grand lady gently, as she proceeded down the ranks, "quite a pity!" No further comment.

Truly an unforgettable moment, particularly for the mortified Cadet.

Prince Alexis Troubetzkoy, Toronto.

DUKE AND DUCHESS OF YORK

In 1987 the Duke and Duchess of York were in Toronto, the first time for the Duchess, for their official welcome to the Province of Ontario

When the official welcome ended and the Duke and Duchess of York began their walkabout, I was sitting in my wheelchair along the west sidewalk at Queen's Park. The Duke made his way along that side. I got up when he came towards me and stood in front of my wheelchair. He spoke to me first and said "Is that bouquet for me?" I said he could certainly have it but I thought the Duchess might appreciate it more. The Duchess was on the other side of the walk talking to people there. The Duke called out, "Sarah! Come here!" and she came over – fast. There had been some newspaper stories about how the Duchess had been kicking up her heels a bit and I wanted to say something that was both sympathetic and cautionary – like a grandmother in fact. But it is hard to do that in a few seconds and she began by saying "Aren't I lucky to have married him?" I made an appropriate reply and then had my opportunity. "We do appreciate so much the fact that you are a great help to our Queen" I told her. "Isn't she lovely?" the Duchess replied, showing genuine admiration for Her Majesty.

Loveday Cadenhead, Toronto.

♔ ♔ ♔

I got in line for the Duke and Duchess of York. When I was in line I thought about what I was going to say. I thought maybe I should say, "Welcome to Canada". They finally came near me. She was very pretty, she had red hair. The Duke wore a sailor uniform. The Duchess shook my hand, I forgot what to say. She said, "I like your hat". Then I remembered my hat. I forgot to take off my hat and by this time the white was dirty, I mean dirty. It was really hot but it was worthwhile. I will always remember that day.

Alex Calley (age 9), Ottawa.

♔ ♔ ♔

A few short words scrawled on a pink notepad are proof enough for Morris and Jacqueline Shumiatcher that Prince Andrew and Sarah are also just ordinary folk.

The Duke and Duchess of York took a break from their whirlwind schedule Tuesday afternoon [25 July 1989] to visit the prominent Regina lawyer's home at 2520 College Avenue.

The royal sojourn, suggested by the Premier, Hon. Grant Devine was considered a private afternoon retreat.

Soon after some "lively" discussion, centring on Shumiatcher's extensive Inuit art collection, Shumiatcher and his wife ducked out for afternoon tea with the royal staff.

Andrew and Sarah, with the exception of her lady-in-waiting and his personal aide, were left to themselves in the picturesque, two-storey house to do as they pleased.

"Yes. We left them the run of the house", Shumiatcher joked in an interview Tuesday night.

When the Shumiatchers returned home about 8 p.m., after the

royal couple had already left for London, there it was, inconspicuously left on a ledge near the Inuit sculptures - the words etched, and forever preserved, in royal ink.

"25, July. 17:50 hrs.", read a short note written out on a tiny pink notepad and signed simply, Andrew, "Jim Randle (sic) – your vet – rang to ask about Maxi's leg".

Shumiatcher said Maxi, a nine-year-old dancing poodle, was operated on several weeks ago by Regina veterinarian Jim Randall. She had a broken leg, but is nearly healed now.

"Well look at this Jacquie. Now this is a story", Shumiatcher said to his wife, after stumbling across the note while explaining some of the Inuit sculptures to reporters.

"They both knew about Maxi and her condition. We introduced her to them right away. It just proves they are real common people with real common sense."

Randall, contacted late Tuesday night, was completely flabbergasted with the news he had spoken to Andrew.

"You're kidding, right?", he said in disbelief. "It sounded like I was talking to an older man, and I noticed the British accent. But I had no idea who I was really talking to.

"I guess I had a thrill of a lifetime and didn't even know it."

Randall said the Duke tried not to let on that the Schumiatchers were away.

"I only wanted him to pass on the message that I had called. At first, I didn't even think he was paying attention to what I was saying. Maybe I woke him up from a nap."

The Duke and Duchess, while catching their breath after a long day of public appearances, also took some time out to eat a light meal of sausage rolls, fruit, sandwiches and tea.

Shumiatcher said his door is always open to the royals.

"Next time, they can bring the whole family. Even grandma, too", he said, referring to the popular Queen Mother.

Kevin Blevins, Regina Leader-Post.

3

A PEOPLE'S KING

While Canada had seen numerous royal tours prior to 1939, including those by future sovereigns, no reigning sovereign had previously set foot in the country. This made the 1939 tour constitutionally as well as emotionally memorable and a watershed in Canadian history. The tour marked the culmination of Canada's evolution to full independence confirmed by the Statute of Westminster in 1931, and was a sequel to Their Majesties' coronation in 1937.

War was an increasing threat in Europe however as the King and Queen arrived in Canada and would come within a few short months. While it provided a sombre backdrop to a colourful and exhilarating six weeks, it could not detract from the event but rather made it more poignant.

The whole country turned out for the tour, beginning with Quebec City, which defied the pessimists, who had doubts about the welcome that would be offered by French-Canadians, and set a standard for loyalty and warmth the rest of the country was challenged to match. It is not surprising then that this tour produced some of the best loved anecdotes and reflections on the Monarchy.

Sailing to Canada for their historic 1939 tour, the King and Queen were delayed by heavy fog. Queen Elizabeth wrote to Queen Mary from the Empress of Australia.

We very nearly hit a berg the day before yesterday, and the poor Captain was nearly demented because some kind cheerful people kept on reminding him that it was about here that the *Titantic* was struck, & just about the same date!

John W. Wheeler-Bennett, King George VI His Life and Reign.

♛ ♛ ♛

Speech of welcome by the Prime Minister, Rt Hon. W.L. Mackenzie King to King George VI and Queen Elizabeth, Quebec City, 17 May 1939.

Today all the Privy Councillors of Canada have been invited to meet Your Majesty, including members of both present and past Administrations. It is the first occasion since Confederation, apart from the meetings of the first Cabinet, on which all members of the King's Privy Council for Canada have been brought together. It is the first time in the history of Canada that the Ministers of the Crown, and, indeed, all members of Your Majesty's Privy Council, have been assembled in the presence of their King. Today as never before the Throne has become the centre of our national life.

Here, too, you will be in the heart of a family which is your own – a family of men and women of varied stock and race and thought, who in free association with other members of the Commonwealth, but equally in their own way, are working out their national destiny. We would have Your Majesties feel that in coming from the old land to the new you have but left one home to come to another; that we are all of one household . . . In your daily lives we see exemplified the things we value most – faith in God; concern for human well-being; consecration to the public service; delight in the simple joys of home and family life. Greater than our sense of the splendour of your state is our affection for two young people who bear in so high a spirit a responsibility unparalleled in the world.

Their Majesties' Visit to Canada, The United States And Newfoundland: A Chronological Record of the Speeches and Broadcast Addresses etc.

♛ ♛ ♛

C'est en français que l'honorable Maurice Duplessis, premier ministre, souhaite la bienvenue à nos souverains; c'est en français aussi que répond Georges VI; et, chose étonnante, mais qui a été bien remarquée,

Sa Majesté parle un français clair, net, sans aucun accent étranger et paraît s'exprimer avec plus de facilité que dans sa propre langue maternelle.

Eugène Achard, Georges VI, Roi Du Canada.

♛ ♛ ♛

Having joined the Non-Permanent Active Militia in 1936, shortly after Hitler's Nazis had crossed the Rhine, I was serving with the Royal Montreal Regiment. My Company Commander, Major Robert Mitchell, M.C., a grizzled veteran of World War I, was well known for both his competence as an officer of Field Rank *and* for his staccato commands.

On this particular Sunday morning Their Majesties were scheduled to proceed, accompanied by the Mayor and various dignitaries, from Church Services to a wreath-laying ceremony. My regiment had been posted on either side of the gently-sloping Côte-St-Luc in Westmount, a surburb of Montreal, quite close to the cenotaph.

Because of the dearth of soldiers, each militiaman was placed at five-pace intervals — and the regiment, accordingly, was stretched out over a considerable distance — much too far for the Commanding Officer's commands to be heard by all ranks over the anticipated sounds of the marching bands, the clippety-clop of the horses' hooves and the cheers of the bystanders anxious to demonstrate their affection for their beloved King and Queen.

Because of this, the decision had been reached to have the various commands issued by each individual Company Commander upon the approach of the Royal entourage. Finally, as the sounds of the oncoming cavalacade intensified, Major Mitchell, resplendent in his scarlet tunic and in his best parade-ground manner, shouted out: " Company — Atten — SHUN! Company — Slope — ARMS! Company — PREsent ARMS!"

At the precise instant of issuing the executive word-of-command "ARMS!" — and as he whipped his sword to the "Present" — his lower denture flew out of his mouth and landed squarely in the middle of the road over which the cavalcade was to pass. And so it happened — the hundreds of mounted horsemen, the marching bands and the Royal horse-drawn landau bearing Their Majesties — all passed directly over the denture lying in their path — and nary a hoof nor a foot stepped on the mouthpiece.

Exhibiting the same sang-froid as ever, when the last of the parade had passed, Major Mitchell, having first brought the Company to the position of "Order Arms", called out loudly: "Sergeant-Major — Denture RecovER!" and, at this point, as the hapless Warrant Officer scampered to retrieve the mouthpiece, the entire Company broke up in merriment

— and in relief that everything had gone off so perfectly in spite of such a totally unplanned yet hilarious incident.

Major G. B. Dionne, (Ret'd), Kelowna, British Columbia.

♛ ♛ ♛

At a moment during the banquet [given in honour of the King and Queen by the City of Montreal at the Hotel Windsor, 18 May 1939] when conversation had flagged somewhat, the King, noticing that Mayor Houde was fidgeting with a piece of paper in his hand, asked, "What's that you have there, Mr Mayor?"– "Sir, it is a list of what I must do and not do this evening." – "May I see it?" – "Yes, Sir, but it will make me blush."

Mayor Houde then handed over the notes, which were in French; and, with the Queen listening, the King read them out, item by item, with great amusement. "Did you do this?" the King asked. – "Yes, Your Majesty, I did." – "But you certainly did not do this", said the King, enjoying himself completely. – "I am afraid you have got me there, Sir", admitted Mayor Houde, "but if you wish, I shall start it over again". And Their Majesties broke into hearty laughter, as did also the Mayor, who added, "I wish I could talk, but I am supposed to wait until I am spoken to". –" Mr Mayor, I am your King, and I order you to tell me what you like." And so, leaving formality aside, Mr Houde kept the royal guests in continuous merriment with his witty sallies and droll stories, some in French and some in English.

Before the dessert, the Mayor proposed the King's and the Queen's health in the two languages.

Outside, in Dominion Square, the immense crowd which had been waiting for over an hour and a half started to chant out, "We want the King! We want the Queen!" Soon the chant grew into a roar so persistent that word of the popular wish was brought to Mayor Houde. He mentioned it to the King, and most graciously Their Majesties agreed at once to make an appearance in public. Accompanied by Mayor Houde and the Prime Minister, they made their way to the balcony overlooking the square. In this vast place was a solid mass of humanity – perhaps a hundred thousand spectators. The instant they appeared on the flood-lighted balcony, the King and Queen were greeted with wave after wave of cheers from that waiting sea of humanity.

On leaving the balcony, the royal party returned to the banquet hall for dessert and coffee, but this time took their seats in the Rose Room in order to give the overflow guests the benefit of their presence. During the dinner, between selections by a string orchestra, English and French folk-songs were sung by a French-Canadian quartet. After a last song in the Rose Room, Mayor Houde rose and said, "Her Majesty has told me that she is teaching Princess Elizabeth and Margaret Rose our song: 'Alouette'. I shall ask the quartet to sing it for the Queen". They did, with great success. The King beat time to the tune, the Queen hummed it with the necessary gestures to nose, head, and arms, and soon the whole company was singing it. The Queen then asked Mayor Houde what was the standing of 'Alouette' in Quebec. 'If Your Majesty allows me to be frank', replied the Mayor, 'I'll say it is our national anthem after midnight'.

Gustave Lanctôt, The Royal Tour of King George VI and Queen Elizabeth in Canada and the United States of America 1939.

♛ ♛ ♛

The story of the mayor and his chain of office seems to be one of those royal anecdotes that are regularly recycled. There is little doubt however that it originated in the 1939 tour. Added proof of this is given in Elizabeth Longford's The Oxford Book of Royal Anecdotes where the tale is related in connection with the 1947 tour of the Union of South Africa by King George VI, Queen Elizabeth and the Princesses Elizabeth and Margaret. H. Willis-O'Connor on the other hand in Inside Ottawa says that the Mayor of Ottawa was the mayor in question and that it was his wife who made the gaffe when asked by the King why her husband did not wear his chain of office.

Their favourite standing joke on the [1947] tour was the question asked of each other whenever they were in gala dress: "Is this a special occasion?" It appears that during the King's tour of Canada before the war, he once noticed that a local mayor was not wearing a mayoral chain. The King, planning to present him with one, asked him whether or not he had a chain.

"Oh, yes, Sir", answered the mayor. "I have."

"But I notice you are not wearing it", said the King.

"O", explained the mayor, "but I only wear it on special occasions".

Elizabeth Longford, The Oxford Book of Royal Anecdotes

♛ ♛ ♛

Their Majesties left [the station on their arrival in Ottawa, 19 May 1939] in the state landau, escorted by the Princess Louise Dragoon Guards, a brave company in their plumed helmets, smart uniforms and riding splendid mounts. Behind the escort came the senior members of Their Majesties' Staff, followed by Lord and Lady Tweedsmuir and myself.

It was a wonderful drive, every foot of the seven miles to

Government House. The people lining the route gave their young King and Queen such a welcome that I felt a lump in my throat. Later, the Marquese Rossi-Longhi, Italian Consul General, said to my wife:

"I never saw anything like it! Indeed, I would not have believed it unless I had seen it – I mean the voluntary cheering on the part of the people! There was love of these simple young monarchs in every voice. I even saw people so deeply stirred that they were weeping".

Willis-O'Connnor and Madge Macbeth,
Inside Government House.

♛ ♛ ♛

The King's address to Parliament, Ottawa, 19 May 1939.

Honourable Members of the Senate and Members of the House of Commons, I thank you sincerely for your addresses received on my arrival in Quebec. The Queen and I deeply appreciate your loyal and affectionate messages. I am very happy that my visit to Canada affords me an opportunity of meeting in Parliament assembled the members of both Houses. No ceremony could more completely symbolise the free and equal association of the nations of our Commonwealth. As my father said on the occasion of his Silver Jubilee, the unity of the British Empire is no longer expressed by the supremacy of the time-honoured Parliament that sits at Westminster. It finds expression today in the free association of nations enjoying common principles of government and a common attachment to the ideals of peace and freedom, bound together by common allegiance to the Crown.

The Queen and I have been deeply touched by the warmth of the welcome accorded us since our arrival in Canada. We are greatly looking forward to visiting each of the Provinces . . . It is my earnest hope that my present visit may give my Canadian people a deeper conception of their unity as a nation . . . may the Blessing of Divine Providence rest upon your labours, and upon my realm of Canada.

Their Majesties' Visit to Canada, The United States and Newfoundland: A Chronological Record of the Speeches and Broadcast Addresses etc.

♛ ♛ ♛

In a letter to his sister, Lord Tweedsmuir, the Governor General, described the scene when the King unveiled the National War Memorial in Ottawa, 21 May, 1939:

The Queen told me that she must go down among the troops, meaning the six or seven thousand veterans. I said it was worth risking it, and sure enough the King and Queen and Susie and I disappeared in that vast mob!–simply swallowed up. The police could not get near us. I was quite happy about it because the veterans kept admirable order. It was really extraordinarily touching; old Scotsmen weeping and talking about Angus. One old fellow said to me, 'Ay, man, if Hitler could see this!' It was a wonderful proof of what a people's king means.

Janet Adam Smith, John Buchan.

♛ ♛ ♛

The state banquet that had caused the Cabinet such long and painful deliberations gave rise to two rather amusing incidents. The banquet took place in the Ball Room at Government House, and never had the room looked so impressive. The Canadian Artillery Association plate adorned the walls and some of it was on the horseshoe table. Red tulips glowered under the light of numerous candelabra and the space in front of Their Majesties was banked with a mass of purple Darwin tulips. The flowers were arranged by Joan Pape, Her Excellency's lady-in-waiting, who had special gifts in that direction. She could make a handful of weeds look like a sumptuous bunch of orchids.

After dinner, Their Majesties' Staff and that of the Governor General lined up on one side of the "long room", and the guests stood opposite. Then the Royal procession entered and the King and Queen shook hands all around. The latter wore a pink tulle crinoline gown lightly spangled with blue and gold. We were told that she had brought out the Koh-i-nor diamond but I did not see it.

She did not wear gloves.

The King walked with the Queen on his right arm and His Excellency had Lady Tweedsmuir at his left. Or maybe it was the other way round. Anyway, conformity was lacking and Eric Mackenzie (who had nothing to do with Court etiquette) took it as a personal affront and worked himself into a temper by the time we got to the table. Then the second incident occurred. The Pipers were five minutes late.

Not that it really mattered. They entered with the dessert, piped all around the table, then from the end of the room where they stood still. Once again around the table, and that was all there was to it. But Eric seemed likely to have a stroke.

No toast was drunk for the King himself was host.

Perhaps I should add a third incident. When dinner was finished and Their Majesties were waiting in the saloon for the reception guests to arrive, Lord Airlie was in the small group surrounding the King and Queen. He was carrying his wand of office, and while chatting Queen Elizabeth took it from him and began to play with it.

He protested in some such words as these:

"Ma'am, hadn't you better let me have my wand again? It's not safe with you. You broke it once before. Remember?"

"Yes", said the King, with his gentle, affectionate smile. "I remember, because I had to pay for it".

Willis-O'Connor and Madge Macbeth,
Inside Government House.

♛ ♛ ♛

In May 1939 the journalist Lotta Dempsey was in St Michael's Hospital, Toronto, having a baby.

At that time King George VI and Queen Elizabeth, now the Queen Mother, were . . . visiting Toronto. It was about the only royal tour here I failed to cover, over a period of thirty years or more. We all listened on the radio to the plummy, breathless purple prose with which announcers of the day described such events. Shortly thereafter Sister Vicentia glided in, wreathed in smiles. She carried a bouquet of tiny white rosebuds, pulled one out, and put it on my bed.

"Her Majesty has been sending bouquets presented to her to patients in hospitals", she said, "and asked that this one especially be distributed to mothers of new babies, in memory of her visit and her own loved little daughters, Lillibet and Margaret Rose". (I pressed my rosebud in one of the books on my bedstead and have the faded, dried petals still.)

One evening, many, many years later, I called a taxi at the *Star*, gathered presents I had for my son on his birthday, and prepared to journey the distance to dinner with him, his wife, and small daughter in the suburbs.

The young cabbie was curt to the point of surliness and began driving at a dangerous speed, swerving in and out of traffic. To slow him down without appearing cross, I said, "Hi, there, could you take it a little easier? I've got some presents here for my son's birthday today, and a couple are breakable".

There was a dull "huh" from the front, then, "It's my birthday today, too, and nobody's giving me any presents". The tone was bitter.

I started to talk, as much to keep him from charging ahead madly as anything, and discovered he was separated, broke, and generally fed up with life. I asked his age. "Why, you're the same age as my son", I said. "Where were you born?"

"Toronto."

Then, "What hospital?"

"St Michael's."

I said excitedly, "then your mother and I were there giving birth to our sons, at the same time. She must have told you . . ."

He broke in acidly, "She didn't have a chance to tell me anything.

She died when I was a baby. My father married again, a woman with kids of her own. I had a rough time. Anyway, you wouldn't have seen my mother. She'd have been in a public ward. We were very poor".

I leaned forward and touched his shoulder. "Would you like to know what it was like the day you were born? My son liked to hear it".

He relaxed a little and nodded. I described the scene, the crowds in the streets because of the royal visit and my concern that the doctor wouldn't make it through the traffic jams. And I told him how Dr O'Leary, who probably delivered his mother, too, and had a wooden leg, said not to worry, he'd hop through waving if necessary. By the time I got to the Queen's bouquet of white rosebuds we had arrived at my son's house. The driver pulled to a stop, turned around, and gazed at me with a strange and wondering look in the hard, narrowed eyes I had seen watching in the rear-view mirror. He said, very, very softly, "Then that's what the dried-up petals are in my mother's Bible. I always wondered".

Lotta Dempsey, No Life for a Lady

♛ ♛ ♛

When Her Majesty Queen Elizabeth The Queen Mother came to Canada in the spring of 1939 with King George VI, she had to come from the Provincial Parliament Buildings in Queen's Park to Hart House at the University of Toronto where the University of Toronto contingent of the Canadian Officer Training Corps was the guard of honour. Most of them were like me – superficially trained because we had only done a couple of hours a week for four or five months of military training as university students. Consequently, the guard looked very clean, shined and well-pressed but their drill was of doubtful quality.

Similarly, the guard commander was equally uncertain. He kept glancing toward the Parliament buildings and suddenly he gave the command, "University of Toronto contingent, Royal Salute! Present arms!" which we raggedly executed and were shocked to see a police constable riding a motorcycle with a lady in a big white hat like the Queen's sitting in the sidecar. As it turned out, the lady for whom the Royal Salute was given was the wife of the Mayor of Toronto who had twisted her ankle!

The guard commander, the guard, the policeman and the Mayor's wife were all so discomfitted that they didn't know what to do until she had been half carried out of sight. Only then did the guard commander remember that we were all standing there at the Royal Salute and he gave the quavering order, "Order arms!" Everything picked up a few minutes later when the Queen and the royal retinue appeared. "The Royal Salute! Present arms!" was again commanded and because of the extra practice it was reasonably well done.

In the three years that I served in the Toronto contingent of the COTC I received no pay whatever, save and except a special cheque for the Royal Parade which was made out in the poetry, "Pay to Gentleman Cadet B.J. Legge the sum of $1.10". Not bad for three years of service and like all students at the time I was so hard up that I had to cash it instead of framing it for posterity.

Major-General Bruce Jarvis Legge, Toronto.

♛ ♛ ♛

Prime Minister Mackenzie King accompanied the King and Queen on the trip and followed them around wherever they went like a faithful terrier. His presence at Mayor [of Winnipeg, John] Queen's party was too much for the commentator who began bravely by saying, "The King, the Queen and Mr King have now arrived at the city hall and Mr Queen is on the steps to meet them. The King is now shaking hands with Mr Queen, and now the Queen is shaking hands with Mr Queen, and now Mr King is shaking hands with Mr Queen. And now the King and Mr Queen and the Queen and Mr King are moving into the reception hall. Now the King and Mr Quing, I mean Mr Keen and the Quing . . . I'm sorry I mean . . ." He floundered on becoming more and more confused and desperate while Their Majesties' loyal subjects in front of the legislative Buildings rocked with laughter.

Florence Bird, Anne Francis:
An Autobiography.

♛ ♛ ♛

There were two receptions [in Winnipeg] that day [24 May 1939]. The first was given by the Mayor, John Queen, and the second by the Premier, John Bracken. We were invited to attend the Premier's party and were required to sit on funeral-parlour chairs in front of the Legislative Buildings for two hours until the King and Queen arrived and went into the rotunda. We had been instructed to get all dolled up for the occasion, the men in striped trousers, cutaway coats and top hats, the women in short cocktail dresses. It was raining so hard that I wore a raincoat over my best dress and held an umbrella over my best hat. J.B. refused to share the umbrella because he didn't think it wide enough for two people. He maintained an unflinching calm while the rain pelted down on the silk hat he had not worn since our wedding – and has never worn again. After we had sat there for half an hour I could see the topper was slowly warping and crinkling and looked as if it might melt away. When I cried out at the spectacle, J.B. said with solemnity, "A plugged hat is the least I can sacrifice for king and country".

Florence Bird, Anne Francis:
An Autobiography.

♛ ♛ ♛

The King's Victoria Day broadcast in 1939 was made from Government House, Winnipeg and carried to all parts of the Empire-Commonwealth. The King concluded by addressing young people.

It is true – and I deplore it deeply – that the skies are overcast in more than one quarter at the present time. Do not on that account lose heart. Life is a great adventure, and everyone of you can be a pioneer, blazing by thought and service a trail to better things. Hold fast to all that is just and of good repute in the heritage which your fathers have left you, but strive also to improve and equalise that heritage for all men and women in the years to come. Remember, too, that the key to all true progress lies in faith, hope and love. May God give you their support, and may God help them to prevail.

Their Majesties' Visit to Canada, The United States And Newfoundland: A Chronological Record of the Speeches and Broadcast Addresses etc.

♛ ♛ ♛

During that tour across Canada in 1939, the royal couple visited Saskatchewan and were seen by thousands. A state dinner was held at Government House. The Honourable Archie McNab was Lieutenant-Governor in residence. In bidding farewell to the royal couple, Mr McNab said "Come again soon and next time bring the kids!" That remark was indicative of the friendly atmosphere the King and Queen Elizabeth were able to engender.

Address by Hon. Frederick Johnson, former Lieutenant-governor of Saskatchewan, at a service of thanksgiving for the 90th birthday of Queen Elizabeth The Queen Mother, St Mary's Church, Regina, 9 September 1990.

♛ ♛ ♛

The procession then drove to the lookout of the British Pacific Properties, fifteen hundred feet above sea level. Their Majesties alighted to enjoy the beautiful sight of Vancouver proudly spreading along English Bay and Burrard Inlet. Indicating the points of interest, Mayor Telford remarked: 'You will have to go a long way to see a more beautiful sight'. The King replied: 'We have come a long way to see it. I have never seen anything like it'.

Then Their Majesties, with Mayor and Mrs Telford, proceeded to the 'Guest Cottage', where they were greeted by Major P.A. Curry. Attended by a maid, the Queen poured tea. At one point the Queen remarked to Major Curry: 'If I wanted to buy a home here, could I do so?'

"By all means", said Major Curry. After a pause, the Queen added: "This seems to me the place to live".

Gustave Lanctôt, The Royal Tour of King George VI and Queen Elizabeth in Canada and the United States of America 1939

♛ ♛ ♛

Retired lawyer Theodore DuMoulin, now 80, was on guard with his militia unit on a street in downtown Vancouver. This meant, says DuMoulin, "that there was nobody between us and the royal vehicle. The Queen was terrific, she just bowled everyone over she was so beautiful". And at the regimental armouries after the procession, an officer mentioned raising a toast to the Queen and suggested the traditional gesture of smashing the glasses into the fireplace, so no lesser person could be toasted from the same vessels. This would have been too expensive, remembers DuMoulin, so they found a large glass bowl in the kitchen, and following the loyal toast "several of us shoved it out the window with the most shattering crash you ever heard in your life".

Tom Suddon, Toronto, from an interview with Mr DuMoulin in July 1989.

♛ ♛ ♛

When the King and Queen came to Stratford
Everyone felt at once
How heavy the Crown must be.
The Mayor shook hands with their Majesties
And everyone presentable was presented
And those who weren't have resented
It, and will
To their dying day.
Everyone had almost a religious experience
When the King and Queen came to visit us
(I wonder what they felt!)
And hydrants flowed water in the gutters
All day.
People put quarters on the railway tracks
So as to get squashed by the Royal Train
And some people up the line at Shakespeare
Stayed in Shakespeare, just in case –
They did stop too,
While thousands in Stratford
Didn't even see them

Because the Engineer didn't slow down
Enough in time.
And although,
But although we didn't see them in any way
(I didn't even catch the glimpse
The teacher who was taller did
Of a gracious pink figure)
I'll remember it to my dying day.

James Reaney, Poems.

♛ ♛ ♛

As a fourteen-year-old patrol leader in the Boy Scouts I was given the privilege of being a member of the Guard of Honour at the entrance to Civic Stadium in Hamilton during the 1939 Royal Tour. As the big Lincoln Continental passed within ten feet of my dipped flag (a salute given only to royalty), the Queen, waving and smiling, stared right at me, and winked.

Wow! I couldn't smile back as we were told to stare straight ahead and remain expressionless. But unknown to anyone, my body swelled up and completely covered in goose pimples. It still happens when I see her on T.V.

Ronald C. Kearns, Collingwood, Ont.

♛ ♛ ♛

On 15 June [1939], Their Majesties sailed for home from Halifax in the liner Empress of Britain. They bade an affectionate farewell to their Canadian subjects, whose hearts they had captured and whose tears were falling. As the King said later: 'I nearly cried at the end of my last speech in Canada, everyone round me was crying'. The tour has been of immense psychological importance to them and they realised it as such. "This has made us", they both said on more than one occasion.

The North American tour was indeed a climacteric in the King's life. It had taken him out of himself, had opened up for him wider horizons and introduced him to new ideas. It marked the end of his apprenticeship as a monarch, and gave him self-confidence and assurance. No longer was he over-awed by the magnitude of his responsibility, the greatness of his office and the burden of its traditions. Now at least, he felt, he could stand on his own feet and trust his own judgement.

John W. Wheeler-Bennett, King George VI,
His Life and Reign.

♛ ♛ ♛

Queen Elizabeth, the Queen Mother, Consort of King George VI. Toronto speech, 29 June 1979.

Forty years ago, when I first came here with the King – a few months before the outbreak of war – I did fall in love with Canada, and my affection has grown with each succeeding visit.

Empire Club Addresses.

♛ ♛ ♛

From coast to coast your people with elation
Have given you gladly all their loyal praise;
At last fades out the welcome of a nation,
And into story pass these noble days.
Taken from our hearts these faithful words in parting,
When from our shore the lordly ship goes free,
While the last, swift Canadian gulls are darting,
And the long harbour opens to the sea.
May many a lovely memory never perish,
Scenes of our glorious country; far above
All the land's peerless beauty may you cherish
The crowning glory of a people's love.
While the King reigns from ocean unto ocean,
Under the wide, serene Canadian sky,
We whom you leave in ageless, deep devotion,
Can never to our Sovereign say goodbye.
Master of life whose power is never sleeping
In the dark void or in the hearts of men,
Hold them, our King and Queen, safe in Thy keeping
And bring them to their western realm again.
And for their Canada be watchful ever,
Grant us this boon if there be one alone,
To do our part in high and pure endeavour
To build a peaceful Empire round the throne.

Duncan Campbell Scott, "Farewell To Their Majesties", a poem broadcast by the CBC on the occasion of the departure of King George VI and Queen Elizabeth from Canada, 15 June 1939, and quoted from The Circle of Affection, and Other Pieces in Prose and Verse.

4

ELIZABETH II OF CANADA

The number of Canadian firsts recorded in the reign of Queen Elizabeth II is staggering. The Queen was the first of the Royal Family to fly to Canada (1951), the first to adopt officially the title "Queen (or King) of Canada" (1953), the first to open Parliament (1957), the first to adopt a distinctive Canadian personal banner (1962). The Queen has also reigned longer than any sovereign since Confederation and is one of the longest reigning monarchs in our thousand year history back to Saxon days.

The Queen is the first monarch to come regularly to Canada. Whereas prior to her accession a reigning monarch had only come to Canada once, the Queen comes about every second year on average. Modern instant communications have also meant that the Queen is fully conversant with events happening in her Canadian realm at all times.

Fluently bilingual and familiar through her travels with all parts of Canada, the Queen brings the passion of personal involvement in and commitment to Canada together with the objectivity of partial detachment in commenting on Canadian concerns. And through all her interventions in Canadian life the observation of her biographer, Lady Longford, shines through, "[The Queen] considers herself Canadian, not just Queen of Canada".

Majestic goings-on affect different royal-plummage watchers in different ways. Like many reporters who have trailed the Royals over long years, I always start out a sceptic. "This time, it won't work. I'll pierce the mystique." I never do. I've seen such seasoned and worldly press photographers as the *Toronto Star*'s Reg Innell turn cow-eyed and putty-voiced when summoned to converse with Queen Elizabeth [II]. I remember Dorothy Kilgallen, the New York-based syndicated columnist and once acerbic chronicler of peccadillos of the high, the mighty, and the wealthy of many lands, standing behind me in a line to be received by the Queen and Prince Philip. It was in Ottawa, and she had twitted some of us over our colonial obeisance to just another woman. "I'll give her some plain talk", she said, eyes snapping.

I turned back to watch the writer, after my own usual tongue-tied moments. She just stood there, mumbled something as she took the Queen's hand, looked into those cool, clear blue eyes, and curtsied. Her "Yes, Your Majesty", and "No, Ma'am", were as respectful as any I have heard. She walked away, bemused. "What is it?" she asked. "What does it do to you?"

Lotta Dempsey, No Life for a Lady.

This is a story of royal duty performed with spunk and a spirit of adventure. When in November of 1951 the then Princess Elizabeth and Prince Philip visited Montreal, they stayed at the venerable old Windsor Hotel across from the square at the corner of Peel and Dorchester. It stood in traditional old-world splendour with its gray sandstone facade, tall windows, high ceilings and archaic plumbing.

After an exhausting whirlwind tour of the city, the royal couple retired to their suite at the Windsor. Hundreds of enthusiastic well wishers thronged the flood-lit square calling for the Princess and the Prince to appear. Some had climbed onto tree branches. Some sang "O Canada". Suddenly there was movement behind the ornamental balcony above the main entrance and the crowd roared when the young couple waved from this postage stamp-sized enclosure. The performance was later repeated to everybody's delight.

Ten years later my company hosted a dinner for a small group of overseas dignitaries. The venue was the royal suite at the Windsor Hotel. The hotel manager confirmed that Princess Elizabeth and Prince Philip had stayed here. It turned out I was the only person present who had been in the square that night. When I recalled the excitement the hotel manager asked if anybody would be interested to see how the young couple got onto the balcony. Our curiosity was aroused. We followed him down a rather narrow hallway into the most private room of the establishment which was adorned with a cast iron water tank near the high ceiling, a long chain with porcelain handle and a lid-less convenience. Behind it was a tall sliding window. A board had covered the seat, it was explained to us, somebody had pushed up the window then assisted the royal couple to climb up and out and, *voilà*, there, in the square below, had been the wildly cheering multitude of their loyal subjects.

Harry Liedtke, Kelowna, British Columbia.

♛ ♛ ♛

Her Majesty was on her first visit to Canada, when she was still Princess Elizabeth and had but lately wed her handsome prince. I was on my first royal tour. That was in October of 1951. I was assigned by *The Globe and Mail*, where I was then a columnist, with two of the finest journalists I know and the most delightful friends and confrères – Kenneth MacTaggart and Bruce West. Around the office we became known as the trembling trio, on this as on many other assignments together because of our constant apprehension when away from home base. I have found this a characteristic of most of the best journalists I know. It's like the skilled actor's stage fright or the great athlete's last-minute sense of panic.

This was to be a month-long tour, most of it by special train, with press cars coupled to the royal coaches. We were to stay with it all the way, from Quebec City to Victoria. We met the Princess all right at Dorval airport, Montreal, and she emerged from the stratocruiser, the Canopus, looking wan and frightened . . .

In Ottawa, Mayor Charlotte Whitton, a firm royalist and fiery little feminist, had arranged for a royal flotilla to sweep along the Ottawa River, so that citizens and thousands of tourists flocking in could line the banks and get a good view of the young couple. Charlotte was in the gaily bedecked flagship with the Royals and their attendants and (I later learned) a radio on which they listened to the running story of their processional cruise. It was a cold November day, and a stranger site than this strung-out, meandering, and motley aquatic parade would be hard to imagine.

The boat for the national press tour party (always a snobbish distinction from local scribes we picked up and dropped regionally) was one of the many power boats of ancient vintage commandeered for the occasion, its pilot a young and obviously inexperienced sailor. No sooner had we coughed and staggered into the procession than there were several clearly dying spasms of the rusty engine and we were adrift midstream. With a Herculean effort on some time-warped oars, men of the party painfully pulled us near shore at a point where a small wooden fisherman's clubhouse offered a rickety wharf.

Twin hazards menaced my next move. First, my eager-beaver instinct to reach the clubhouse and to telephone ahead of the others and file from notes I had made earlier. So near-sighted Dempsey outsmarted herself, because the second hazard was that unbeknownst to this Torontonian, the Eddy Match Company up river spewed shavings from its product into the water. At the spot where we were attempting to land, they had eddied into a curve in the shoreline, forming a sawdusty mat. Thinking it was solid ground, I leapt from the boat while others waited for it to touch the wharf. Alas, it was not solid ground. Slowly I sank up to my shoulders in icy murk. An empty beer carton surfaced as I went down.

The roars of laughter from my fellow reporters, richly deserved, soon were stifled in concern, and I was hauled out, cold and singularly unlovely, webbed in matchwood and slime. A photographer of a rival paper snapped the sorry scene, but graciously did not send it in, due to my venomous threats. My friends hauled me to the clubhouse, where a fire was burning in a pot-bellied stove. There was no telephone, and so the others rushed off. A lone attendant tried to comfort me – none of the waiting taxis would take me in, quite wisely – and in a few moments a man who had been duck hunting drove up. Grudgingly he agreed to return me to the Lord Elgin hotel. My heavy camel's-hair coat was crusted and sopping, and my plight was not eased by the fact that the hunter had covered his back seat with canvas (the only reason, I imagine, he agreed to a Samaritan gesture), strewn with the corpses of a dozen or so bloody wild fowl. By the time we arrived at the hotel, where he dropped me and fled, I looked like something out of a nightmare (or an Alice Cooper performance today). As I slunk through the lobby, the cluster of built-in paper-reading sitters who always populate such places glanced up, startled. Some hastily decamped. Several disappeared into the recesses of the beer parlour.

In the elevator, the operator stopped and stared as I stood, dripping water forming a pool at my feet. I said crossly, "Well, get me to the tenth floor. Have you never seen a wet woman before?"

Back in the gala procession, I was to find later, the Princess and Duke of Edinburgh heard this startling break in the flow of glowing description of golden-agers, some in wheelchairs, waving handkerchiefs; Scouts and Guides, Wolf Cubs and Brownies, marching ashore in pace with the onward convoy; crowds shouting and waving flags . . . "We interrupt this broadcast to report that one of the women reporters covering the royal flotilla from the press boat has just fallen into the river. This is all we have for now. So back to the Princess, who is looking radiant (I imagine she was stung with the stiff winter wind) . . .

And there the radio people left me. But word soon spread, and Bruce West and Kenneth MacTaggart, off on other aspects of the tour, rushed to a telephone. When they found me in my room, just emerging from a shower and wondering what I would wear to a reception later in the day (I had another dress, but just one coat), Bruce said, "But Lotie, you had a cold already".

"Well, it's gone now", I answered. And oddly it was.

Next scene: a borrowed coat and word at the reception that the Princess would like to speak with me. She had ascertained the identity of the soggy reporter. Having learned from me that I was all right, Her Royal Highness allowed herself a mischievous smile. "Will you be coming with us on the whole tour, Miss Dempsey?" she asked, innocently.

"Yes, Your Highness, I will."

She appraised me for a moment. "Might you not find it rather strenuous?" There were smiles all around, and so I gathered my courage and said, knowing she was new to our big and often astonishing country, "Not any more strenuous, ma'am, if I may be so bold as to suggest it, than you will".

I'm sure, if she later reflected on this observation, she would agree with it – after going down the mines, up the mountains, through the dust, and under the tent flaps of Canada. Not to mention unintentional confrontations with this reporter, such as the time I tripped, curtsying, and fell on Prince Philip. But that, later.

There was a postscript to my misadventure in the Ottawa River. My husband, who had been sitting at home reading while my small son listened to the tour report on the radio, was roused from his preoccupation with the child's remark, "Daddy, they say one of the women reporters just fell off the press boat into the river".

Without taking his eyes from his newspaper, my husband replied, "That will be your mother".

Lotta Dempsey, No Life for a Lady.

♛ ♛ ♛

In 1951, the present Queen Elizabeth II, then Princess Elizabeth, visited Canada, including Prince Edward Island. The staff at the Experimental Farm in Charlottetown were royally amused during a part of her tour of the Farm. She was guided into almost every part of the Farm's work including the pig barn. In conversation with her, the man in charge of the pigs, Lloyd Yeo, said to her "It seems very strange to be taking a princess into a pig barn and showing her around". She responded in her beautiful sophisticated British accent, "Oh, I don't mind at all. We have pigs over home".

The staff could have easily believed that her father was a farmer.

Christine Shaw, Winnipeg, formerly of Prince Edward Island.

♛ ♛ ♛

In St Boniface [in 1951], nine-year-old Robert Painchaud presented the Princess with a golden rose on behalf of the boys and girls of St Boniface. The rose had been made by the Oblate Sisters of St Boniface and had nine petals, on each of which was a picture of one of the nine members of the Royal Family: the King and Queen, the Queen Mother (Queen Mary), Princess Elizabeth, Princess Margaret, the Duke of Edinburgh, Princess Alice of Greece (mother of the Duke of Edinburgh), Prince Charles and Princess Anne.

Larry Krotz, Royal Visits, a Manitoba album/ Visites royales, un album–souvenir du Manitoba.

♛ ♛ ♛

I remember once in Fort William (now Thunder Bay) at the Lakehead, a cold Sunday morning in November. They [the Princess and Duke] had not been married long, but were guardedly formal in public. They were booked in one floor of the hotel, and I had made an appointment to see the Princess's lady-in-waiting that morning to get some data on her British-designed wardrobe . . . We lingered longer than either of us had intended, and as I went to leave, the Princess and Prince Philip emerged from their suite down the hall. To shut the door would catch their attention, and my informant was not happy to have the royal pair know she had received me on this hallowed ground. So she put her finger to her lips, and we stood just inside, but able to watch them. As they moved along, Philip looked at Elizabeth's feet, then pointed with an accusatory cluck-cluck. She had no rubbers or overshoes, and so he left her there and went back. Unaware she was being observed, Elizabeth toed and heeled along the corridor like a happy child, swinging her purse and with eyes so full of love I felt guilty for watching. Philip came up, knelt, and put the rubbers on with the grace with which I later saw him pledge his fealty to his monarch at the coronation. Then they moved, arms entwined, to the elevator.

Lotta Dempsey, No Life for a Lady.

♛ ♛ ♛

As Princess at the Guildhall, London, 19 November 1951, following her first Canadian tour.

I would like [the Canadian people] to know once again that they have placed in our hearts a love for their country and its people which will never grow cold.

♛ ♛ ♛

Each time we [the Queen and Lotta Dempsey] would meet, the matter of my falling in the Ottawa River on her first Canadian visit would come up. Last time she said to me, mischievously, "I've wondered, Miss Dempsey, did you fall or were you pushed by fellow reporters?"

"No, ma'am. I was rushing to file my copy in the telegraph office."

She interrupted, "And you filed it in the river instead".

Lotta Dempsey, No Life for a Lady.

♛ ♛ ♛

Ken MacTaggart, Bruce West, and I, then columnists and staffers at *The Globe and Mail*, had been sent to London for the coronation of Queen Elizabeth II. Bruce arrived early to do "atmosphere" stories. Kenny and I came on a later plane. At the airport, Bruce met us very excited about the beauty of London, preening herself with flags, lights, flowers, and lavish street decorations of all kinds to mark this great event. "We'll check you in quickly", he said, "and then you must come out and see London by moonlight. We may never get another night like this". (He was right. It rained steadily afterwards.)

So when we got to the hotel, Kenny said, "You register and Bruce and I will gather up the luggage so that we can get out as soon as possible". It was now close to midnight.

I went to the desk, and what appeared a very proper and stiff-lipped English lady handed me cards. "You have reservations for Miss Dempsey and Mr MacTaggart from Toronto, Canada", I said, pleasantly, "and we asked for three adjoining rooms. I'd like to be in the middle, if possible". She looked not only disapproving but also astounded. I'm not really the sexy type, and both gentlemen looked highly respectable. So I thought further explanation was forthcoming and, as Ken and Bruce were telling me to hurry up, I added, "You see, we have to have access to each other at all hours of the day and night; me, especially with both of them".

This was quite true, as always with a "team" of writers from one newspaper working on an out-of-town assignment. Time is of the essence, and there is need to report areas or events covered or unusual news items discovered, so that we wouldn't overwrite one another. This was expected at home base, as the speed with which copy must be moved might mean different editors would handle individual stories. I grabbed the keys, we threw our things in the rooms, and we were out and about London town.

Throughout my stay in London the proper Englishwoman at the Cumberland Hotel kept a rather wary eye on me, nodding without smiling whenever I came to get my key. We were on close to a 24-hour routine, and I took time out only to call my husband in Toronto and beg him to get over in time for Coronation Day. He had been planning to join me afterwards, and we were going to Italy and France on holiday. "You must come", I said. "It's just something you've got to share. I've never seen anything so exciting or so beautiful. Flowers are arriving from countries around the world and the streets are like great gardens, and the lights and decorations, and the people . . ."

He got the last seat on the last plane out of Toronto, bringing, as requested, some "stay awake" pills by prescription from our doctor. None of us on the *Globe* team was accustomed to taking anything like this; but we had decided the pressures of work, especially as the big day drew near, might require special medication to keep us on our toes.

As usual, I had forgotten one small item – to mention to the woman at the desk that I was married or that my married name was Fisher. On news jobs I always register as Miss Dempsey to save confusion when calls are being returned and for the home office making contact. I had also neglected to mention that my husband would be arriving to share my room. The one in the middle.

As so often happened, Dick arrived to check in, and there was no answer in my room. So he simply explained, "My name is Fisher. I'll be sharing Miss Dempsey's room". Now the woman was really shaken to her marrow. As I say, she hadn't considered me the ménage-à-trois type, but a foursome?

Dick sighed, explained the situation, and finally achieved access.

Lotta Dempsey, No Life for a Lady.

Monday, October 14 [1957], began with a cabinet meeting at 10 a.m. in the dining-room of Government House. It is the only time in my experience when a cabinet meeting was ever held at Government House in Ottawa. But of much greater importance was the fact that it was attended by the Queen. Her father, King George VI, had attended a meeting of the Canadian cabinet in Ottawa in 1939 during the course of the royal visit of that spring. Ministers were attired in morning dress for this great occasion. Her Majesty sat at the head of the long table with Mr Diefenbaker on her right and I next to him. It had been arranged that after formal presentation of the ministers one item of business would be transacted. I was given the unique honour of presenting it to Her Majesty. It involved only giving approval to some new regulations relating to old-age pensions. In addressing the Queen, I explained briefly the statutory authority for the regulations and the effect they would have when brought into force. I then said that I had the honour on behalf of cabinet to advise that they be approved. She listened very attentively to the explanation. What she was about to do might be a unique historic act; she did not, however, treat it as a mere formality, but a serious exercise of royal power on the advice of her constitutional advisers, and she applied her mind and attention to every word. The Prime Minister then requested her to sign the order-in-council. In a gentle voice she replied, "I usually just initial these orders-in-council". She then proceeded to pen the initials "E.R." to this simple but unique document which thereupon found its permanent place in the records of Her Majesty's Privy Council for Canada.

The cabinet had desired to pay Prince Philip some Canadian honour. That morning on the advice of the cabinet conveyed through the Prime Minister he was sworn in as a member of Her Majesty's Privy Council for Canada. He took the oath of allegiance to his royal wife as Queen of Canada, then the Privy Council oath, in the same form as my colleagues and I had taken it on June 21. The initials P.C. have followed His Royal Highness's name and honours since.

Donald Fleming, So Very Near: The Political Memoirs Of The Honourable Donald M. Fleming.

♛ ♛ ♛

When the Queen was at Government House in 1957, a telegram came from Halifax that a trawler had caught a very large sturgeon. The owners, who understood, correctly, that sturgeons by tradition belong to the Crown, asked in their message whether they might send it on to Her Majesty. The answer was yes, and this 350-pound monster was brought by air from Nova Scotia. An A.D.C. came into the drawing-room to say that the sturgeon had arrived, and the Queen said she would like to see it; so she, Prince Philip, and I and some others went downstairs through the kitchens, where an astonished staff looked on, to the service centre where the ugly brute lay in the crate in which he had travelled.

Vincent Massey, What's Past Is Prologue.

♛ ♛ ♛

The Queen and Prince Philip were to visit, and there we stood on the wide, blue-domed prairie. A ridiculous little strip of carpet was laid out, leading to a flat square surrounded by fields of wild grasses and low stunted bush, and a sweet scent of wolf willow was on the wind. First a speck, then a winged shape, then a plane coming down until we could see the little royal standard blowing on the bow. The door opened, a colonel snapped to salute, and out stepped the smiling, perfectly groomed young woman whose ancestors had led troops in the Wars of the Roses and welcomed Wellington back from the Battle of Waterloo. Somehow it was to shiver, as though old and sceptred ghosts stirred in the new, raw country.

But here, too, is the untouchable, unreachable status. Like it or not, you can't buy or work or build your way to queenhood or kinghood. No amount of image-making, entrepreneuring, tub-thumping, or manipulation can give you access to the throne of the Monarch of the Commonwealth.

Lotta Dempsey, No Life for a Lady.

♛ ♛ ♛

In 1959, when she was six years old, Marjorie Chochinov (née Lum), along with her parents, Alec and Foon Lok Lum, was chosen to present a vase as a gift to Queen Elizabeth II.

I think the presentation made us feel more Canadian. I remember going back to school and feeling, I've done something important, you can't tease me or make fun of me, I did something important that none of you did. For the Chinese community to be asked to make a presentation meant that we were worthwhile citizens.

Larry Krotz, Royal Visits, a Manitoba album/ Visites royales, un album–souvenir du Manitoba.

♛ ♛ ♛

1967 tour by the Queen

Once I saw her [the Queen] laugh so unexpectedly and so infectiously that we all roared. It was at the opening of Expo in 1967 in Montreal. The Queen had had some very iffy times in Montreal and Quebec City, during a tour when the French-English problem was very tense, and there were complaints that people couldn't see enough of her because of a close guard, in addition to the usual flock of officials. Thus she suddenly decided to ride the overhead open cable car so that everyone could see her. By lucky accident, I was with an aide when the decision came and followed him to sit in the little car just behind the Royals. Away we went, swooping over the cheering throngs.

There had been no announcement, and so people in the buildings were not aware of the adventure. At one point, the car track swung right beside a roof-top restaurant in one of the Fair buildings. We happened to stop there for a minute. A man and woman were eating hot dogs and drinking pop at a window table, and the woman looked up to see the face of her Queen smiling on the other side of the glass. She choked and shook the man's arm. He waved a hand at her "joke" when you could see she was telling him of the sight outside. Then he turned and looked, blanched, dropped his paper cup, jumped to attention and, so help me, curtsied. That was when the Queen roared – and waved with a regal nod.

Lotta Dempsey, No Life for a Lady.

♛ ♛ ♛

CBC Radio's Expo 67 broadcast host Bob MacGregor came up with what he considers his worst ever pun during the visit of Her Majesty and Prince Philip to the Expo site.

The royal couple took an unscheduled ride on the fair's minirail sightseeing trains leaving the CBC broadcasters to fill about twenty minutes on the full cross-Canada network.

MacGregor described his broadcast location which was within just a few feet of the Royal Yacht Britannia. "Usually, broadcasters are not allowed to be so close to the Britannia" he explained, "but in our case, Britannia Waives the Rules".

Bob MacGregor.

♛ ♛ ♛

The 1970 royal tour took Her Majesty on an unprecedented visit to the Northwest Territories.

At the Resolute village, the Eskimo people were almost distressingly shy, unable to dare a close approach to the Queen or Princess. Alone, the Queen stepped forward to the first of the groups of people who had arranged themselves in a horseshoe of small tableaux, each demonstrating some traditional Eskimo skills or craft. As she left, Her Majesty turned and spoke to all of these people: "Thank you" she said, "for being just the way you are".

Pat Carney, Tiara and Atigi: Northwest Territories 1970 Centennial – The Royal Tour.

♛ ♛ ♛

One lady was inadvertently pushed aside by the security guards. "She's my Queen, too" she said, her eyes brimming with tears. Commissioner Hodgson spoke to her gently. "Madame" he said, "if my mother were here, I would present her to Her Majesty. But my mother is in Vancouver. Will you be my mother for the day, so I can present you to the Queen?" She accepted, and he did, and she cried.

Pat Carney, Tiara and Atigi: Northwest Territories 1970 Centennial – The Royal Tour.

♛ ♛ ♛

To complement the festivities of the Northwest Territories centennial [in 1970] and to honour Her Majesty The Queen's visit, the Canadian Eskimo Arts Council arranged the first Northwest Territories competition/exhibition of Eskimo carvings. The exhibition opened in Yellowknife in the Franklyn High School at the time of the visit. Her Majesty graciously consented to be present at the opening.

My husband John was chairman of the exhibition and James Houston was a member. Not being members of the royal party, Alice Houston and I, dressed in our best, waited outside the school to cheer the royals on their departure from the exhibition. A small crowd gathered, perhaps two deep, from the steps where the royal party were to emerge. In Yellowknife, at 11 a.m. everyone who could write, could work. Most did.

Her Majesty and the Duke of Edinburgh appeared and were whisked off in their limousine (flown up from Edmonton for the occasion). The Prince of Wales and Princess Anne appeared. They stood on the school steps, relaxed and smiling in the coolish northern sunshine. A woman, standing close to the steps took a picture of the royal brother and sister. She was using a polaroid camera. Prince Charles asked if he could watch the photograph emerge. The woman gave him the camera. He watched with interest, took a good look at the print and returned the camera to its owner with easy warm thanks.

The aspect of the incident which caught our attention was that the woman, who had come out to see the Queen of Canada, had *her hair in curlers.* The occasion was probably the only time in this person's life when she could expect to see four members of the Royal Family in her home town. In Yellowknife crowds are small. She could not have expected to go unnoticed. *Hair in curlers to meet the Queen!* I was embarrassed for her.

Later at lunch our hostess, Barbara Ballantyne enlightened me. "You don't understand" she said, "in Yellowknife, having your hair in curlers at 11 a.m. is a sign of prestige—you can afford not to have a job".

Mary Robertson, Woodlawn, Ontario.

♛ ♛ ♛

In Thompson, Manitoba a six-year-old member of the Thompson Brownie troop was reported to say, "I'd sooner have the Queen than Santa Claus".

Royal Visits, a Manitoba album/
Visites royales, un album–souvenir du Manitoba.

♛ ♛ ♛

When I was in the navy I was picked to be in a guard of honour for a visit from Queen Elizabeth II. Being an ardent monarchist, I was in my glory. For three weeks we were on the parade square six hours every day. My uniform was brand new, dry cleaned three times in a row. My forage cap was totally spotless and remained so. My rifle was torn apart and cleaned with Q-tips and a magnifying glass. I took the time to blue every part. My boots were the pride of the squad. I could smile and see the reflection in them. The final day came about. We all put our white gloves on, gave a final polish to our chrome bayonets and off we marched. We first had an inspection by our warrant officer who was meticulous in looking for loose threads, scuffed boots, smudged buttons and finger prints on forage caps. I passed with a "you will do!" At that point my heart was in my mouth as I stood there. Two minutes later the motorcade came down the road. At this time fate dealt a cruel blow! A passing seagull decided to dislodge his yesterday's meal from twenty feet in the air. His or her marksmanship was perfect. I was hit from the waist up to my neck and part of my shoulder. The warrant officer who watched everything saw this, pointed at me and said "You, out!" I was replaced just as the motorcade came through the gate. I was so close yet so far. I didn't quite get to meet the Queen but to this day I can't look at a seagull without wanting to pick up a rock.

Tim Reid, Port Clements, B.C.

♛ ♛ ♛

In 1977 when the Queen was in Canada as part of her Silver Jubilee Tour, one of the official dinners given in Ottawa was to honour young achievers of under thirty. A Montreal artist of my acquaintance received an invitation and duly, but not too enthusiastically, went along. The guests were given their instructions for the reception following the dinner, being told that Her Majesty would retire from the banquet room for a short while, during which time the guests would move into the ballroom. At a given moment Her Majesty would join her guests and spend a short while moving around the room to speak to individuals.

At first my friend was a little blasé about the whole thing, even sitting below the Queen herself in the banquet room, but when Her Majesty actually appeared on the same level as the guests and began moving among them he became more interested and decided that he very much wanted to speak to her. With this in mind he carefully watched the pattern of Her Majesty's movement down the room and positioned himself where he was certain she would eventually arrive.

I was told on good authority that at this point an official tugged at my friend's arm, saying: "There is someone here who would like to meet you". My friend turned to see Prime Minister Pierre Trudeau standing near waiting for my friend to be presented. My friend was uninterested. He said a quick hello, with the thought, he told me later, that he could probably see the Prime Minister at any time whereas this would probably be the only occasion on which he would be able to speak to Her Majesty.

His calculations were correct, in a short time the Queen was standing before him. He immediately subjected her to the most detailed examination, so that he could later describe to us every aspect of her dress and jewels. While this was taking place he was also answering a question which Her Majesty had made the mistake of asking him, and that was what his materials were. My friend, having forgotten that it was not appropriate to answer in more than a monosyllable or two, then proceeded to astonish Her Majesty with a long dissertation on the make-up, properties, uses and idiosyncrasies of pigmented fibreglass reinforced polyester resin.

At the end of this Her Majesty, dazed and glassy-eyed, and with, no doubt, visions of Michaelangelo in her head, remarked politely: "Oh, so it is not all just chipping away then!"

Patricia Smith, Duncan, British Columbia.

♛ ♛ ♛

Some months ago [October 1977] I had the great honour and privilege of hosting a luncheon for Her Majesty the Queen, in Ottawa. At that luncheon we had about six hundred leaders of the ethnocultural communities from right across Canada. I had the privilege at that time of proposing a toast and making a few comments. I spoke of the Canadians of many cultural backgrounds and of the contribution they have made to this country. I also spoke of the nature of our policy of multiculturalism.

Her Majesty showed herself, through her questioning of me, to be quite impressed with this new policy, and felt that it had a tremendous application in Great Britain, in relationship to the cultural plurality that exists in that country. She asked me if I would be prepared to meet with some of her advisers, some of her Cabinet in England, to discuss the policy. She also indicated that the policy, although it has not been formalised within the Commonwealth, really is very much like the Commonwealth itself which is made up of many lands, cultures, languages, traditions and histories. In a way, the Commonwealth is probably a precursor of the policy of multiculturalism. It brings together various nations under one common banner and one common allegiance to work together in human terms to create understanding among themselves, to work together for their own economic, social and cultural benefit and to share that example with the rest of the world.

The Empire Club of Canada: Addresses 1977–1978, "Multiculturalism, National Unity and the Canadian Economy", Hon. Norman Cafik, speech to The Empire Club of Canada, 8 April 1978.

♛ ♛ ♛

It was one of those gorgeous sunny autumn Saturdays in Ottawa - Queen Elizabeth II and Prince Philip were here on a tour. Frank and I heard on the CBC Radio that the royal couple would be driving through the Experimental Farm that day so we decided to venture forth for a peek. Going to the Farm could be much quieter than the crowds downtown.

That morning happened to be the day our scruffy dog, an airedale terrier, had been booked in to the groomers so we picked him up at the stated time and headed out. We got the car parked and walked out to the road to wait - not many people at all. Eventually the advance party came by. Then the open car with the royals in it. The car was actually going slowly - perhaps they were ahead of schedule or were just enjoying the fall scenery and the lovely day.

We saw them coming along - the Queen looked lovely and was waving as royalty does. Suddenly, her whole face lit up - there was a gorgeous smile and even her nose crinkled up! She slyly nudged Prince Philip and delicately pointed out our dog. You could barely see her hand move to point him out. They both beamed at us and the car went on. I have read that the Queen is a dog fancier. Of course the dog looked his best as he had just been hand-pulled, bathed and all brushed up. I think airedales are most popular in the British Isles. We never forgot the incident and used to tell old Bakov (now deceased) that he was recognised by royalty.

Miriam McManus, Nepean.

♛ ♛ ♛

On one occasion a tour came about as a result of popular demand.

Newfoundland's Declaration of Loyalty in 1977 was born of two things: the federal government's continued refusal to allow a royal visit to Newfoundland; and the marvellous feeling Newfoundland gave me by proudly proclaiming itself "England's oldest colony" and its people "the Queen's most loyal subjects". The Queen was part of their lives, a member of the family whose picture hung in many houses. Newfoundlanders proudly showed carefully kept souvenirs of royal occasions. If the Queen could not come to Newfoundland, then we would take Newfoundlanders to the Queen!

The Declaration of Loyalty's heading proclaimed in old English lettering, "We the undersigned Newfoundlanders wish to reaffirm our loyalty to Your Majesty on the occasion of Your Silver Jubilee". I circulated the Declaration to the small outport post offices all around the island, as places most people went, and the response was immediate and overwhelming. Each day the postman, who got as much of a thrill as I did as the signatures came in, would say: "We only got about 2,000 today"; or, "Today it must be at least five or six thousand!" And it was!

Deadlines came and went. After the first 100,000, Mrs Nellie Carter started circulating Declarations to the churches and Judge Jack White to the schools. The numbers grew and grew, and I damaged my eyes counting and double checking to make sure nobody was counted twice. For instance, Dorothy Wyatt, Mayor of St John's, signed four different ones. And still they came, many accompanied by heart warming notes of good wishes and thanks for being allowed the honour of signing.

Finally, over 400,000 signatures, assembled and bound in red, white and blue binders, showing such place names as Heart's Content, Little Heart's Ease, Witless Bay, Blow Me Down, Flower's Cove, Grand Bruit, were ready and packaged and bound with a gold cord, for their journey to Her Majesty. With them went the map of Newfoundland on which I had underlined each place name as signatures from it came in.

The box weighing fifty-five pounds went to England with Newfoundland's 166th Regiment of the Royal Artillery, who were going to London for a reunion. It actually travelled under the pilot's seat and Harold Lake delivered it to my daughter waiting at Heathrow. As the plane took off, I remarked to Elva Clark, Secretary of the Monarchist League, that the plane looked heavy. "No wonder" she said, "there go 400,000 Newfoundlanders!"

In London, my daughter Persephone drove the precious box in her ancient Mini car to Buckingham Palace, to be delivered to the Queen at Balmoral the next day. A week later the following letter arrived from the the Queen's Private Secretary, Sir Philip Moore.

Balmoral Castle
1 October 1977

Dear Lady Barlow,

I am commanded by The Queen to thank you most warmly for the Declaration of Loyalty from the people of Newfoundland which was delivered to Buckingham Palace by Mrs Robert E. Booth. The Queen was greatly touched by this expression of loyalty on the occasion of her Silver Jubilee by so many of the people of Newfoundland and I should be grateful if you would express Her Majesty's deep appreciation to all concerned.

Yours sincerely,
Philip Moore

As a result of the Declaration containing signatures of four fifths of the population of Newfoundland, Ottawa could no longer avoid a royal visit to Newfoundland. The Queen came to her Newfoundland people the following year, 1978. Her staff said that they had never seen her so relaxed and happy anywhere. But she knew how Newfoundland felt. The first paragraph of her speech at the dinner in her honour in St John's went

"I have been very touched by the sentiments you have expressed on behalf of Newfoundland and Labrador and I want you all to know that I was deeply moved by the Declaration of Loyalty signed by four hundred thousand Newfoundlanders in my Silver Jubilee Year".

When I was presented to the Queen by the Lieutenant-Governor, Hon. Gordon Winter, who mentioned the Declaration, she remarked "It was a jolly good effort". In fact it was the most rewarding thing I have ever done. Later when chatting with her Private Secretary, (who had been looking for me and said it took the Queen to point me out), he told me he would let me know where and when I might expect a Labrador puppy bred by the Queen (we had talked of dogs).

The following year an enchanting three months old puppy arrived, knowing very well who bred him. His name – Sandringham! He had television interviews, where he barked back at the puppy on the monitoring TV set who barked back at him, and he chewed through some important wires. His picture made the first page of the *Daily News*, and the front of the *Labrador Quarterly* in the United States. Over the years he has been interviewed in the garden several times, once making the evening news ahead of the arrival of the royal yacht *Britannia*.

Prince Charles said to "watch him or he will get above himself!" He walked with Prince Philip in 1989 as the Prince took exercise at St John's Airport while his plane refueled. He has been painted four times by the American artist John Weiss, and one of the pair of miniatures was given to the Queen who was pleased. Each year his picture goes on a Christmas card to the Queen so that she can see how he does, and her current private secretary, Sir William Heseltine, wrote: "It would be nice to have so few doubts about one's position in the universe". Sandringham just grins and you can't help grinning back. God bless him!

Jacqueline Barlow (Lady Barlow), St John's.

♛ ♛ ♛

Comment in a speech by the Queen in Edmonton, 2 August 1978.

I am getting to know our country rather well.

♛ ♛ ♛

For the Queen, in particular – a woman of natural reserve and not given to effusive expression – each arrival in Canada is a welcome into the bosom of an overseas family; each departure something of a domestic wrench even after the days, sometimes weeks, of unveiling plaques, planting trees, making speeches, shaking hands, receiving bouquets and the endless, endless travelling which makes privileged routine no less routine for being privileged. The strength of that familial pull is constantly expressed by the Queen's insistence that she is, after all, Queen of a family called Canada. But now and again, she lets slip a more personal comment – much more telling because of its comparative rarity and spontaneity – as she did on leaving west-coast America for British Columbia in March 1983: "'We're going home to Canada tomorrow'."

Trevor Hall, Royal Canada.

♛ ♛ ♛

My husband was waiting at the front of the crowd as the Queen came to visit Nanaimo in the Royal Yacht in 1983. A smaller boat had brought her to shore and as she stepped onto the dock she was met by Mayor Ney. The band, which was assembled some distance away, was supposed to play the Royal Anthem at that moment. There was silence. Everyone waited and waited. Finally, "God Save the Queen" rang out. After it had finished, Mayor Ney was heard to apologise to the Queen for the delay, and then remarked in a humorous tone "That must have been organised by the city council!".

Zena Dumbleton, Ladysmith, British Columbia.

♛ ♛ ♛

When I was a boy, I became convinced that the force that propelled my mother through each day was her belief that if she and the Queen ever met, they would become best friends. Mother believed, I thought, that what Her Majesty really wanted more than anything - more than charades at Balmoral, more than Welsh corgis on the moors, more than folk dances in Bali - was a cup of tea and a chat at our kitchen table. I settled on this notion as the only logical explanation as to why Mom was so concerned about the state of my room and my manners. It seemed to me, at the time, that you would only worry about those things if you feared the Queen herself might drop by at any moment.

It was her fantasy, not mine. More correctly, I suppose, it was my fantasy about her fantasy. Whatever. Ever since I was a teenager, whenever I face a driveway full of snow, I become my mother's son. Every drift I dig into, each bank I bear down on, I do for Her Majesty. I shovel with the certain knowledge that soon the Queen will arrive. And I shovel knowing that before she comes, a member of the royal staff will be dispatched to examine my work, to see if it is up to snuff. That is why I fuss over the edges of the banks, the angles, the smoothness, the evenness under foot. And that is why, when I have finished, I stand and survey my work with such pleasure. For me and my walk, both the form and the function of the job are important. Because they would both be important to Her Majesty.

Stuart McLean, The Morningside World of Stuart McLean.

5

ROYAL PRIVY COUNCILLOR OF CANADA

If one were to name the single member of the Royal Family, excluding monarchs, who has been the most prolific and perceptive observer of the Canadian scene, it could only be His Royal Highness Prince Philip, Duke of Edinburgh, consort of Queen Elizabeth II. The Duke has been to Canada more often than any other member of the Royal Family in history and his many private interests such as the Duke of Edinburgh's Award Scheme, the World Wildlife Fund and the Duke of Edinburgh's Study Conference have brought him to Canada and involved him in Canadian affairs in a unique way. In 1957 the Queen appointed HRH to be a member of the Queen's Privy Council for Canada, a body of which he is now one of the most senior members.

In his remarks to Canadians and observations on Canadian life the Duke has praised the country but he has also challenged it – challenged it to be what it is capable of being. An asset which His Royal Highness has made full use of is that being only distantly in line to the Throne himself, he need not take constitutional advice from the government as the Sovereign and her immediate heirs are bound by tradition to do. Thus, while the Queen speaks her own mind on issues, she would never publicly contradict her government. The Prince is bound only by his good judgement in not putting the Sovereign in an awkward constitutional position by his remarks, a judgement which cannot be faulted on its record and has yet allowed him to be controversial when necessary and always relevant.

Prince Philip's active service during World War II brought him in touch with Canadians on several important occasions. He recalled in a speech to the Canadian War Correspondents' Association that his ship was berthed alongside a Canadian destroyer at Scapa Flow.

I am afraid this situation did not last very long, but I think it may have been a good thing for the health of all concerned, as we very soon lost track of where one hangover ended and the other began.

Peter Butler, The Wit of Prince Philip.

♛ ♛ ♛

In his first major Canadian speech which was delivered to the Toronto Board of Trade, 13 October 1951, the Duke left Canadians in no doubt that he would always speak his mind to them.

I made some enquiries about commerce and science in Canada. I was overwhelmed . . . with every sort and kind of information. Reading the material I was struck by the insistence that Canada was a young country full of promise. Meaning no disrespect to the Canadian who wrote this, I beg to differ.

To me youth means the absence of history or background, a catalogue of untapped resources, and in culture and science a reliance upon others for original thought. But coupled with this statement that Canada is a young country was a series of achievements in every branch of national life which would make many an older country feel proud.

Youth means inexperience and lack of judgement, and an inability to look after one's own affairs. I do not see how these descriptions can be made to fit a nation that drove a railroad through the Rockies, developed the prairies, and exploited the vast natural resources of timber, oil and water power, and is steadily pushing the last frontier northward.

♛ ♛ ♛

Radio broadcast from Yellowknife, 10 August 1954.

Like many other boys, I read stories about Canada's North West and I have long had the ambition to see what it looked like.

♛ ♛ ♛

In Ottawa, October 1958

Just over a year ago the Queen and I attended a banquet given by the English-Speaking Union of the United States in New York. Tonight, here in Ottawa, it gives me the greatest pleasure as President of the English-Speaking Union of the Commonwealth to welcome the representatives of our sister Union. Next month, on 26 November, I hope to preside at a dinner in the Guildhall in London in honour of Vice-President Nixon. That, I think, puts the Commonwealth one up!

Peter Butler, The Wit of Prince Philip.

♛ ♛ ♛

In the same address he referred to English as

A commonly misunderstood language which can do so much to encourage the cohesion of that wide community who are fortunate enough to be in the Commonwealth, and those less fortunate people who are not members.

Applications for membership will receive sympathetic consideration.

Peter Butler, The Wit of Prince Philip.

♛ ♛ ♛

The 1959 tour by the Queen and Prince Philip included our Canadian northland. While in the Yukon Prince Philip stopped at a small Indian village and was chatting with one of the natives. "And tell me, where were you born?" asked the Prince. Without a moment of hesitation, the Indian replied: "Under a spruce tree".

Percy and Judy Buchanan, Lac du Bonnet, Manitoba.

♛ ♛ ♛

As president of the Canadian Medical Association in 1959, Prince Philip told Canadians they were not physically fit. Much criticised at the time, his speech became a landmark in the development of national awareness in this area.

There is evidence that, despite everything, people in Canada are not as fit as they might be. Four things are necessary to change this state of affairs. Proper physical education in schools, adequate recreational facilities for all ages and sections of the community, an extension of the work of youth organisations both in scope and age, and finally an organisation to publicise sports and recreational activities and to encourage people to take part in them.

♛ ♛ ♛

He began his speech to the Canadian Medical Association in typical fashion.

I cannot help feeling that I am in a very quaint situation. Here I am, a layman, at their invitation as joint President of the Canadian and British Medical Associations, the professional holy of holies of medical men.

In recent months I have frequently speculated on the reasons for this invitation without much success; but, for my part, I accepted the invitation as a great honour and privilege and as a gracious gesture on the part of the medical profession to their victims.

However, I also accepted for two reasons. In the first place it would enable me to say something nice to the medical profession as a whole, on behalf of the thousands of millions of past and present patients who owe so much to the tireless and selfless work of doctors and nurses.

Secondly it seemed a perfectly marvellous opportunity to do a little preaching to the preachers.

For once, a patient, although not currently suffering from anything more serious than nervous prostration, has got the medical profession or a sizeable part of it in Canada and the United Kingdom at his mercy.

Peter Butler, The Wit of Prince Philip.

♛ ♛ ♛

He quoted from a Canadian Medical Association Report on public health later in the same speech.

"The definitions of physical fitness are presently unsatisfactory and often are enunciated by persons who do not base their statements on scientific observations."

That last sentence must have been specially put in for my benefit.

Peter Butler, The Wit of Prince Philip.

♛ ♛ ♛

Prince Philip was not so amused the day I tripped on my own curtsy and fell against his shoulder. That can be explained, too. I was flustered when I was announced in a receiving line at Rideau Hall, the residence of the Canadian Governor General and his wife in Ottawa. I always carry a purse with open sides, so that I can reach a notebook and pencil and any needed invitations without the fuss of opening the bag. I had tucked my presentation card in there, ready to be handed to the aide for announcement. But that day, just before coming to the reception, I'd gone to the beauty salon recommended by then Secretary of State Judy LaMarsh. I was pleased with the job and asked for the hairdresser's business card so that I could telephone next time I was in Ottawa. She gave me one – it was the Martha Gray Beauty Salon or something such – and, fearing to be late, I dropped it in the open pocket.

So of course I handed the aide that card in the line-up, and he announced sonorously, "Martha Gray Beauty Salon". That's what threw me.

Lotta Dempsey, No Life for a Lady.

♛ ♛ ♛

To Canadian War Correspondents, May, 1960.

The point of my visit to Canada is to discuss the arrangements for a second Commonwealth Conference on the Human Problems of Industrial Communities, which is to be held in Canada in two years' time.

Now I cannot think of any more unsuitable subject for an after-dinner speech, even if everyone present were madly interested in it. But my orders were to tell you about this Conference, so whether you like it or not you're going to hear about it. If anyone feels like throwing tomatoes please throw them at the chap who suggested this subject.

Peter Butler, The Wit of Prince Philip.

♛ ♛ ♛

To the Duke of Edinburgh's 2nd Commonwealth Study Conference, Vancouver, June 1962.

Efficiency is merely another name for tyranny unless it is consciously achieved by the voluntary actions of groups of human beings.

Leslie Frewin, More Wit of Prince Philip.

♛ ♛ ♛

To the American and Canadian Chambers of Commerce, February, 1969.

Professionalism has now reached such a standing that, provided you are paid to comment or to criticise or even to teach, no one really cares whether you make any sense.

Leslie Frewin, More Wit of Prince Philip.

♛ ♛ ♛

When addressing the Canadian Council of Christians and Jews, Incorporated, in October, 1969.

It may be a little indelicate in this egalitarian age to suggest that it was the generations of wealthy and privileged people whose only concern was to fill their leisure, who discovered all sorts of interesting and enjoyable activities. From stamp collecting to yachting, from judo to music and from riding to poetry, it's all been tried and there is something for every taste.

Frankly, I would like to see the day when a person's work may decide their income, but where they leisure activity and their voluntary work decides their social standing.

Leslie Frewin, More Wit of Prince Philip.

♛ ♛ ♛

On the monarchy, Ottawa, 18 October 1969.

It is completely a misconception to believe that the Monarchy exists in the interests of the Monarch. It exists solely in the interests of the people. We don't come here for our health. We can think of other ways of enjoying ourselves.

♛ ♛ ♛

Prince Philip's spontaneity of response also means that he offends some of the people for some of the time. During his Canadian tour of 1969, for example, he said, when presented with a cowboy hat at Calgary Alberta, "Not another one?" He later made a public apology. Then in Vancouver he forgot the name of the new annex to the city hall that he was opening: "I declare this thing open – whatever it is". More apologies: "It was raining and I wanted to get on with it: especially as the total audience was about fifteen passing shoppers under umbrellas". The annex, however, has never recovered, and is known as the "East Thing". In Toronto he offended yet more people by suggesting that the traditional Christmas broadcast to the Commonwealth should be dressed up and called "The Queen Show".

Denis Judd, Prince Philip.

♛ ♛ ♛

At the Royal Agricultural Winter Fair, Toronto.

Perhaps if they introduced polo I might come again, provided I'm not made to ride a pony made entirely of butter [referring to a horse sculpted entirely of butter].

We are much given to using that cliché about the 'have' and the 'have-not' nations, but people seldom specify what it is exactly which some have and some have not. If it refers to the material comforts and gadgets, then the world is destined to be divided a very long time because by no stretch of the world's resources can every nation enjoy the same material standard of existence as North America today. Just imagine the traffic problem alone!

Leslie Frewin, More Wit of Prince Philip.

♛ ♛ ♛

Explaining Canada to Americans on the TV/radio show "Meet The Press", Washington, 8 November 1969.

I think Canada is in a totally different situation [from Australia and New Zealand]. As you know, it has the added difficulty of having the state of Quebec, or the province of Quebec, which is French-speaking and Roman Catholic, and really in a sense different in many respects from the rest of Canada. And this is the thing which up until recently was wholly a Canadian problem, and really, I think that the Canadians had got this well under control. At the moment it is not well under control.

Leslie Frewin, More Wit of Prince Philip.

♛ ♛ ♛

The Queen came to Duncan in 1971 to lay the foundation stone of the new library. She and Prince Philip were chatting to various dignitaries who were lined up in a three-sides-of-a square formation. On one side were the men of the Royal Canadian Legion and on the other the Ladies Auxiliary. When Prince Philip got to the ladies (close to where I was standing so that I could overhear), he did a sort of double take, looked back across the square at the men he had just inspected, and, with a twinkle in his eye, asked one of the ladies, "What's the matter. Aren't you speaking?" This caused quite a titter among the ranks. The men, who were still standing rigidly at attention, had twigged that the giggle had concerned them, because of Prince Philip's backward glance, and one could see they were bursting to find out what all the giggling was about - but they had to wait till later.

Zena Dumbleton, Ladysmith, British Columbia.

♛ ♛ ♛

Many years ago when my children were very young, Queen Elizabeth II and Prince Philip had a brief stop-over in Chilliwack. They were travelling on the Royal Train so at the station a small raised platform had been built where the dignitaries of the city were waiting to greet the Queen and the Prince.

All went as scheduled and the Queen was invited to sit at a small table to sign the city guest-book. But there was no pen. Suddenly Prince Philip turned towards my two oldest children who were right at the edge of the platform. He pointed his finger and said, "Who snitched the pen?" The crowd burst into laughter and a big round of applause for Philip followed. A lady in the crowd produced a pen and Philip saved the day - a day to remember for two now forty and forty-three years old "kids".

Margaret Snell.

♛ ♛ ♛

In St John's at the beginning of the 1978 royal tour there was the usual reception for the media. When John Aimers, Dominion Chairman and Founder of The Monarchist League of Canada, was presented to the Duke of Edinburgh as the representative of *Monarchy Canada*, the League's magazine, His Royal Highness remarked,

"Competition, eh!"

♛ ♛ ♛

A March visit to St John's, 1989.

His Royal Highness presented gold awards in the Green Room at Government House to twelve recipients from the province. "Did you hit anything?" the Duke asked one achiever who had told him that one of his activities had been rocketry.

Monarchy Canada.

6

KINGS AND QUEENS OF CANADA

As the Duke of Edinburgh has noted, Canada is often thought of and referred to as a young country, and in some ways it is. But at 124 years of age the Dominion of Canada's existence as a state makes it one of the older states in the modern world. Nor did Canadian history or the name Canada begin with Confederation. For nearly four hundred years before that there had been European discovery and settlement in Canada and thousands of years of Amerindian history before that.

While the values, traditions, ancestry and of course authority of the Canadian Monarchy go back to Europe and beyond to antiquity and pre-history when Canada's European and Aboriginal peoples were one in Eurasia, the Canadian Monarchy may be considered as beginning in 1497 with the arrival of John Cabot on behalf of King Henry VII of England.

Our Kings and Queens (English, French, British and Canadian) since 1497 have not played a mere passive role but have actively and decisively altered Canadian history by their encouragement of discovery, settlement and constitutional development. The story of Canada is to a great extent inseparable from the story of its Kings and Queens.

HENRY VII

Then, seeing the English nation only hath right unto these countries of America from the Cape of Florida northwards by the privilege of first discovery, unto which Cabot was authorised by regal authority, and set forth by the expense of our late famous King Henry the Seventh...it may greatly encourage us upon so just ground, as is our right...to prosecute effectually the full possession of those so ample and pleasant countries appertaining unto the Crown of England...

Richard Hakluyt, Hakluyt's Voyages.

FRANÇOIS I

Marguerite, Queen of Navarre, sister of King François I, writes the first story set in Canada.

The King [François I] having given the command of a small squadron to Roberval for an expedition he had resolved to make to the island of Canada, that captain intended to settle in the island, in case the air proved good, and to build towns and castles there. Every one knows what were the beginnings of this project. In order to people the country with Christians, he took with him all sorts of artisans, among whom there was one who was base enough to betray his master, so that he was near falling into the hands of the natives. But it was God's will that the conspiracy should be discovered; and so did no great harm to Captain Roberval, who had the traitor seized, intending to hang him as he deserved. He would have done so but for the wife of this wretch, who, after sharing the perils of the sea with her husband, was willing to follow his bad fortune to the end. She prevailed so far by her tears and supplications, that Roberval, both for the services she had rendered him, and from compassion for her, granted what she asked. This was, that her husband and herself should be left on a little island in the sea, inhabited only by wild beasts, with permission to take with them what was necessary for their subsistence.

The poor creatures, left alone with fierce beasts, had recourse only to God, who had always been the firm hope of the poor wife. As she had no consolation but in her God, she took with her for her preservation, her nurture, and her consolation, the New Testament, which she read incessantly. Moreover, she worked along with her husband at building a small dwelling. When the lions and the other wild beasts approached to devour them, the husband with his arquebuse, and the wife with stones, defended themselves so well, that not only the beasts durst not approach them, but even they often killed some of them which were good to eat. They subsisted for a long time on such flesh and on herbs after their bread was gone. However, in the long run, the husband could not resist the effects of such diet; besides, they drank such unwholesome water that he became greatly swollen, and died in a short while, having no other service or consolation than his wife's, who acted as his physician and his confessor; so that he passed with joy from his desert to the heavenly land. The poor woman buried him in a grave which she made as deep as she could; the beasts, however, immediately got scent of it, and came to devour the body, but the poor woman firing from her little dwelling with her arquebuse, hindered her husband's body from having such a burial. Thus living like the beasts as to her body, and like the angels as to her spirit, she passed the time in reading, contemplation, prayers, and orisons, having a cheerful and contented spirit in a body emaciated and half dead.

But He who never forsakes His own in their need, and who displays His power when all seems hopeless, did not suffer that the virtue with which this woman was endowed should be unknown to the world, but that it should be known there for His glory. After some time one of the vessels of Roberval's fleet passing before the island, those on deck saw a woman, who reminded them of the persons they had put ashore there, and they resolved to go and see in what manner God had disposed of them. The poor woman, seeing the vessel approach, went down to the sea-beach, where they found her on landing. After thanking God for their arrival, she took them to her poor little hut, and showed them on what she had subsisted during her melancholy abode there. They could never have believed it, had they not known that God can nourish His servants in a desert as at the finest banquets in the world. As she could not remain in such a place, they took her straightway with them to Rochelle; and there, when they had made known to the inhabitants the fidelity and perseverance of this woman, the ladies paid her great honour, and were glad to send their daughters to her to learn to read and write. She maintained herself for the rest of her days by that honourable profession, having no other desire than to exhort every one to love God and trust in Him, holding forth as an example the great mercy with which He had dealt towards her.

Queen Marguerite of Navarre, The Heptameron.

HENRI IV

A very persistent nobleman of Britanny, Troïlus de Mesgouez, Marquis de La Roche, actually tried to colonise Sable Island with convicts . . . In 1598, armed with a commission from Henri IV . . . [he] combed the prisons for colonists, but took only sixty with him. His curious choice of Sable Island for a colony, from all his vast domain which extended from Cape Chidley to Cape Cod, seems to have been due to a fear that the convicts would run away if they settled on the mainland – which doubtless they would have done. La Roche returned to France in October 1598, leaving his settlement to its own devices for five years. The ex-convicts hunted cattle, wolves, seal, and fox, fished, built huts from the timbers of a wrecked vessel – possibly Gilbert's – and quarrelled among themselves. La Roche having sold out, it was [Thomas] Chefdhostel who annually brought provisions to Sable Island and returned to France with peltry and fish oil. During his visit in 1603 he found only eleven colonists, all men, alive. Those he repatriated, and Henry IV summoned them into his presence. Clothed in shaggy skins and with beards of prodigious length, they looked like ancient river gods. Chefdhostel had robbed them of the peltry that they had accumulated, but the king forced him to disgorge and also gave each man a generous gift.

Samuel Eliot Morison, The European Discovery of America – The Northern Voyages A.D. 500–1600.

♛ ♛ ♛

In 1605 ten crystals [of amethyst] were sent by the first colonists in Acadia to Henri IV of France, and one from Cape Blomidon was among the French royal jewels.

Encyclopedia Canadiana, 1966.

HENRY VIII

Captain John Rut ... wrote the first letter from North America to Europe and sent it home to King Henry VIII by an English ship that was returning with a load of codfish.

L.E.F. English, Historic Newfoundland And Labrador.

ELIZABETH I

Frobisher departs on his first voyage of discovery to Canada, 1576.

The 8th day, being Friday, about 12 of the clock we weighed at Deptford and set sail all three of us, and bore down by the Court, where we shot off our ordnance and made the best show we could. Her Majesty, beholding the same, commended it, and bade us farewell with shaking her hand at us out of the window. Afterward she sent a gentleman aboard of us, who declared that Her Majesty had good liking of our doings, and thanked us for it, and also willed our Captain to come the next day to the Court to take his leave of her. The same day towards night Master Secretary Wolley came aboard of us, and declared to the company that Her Majesty had appointed him to give them charge to be obedient and diligent to their Captain and governors in all things, and wished us happy success.

Richard Hakluyt, Hakluyt's Voyages.

♛ ♛ ♛

The Queen herself named the territory [Frobisher] had found, *Meta Incognita*, the unknown bourne. It is still so called today.

Samuel Eliot Morison, The European Discovery of America – The Northern Voyages A.D. 500–1600.

JAMES I & VI

Despite the money he did make from the sale of fish and furs brought back in his ships, [Sir William] Alexander realised that he could not possibly hope to continue to finance the enterprise out of his own pocket. Early in the new year (1624), he published "An Encouragement to Colonization", a tract designed to interest and elicit the support of capitalists and arouse in them an interest in the "remunerative character, the feasibility and even the moral grandeur and Christian duty of planting colonies in the New World". The tract was aimed at the Scottish gentry whom Alexander hoped to attract as potential landholders and backers for the enterprise.

The most productive response came from King James VI himself. On October 18, 1624, James wrote the Privy Council of Scotland suggesting that, as a symbol of his support for New Scotland, he would be prepared to create an Order of Baronets of Nova Scotia. The honour of Baronet of Nova Scotia would be given to any Scot who would agree to finance and send out a certain number of settlers to Nova Scotia. The new baronet would also receive title to 30,000 acres of land in Nova Scotia. The Privy Council replied in November by issuing a proclamation setting out the terms and conditions of the award and welcoming not only Scots, but English, as well, to join the Order. Initially, there was to be a maximum of one hundred knights baronet in the Order. Moreover, they would have precedent over all knights of the realm (the Scottish realm, that is). In return, the prospective knight baronet would have to pay 1000 Scottish "merks" to Sir William Alexander, and send six men to settle on his land, fully armed, clothed and provisioned for two years, all this to be done within one year of his having accepted the title.

Peter L. McCreath and John G. Leefe, A History of Early Nova Scotia.

CHARLES I

Eight years after Baltimore vacated Ferryland [the settlement he established in Newfoundland in 1622], Sir David Kirke took over the property under charter from the Crown....Kirke, like Baltimore, was a staunch Loyalist and during the struggle between King and Parliament he offered Charles [I] a refuge at Ferryland. He fitted out a fleet of ships manned with heavy guns to make an invasion of England in conjunction with Prince Rupert of the Rhine. The plan did not eventuate, and the victorious Parliament called Kirke home to England to answer the charge of rebel. As he had not actually taken part in the war, he was allowed to return to Newfoundland, but as a precaution Oliver Cromwell sent a British fleet to take every gun out of Ferryland.

L.E.F. English, Historic Newfoundland And Labrador.

♛ ♛ ♛

The Coat of Arms of Newfoundland was granted by Charles I in 1637, some twelve years before he lost his head in the altercation with Cromwell. Its existence appears to have been forgotten until 1927 when the Newfoundland government was made aware by Sir Edgar Bowring, who was in London, that there were certain records in the College of Arms relating to the grant of a Coat of Arms to Newfoundland by King Charles I. After a thorough investigation the Coat of Arms, showing two Beothuck Indians holding up a red shield containing a white cross, two lions rampant and two unicorns rampant, surmounted by a moose (frequently mistaken for a caribou) was officially adopted by the Newfoundland government, 1 January 1928.

Paul O'Neill, A Seaport Legacy -
The Story of St John's, Newfoundland.

LOUIS XIV

In 1661 the inhabitants of New France sent Pierre Boucher to Paris to seek royal help for the settlement in Canada which was in desperate straits. This led to Quebec being made a royal province in 1663. Pierre Boucher later recalled his mission:

I had the honour of speaking to the King, who questioned me about the state of the country, of which I gave him an accurate account, and His Majesty promised me that he would help the country and take it under his protection.

♛ ♛ ♛

The expected reinforcements finally arrived; on November 9th, 1684, the whole population of Quebec, assembled at the harbour, received with joy three companies of soldiers, composed of fifty-two men each. The Bishop of Quebec [François de Laval-Montmorency] did not fail to express to the king his personal obligation and the gratitude of all: "The troops which your Majesty has sent to defend us against the Iroquois", he wrote to the king, "and the lands which you have granted us for the subsidiary church of the Lower Town, and the funds which you have allotted both to rebuild the cathedral spire and to aid in the maintenance of the priests, these are favours which oblige me to thank your Majesty, and make me hope that you will deign to continue your royal bounties to our Church and the whole colony".

A. Leblond de Brumath, Bishop Laval.

♛ ♛ ♛

Frontenac's parliament scheme of "estates" fell through. King Louis XIV struck it out. Frontenac was only King when the ice was there. With the spring ships, the rule of Louis XIV came back. Nor was ever any king more industrious or more watchful. He read all the dispatches from Canada. He made little notes on the side: "The King thinks this ... The King wishes that". And what he wished was done. Our English history, as full of the odour of prejudice as an old cask, presents us a Louis XIV as a butterfly among ladies all in silk, slowly turning to a crooked old man among ladies all in wigs. In reality Louis was industry itself, sagacity. He knew men like Colbert and Frontenac when he saw them. But with peace established, complaints from New France reached the King right and left, and Frontenac had to go.

Stephen Leacock, Leacock's Montreal.

♛ ♛ ♛

It was Louis XIV, his ministers, and their appointed officials who had harnessed the latent energies of the Canadian people, given them direction and the necessary means to pursue the aims of the French Crown in North America. Had Canada, after 1663, had to rely solely on its own resources in capital, manpower, and administrative talent it might have survived a while longer; but then again, it might not. In short, Canada in 1701 was yet a colony, a royal province of France, albeit a unique one. Although its achievements, its aspirations, its very flaws were to a considerable degree the product of the Canadian people and their environment, Canada still bore the unmistakable impress of one man, Louis XIV.

W.J. Eccles, Canada Under Louis XIV 1663–1701.

CHARLES II

Within a year, [in 1657] Thomas Temple arrived in the new world and formally took possession of Acadia. Not only did he hold a commission as governor of Nova Scotia from Cromwell, but he had somehow managed to obtain one from King Charles II, who was residing in France [in exile, waiting to be restored to the throne that had been his by law since his father's execution in 1649].

Peter McCreath and John Leefe,
A History of Early Nova Scotia.

♛ ♛ ♛

In the meantime [summer of 1665], the commissioners of the King [Charles II] of Great Britain arrived in that place, and one of them would have us go with him to New York, and the other advised us to come to England and offer ourselves to the King, which we did . . . We arrived in England at a very bad time for the plague and the wars. Being at Oxford, we went to Sir George Carteret, who spoke to his mate, who gave us good hopes that we should have a ship ready for the next spring and that the King did allow us forty shillings a week for our maintenance, and we had chambers in the town by his order, where we stayed 3 months. Afterwards the King came to London and sent us to Windsor, where we stayed the rest of the winter."

Arthur T. Adams, The Explorations of Pierre Esprit Radisson.

ANNE

Address of the four Indian 'Kings' (one of whom was the grandfather of Joseph Brant the Loyalist) presented to Queen Anne, 19 April 1710.

GREAT QUEEN!

We have undertaken a long and tedious Voyage, which none of our Predecessors could ever be prevail'd upon to undertake. The Motive that induc'd us was, that we might see our GREAT QUEEN, and relate to Her those things we thought absolutely necessary for the Good of HER and us Her Allies, on the other side the Great Water...

We were mightily rejoiced when we heard by *Anadagarjaux*, that our Great Queen had resolved to send an Army to reduce *CANADA*; from whose Mouth we readily embraced our Great Queen's Instructions; and in Token of our Friendship, we hung up the *Kettle*, and took up the *Hatchet*: ... The Reduction of *Canada* is of such Weight, that after the effecting thereof, We should have *Free Hunting* and a great Trade with Our *Great Queen's* Children: and as a Token of the Sincerity of the Six Nations, We do here, in the Name of All, present Our *Great Queen* with these BELTS of WAMPUM.

We need not urge to our *Great Queen*, more than the necessity we really labour under obliges us, that in the Case our *Great Queen* should not be mindful of us, we must, with our Families, forsake our Country and seek other Habitations, or stand Neuter; either of which will be much against our Inclinations.

Since we have been in Alliance with our *Great Queen*'s Children, we have had some knowledge of the *Saviour* of the World; and have often been importuned by the *French*, both by the insinuations of their Priests, and by Presents, to come over to their interest, but have always esteem'd them *Men of Falsehood*: But if our *Great Queen* will be pleas'd to send over some Persons to instruct us, they shall find a most hearty Welcome.

We now close all, with Hopes of our *Great Queen's* Favour, and leave it to Her Most Gracious Consideration.

Quoted in Richmond P. Bond, Queen Anne's American Kings.

♛ ♛ ♛

The Mohawk garrison, enclosing the chapel and manse [as ordered built by Queen Anne] on the south bank of the Mohawk River as it accepts the Schoharie, was completed in August of 1712 despite an Indian assault on the carpenters, and the Governor stationed at the future Fort Hunter "20 private men and an officer". In October Mr [Rev'd Thomas] Barclay went from Albany to the new church; he chose Matthew XXI. 13 as his text, following the desire of the sachems that he preach against the profanation of God's house, "some being so Impious as to make a Slaughter House of it". Nothing remains today of the original group of buildings, but the site is marked with a metal plaque and in season by the concourse of a wild flower uncommonly well-named for this history - Queen Anne's Lace...

For Queen Anne's Chapel Her Majesty sent, as was her way, a set of rich communion plate - a salver, a bason, a chalice, a paten, and two flagons - inscribed with the royal cipher and coat-of-arms and bearing the almost regal hallmark of the silversmith Francis Garthorne. The Queen also sent sumptuous furniture - an altar cloth, pulpit cloth, communion table cloth, two damask napkins, carpet for the communion table, large cushion with tassels for the pulpit, and small cushion for the desk - as well as a Holland surplice, one large Bible, two Common Prayer Books, one book of homilies, and a painting of Her Majesty's arms on canvas.

Richmond P. Bond, Queen Anne's American Kings.

♛ ♛ ♛

From Schenectady [4 July 1783], Mr [Rev'd John] Stuart hears the Plate belonging to the Mohawk Chapel is yet safe; as also the Furniture of the Reading Desk and Communion Table. The Pulpit-Covering was stolen, when the Church was plundered...The Plate and Books belonging to the Mission he has thought proper to order to be sent to Montreal, by the first safe conveyance; ...

Quoted in Charles M. Johnston, The Valley of the Six Nations.

LOUIS XV

Building the fortress of Louisbourg on Cape Breton Island was a large and expensive undertaking for the government of France. Louis XV is reported to have said one day while gazing absent-mindedly from a window in his palace in Versailles "The walls of Louisbourg; they have cost so much I should be able to see them from here".

♛ ♛ ♛

It is quite remarkable that I have never heard a man of the people blame Louis XV for the disasters that befell Canadians after the colony was left to its own resources. If anyone accused the monarch, Jean-Baptiste would retort, "Bah! It was La Pompadour who sold the country to the English!" And he would launch into abuse of the lady.

A Man of Sentiment, The Memoirs of Philippe-Joseph Aubert de Gaspé 1786-1871.

LOUIS XVI

Although Louis XVI became King after Quebec fell to the English and never reigned over Canada he was honoured by French Canadians.

Most intriguing of all [Jean Antoine] Aide-Créquy canvases is *Saint Louis tenant la couronne d'épines*, painted in 1777 to honour Louis XVI's accession to the French throne three years earlier. St Louis stands poised in a marble hall like an actor imitating royalty. The canvas hung formerly in the Ile-aux-Coudres church where Aide-Créquy was curé; it was discovered in a nearby garret during the present century, and now hangs in the episcopal palace of Chicoutimi. The theme of the painting is a subtle allegory in which the newly crowned French king becomes identified with St Louis by bearing in his hand the nails and crown of thorns that the saint normally carried, but these are simply transparent guises which do not really hide the monarch's identity. His flowing robes are like those of Louis XIV in an engraving of Rigaud's handsome portrait now in the Louvre. Aide-Créquy painted the canvas to express his continuing fealty to France and the French crown; it hung in his church as a reminder to parishioners of their racial origins, and yet he and they avoided all danger that the British could question their loyalty; if anyone raised such a question, it could be pointed out that the portrait honoured the patron saint of Ile-aux-Coudres.

A.J. Russell Harper, *Painting in Canada – A History.*

GEORGE II

In 1749 the King commissioned Edward Cornwallis to establish a settlement in Nova Scotia, a move which resulted in the founding of Halifax.

George the Second, by the Grace of God of Great Britain, France and Ireland, King, Defender of the Faith, etc. To our trusty and well-beloved, the Honourable Edward Cornwallis, Esquire, Greeting ... know you that we are reposing special trust and confidence in the prudence, courage, and loyalty of you, the said Edward Cornwallis, ... have thought it fit to constitute and appoint you, the said Edward Cornwallis, to be our Captain General, Governor in Chief in and over our Province of Nova Scotia or Acadie in America, with all the rights, members, and appurtenances whatsoever thereunto belonging, and we do hereby require and command you to do and execute all things in due manner that shall belong unto your said command ...

And for the better administration of justice, and the management of the public affairs of our said Province, we hereby give and grant unto you, the said Edward Cornwallis, full power and authority to chuse, nominate, and appoint such fitting and discreet persons as you shall either find there or carry along with you not exceeding the number of Twelve, to be of our Council in our said Province...

And we do hereby give and grant unto you full power and authority, with the advice and consent of our said Council, from time to time as need shall require, to summon and call General Assemblys of the Freeholders and Planters within your Government according to the usage of the rest of our Colonies and Plantations in America ...

And we do by these presents give and grant unto you the said Edward Cornwallis full power and authority, with advice and consent of our said Council, to erect, constitute, and establish such and so many Courts of Judicature and Publick Justice ... as you and they shall think fit and necessary.

Quoted in Norman Ward, Government In Canada.

♛ ♛ ♛

When the Duke of Newcastle, the King's whig prime minister, remarked that General James Wolfe, who had just been appointed to command the expedition of 1759 that took Quebec, was mad, King George II is reported to have replied,

"Mad, is he? If so, I hope he bites some of my generals!"

GEORGE III

King George III was always said to have a prodigious memory for faces. Apparently he only needed to see a man once (and sovereigns see a great many men) to recall him for the rest of his life. The following anecdote seems to confirm this observation.

Monsieur Charles de Lanaudière, while still serving in France, had accompanied his uncle, the Comte de Boishébert, on a diplomatic mission to the English court. Here he was presented to George III. Fifteen years after this first interview with the monarch of Great Britain, he was again presented, this time as a British subject. The king recognised him immediately and said in French, "You were formerly introduced to me as a French subject, but I am happy that today you're presented as one of mine". He then added in English, "But I forget that you speak English fluently", and continued the conversation in this language.

A Man of Sentiment, The Memoirs of Philippe-Joseph Aubert de Gaspé 1786-1871.

♛ ♛ ♛

In 1766 King George III sent a full-figure statue of himself to Montreal as a gift to his new subjects. When the statue was desecrated at the beginning of the American Revolution, the future Bishop Verreau made clear that he believed it was English-speaking Montrealers hostile to the Crown's policy of upholding the rights of French-speaking Canadiens and sympathetic to the rebels in the thirteen colonies who perpetrated the deed not French Canadians.

Le premier May 1775, - les mauvais sujets commencèrent à insulter le buste de Sa Majesté qui était sur la place de la ville à Montréal - On trouva le matin le buste barbouillé de nois avec unchapelet de patates passé dans le cou et au bout une croix de bois avec cette inscription - VOILA LE PAPE DU CANADA ET LE SOT ANGLOIS. Aussitôt le Général Guy Carleton - Gouverneur de la Province à Québec - fut instruit de l'insulte fait au buste de Sa Majesté - Les Canadiens indignés et mortifiés d'une telle insulte - à quoy ils n'attendoient pas - eurent quelques difficultés avec plusieurs anglois à ce sujet. Monsieur de Belestre - ancien capitaine et chevalier de St Louis fut frappé par un nommé Frinke, et le Sr Lepailleur par le nommé Solomon. Il y avoit quelques indices que c'étoient des Juifs et des mauvais sujets anglois qui avoient commis cette insulte - sans qu'on ait put decouvrir les criminels, - Cependant le Général Guy Carleton fit une proclamation pour découvrir les coupables.

L'Abbé H.A. Verreau, Invasion du Canada Par Les Americains en 1775.

♛ ♛ ♛

A "Petition of divers of the French inhabitants of the Province of Quebec to the King's Majesty". The petition was signed about December 1773 and presented to George III about February 1774.

Sir,

Your most obedient and faithful new subjects in the province of Canada take the liberty to prostrate themselves at the foot of your throne, in order to lay before you the sentiments of respect, affection, and obedience towards your august person, with which their hearts overflow, and to return to your Majesty their most humble thanks for your paternal care of their welfare.

Our gratitude obliges us to acknowledge, that the frightful appearances of conquest by your Majesty's victorious arms did not long continue to excit our lamentations and tears. They grew every day less and less as we gradually became more acquainted with the happiness of living under the wise regulations of the British empire. And even in the very moment of conquest, we were far from feeling the melancholy effects of restraint and captivity. For the wise and virtuous general who conquered us, being a worthy representative of the glorious sovereign who entrusted him with the command of his armies, left us in possession of our laws and customs; the free exercise of our religion was preserved to us, and afterwards were confirmed by the treaty of peace; and our own former countrymen were appointed judges of our disputes concerning civil matters. This excess of kindness towards us we shall never forget. These generous proofs of the clemency of our benign conqueror will be carefully preserved in the annals of our history; and we transmit them from generation to generation to our remotest posterity. These, Sir, are the pleasing ties by which, in the beginning of our subjection to your Majesty's government, our hearts were so strongly bound to your Majesty; ties which can never be dissolved, but which time will only strengthen and draw closer.

In the year 1764, your Majesty thought fit to put an end to the military government of this province, and to establish a civil government in its stead. And from the instant of this change we began to feel the inconveniences which resulted from the introduction of the laws of England, which till then we had been wholly unacquainted with. Our former countrymen, who till that time had been permitted to settle our civil disputes without any expense to us, were thanked for their services, and dismissed; and the militia of the province, which till then had been proud of bearing that honourable name under your Majesty's command, was laid aside. It is true indeed we were admitted to serve on juries; but at the same time we were given to understand, that there were certain obstacles that prevented our holding places under your Majesty's government. We were also told that the laws of England were to take place in the province, which, though we presume them to be wisely suited to the regulation of the mother-country for which they were made, could not be blended and applied to our customs without totally overturning our fortunes and destroying our possessions. Such have been ever since the era of that change in the government, and such are still at this time, our just causes of uneasiness and apprehension; which however we acknowledge to be rendered less alarming to us by the mildness with which your Majesty's government has been administered.

Vouchsafe, most illustrious and generous sovereign, to dissipate these fears and this uneasiness, by restoring to us our ancient laws, privileges, and customs, and to extend our province to its former boundaries. Vouchsafe to bestow your favours equally upon all your subjects in the province, without distinction! Preserve the glorious title of sovereign of a free people: a title which surely would suffer some diminution, if more than an hundred thousand new subjects of your Majesty in this province, who had submitted to your government, were to be excluded from your service, and deprived of the inestimable advantages which are enjoyed by your Majesty's ancient subjects. May heaven, propitious to our wishes and our prayers, bestow upon your Majesty a long and happy reign! May the august family of Hanover, to which we have taken the most solemn oaths of fidelity, continue to reign over us to the end of time!

We conclude by entreating your Majesty to grant us, in common with your other subjects, the rights and privileges of citizens of England. Then our fears will be removed, and we shall pass our lives in tranquility and happiness, and shall be always ready to sacrifice them for the glory of our prince and the good of our country.

We are, with the most profound submission,

Your Majesty's most obedient, most loyal,

and most faithful, subjects,

FR. SIMONNET, &c., &c.

Arthur Barriedale Keith, Speeches And Documents On British Colonial Policy 1763-1917.

♛ ♛ ♛

His determination during the American Revolution not to lose Canada.

I will never consent that in any treaty that may be concluded a single word be mentioned concerning Canada, Nova Scotia, or the Floridas, which are Colonies belonging to this country, and the more they are kept unlike the other Colonies the better.

Letter of George III to Lord North, 26 March 1778, quoted in Beckles Willson, George III As Man, Monarch And Statesman.

♛ ♛ ♛

Additional instructions received by Haldimand in mid-November 1783 about allotting lands to Loyalists.

Whereas many of Our Loyal Subjects Inhabitants of the Provinces now the United States of America, are desirous of retaining their Allegiance to Us, and of living in our Dominions, and for this purpose are disposed to take up and improve our lands in our Province of Quebec; And We being desirous to encourage our said Loyal Subjects in such their Intentions, and to testify our approbation of the loyalty to Us, &

Obedience to our Government, by alloting Lands for them in our said Province; and whereas We are also desirous of testifying our approbation of the Bravery and Loyalty of our Forces serving in our said Province, and who may be reduced there, by allowing a certain quantity of Land to each of the Non-Commissioned Officers and private Men of Our said Forces, who are inclined to become settlers therein. It is Our Will and pleasure, that immediately after you shall receive this Our Instruction, you do direct our Surveyor General of Lands for our said Province of Quebec, to admeasure & lay out such a quantity of Land as you with the advice of our Council shall deem necessary & convenient for the Settlement of our said Loyal Subjects, the Non Commissioned Officers and private Men of our Forces which may be reduced in our said Province, who shall be desirous of becoming settlers therein; etc.

E. A. Cruickshank, The Settlement of the U.E.L. on the Upper St Lawrence and Bay of Quinte in 1784: A Documentary Record.

♛ ♛ ♛

[William] Smith attended a royal levée with Sir Guy Carleton [on 24 January 1784], and was able to observe George III at close quarters: "His Heighth about 5 Feet 9 Inches, very far from the Corpulence given to him in Pictures. Complexion fair, Large Whitish Eyebrows, Forhead a little roughened and upon the Whole a Face of Care". When he was presented to the King, rheumatism and the sword Smith was wearing (presumably for the first time) prevented a proper obeisance. Apparently, the King was not perturbed. "You continued with us to the last?", he said, and, looking at Sir Guy, he observed, "They would not suffer Men of Talents to remain." The afterglow of that royal commendation would have to warm Smith through many bleak months to come.

L.F.S. Upton, The Loyal Whig: William Smith of New York & Quebec.

♛ ♛ ♛

In York [Toronto] there was vastly less social life than there had been in Quebec, or even in Niagara the previous winter. The only ball of importance was on January 18th, the birthday of Queen Charlotte, wife of George III. There were not many ladies in York, but those who attended were, Elizabeth [Simcoe] noted, "much dressed".

Florence McLaughlin, First Lady of Upper Canada.

♛ ♛ ♛

For his brilliant capture of Detroit on August 16th of the same year [1812] King George III knighted Brock, but the General was in his grave before the news reached Canada. The King took a novel way of informing the

Hero of Upper Canada of the honour conferred on him. He sent him a very large and beautifully executed gold medal, made to suspend from the neck. On the obverse is "Detroit" exquisitely engraved; on the reverse, the figure of Britannia, and round the rim "Major-General Sir Isaac Brock". In the summer of 1913, when the writer saw the medal it was in the possession of the Misses Tupper of Guernsey, great-nieces of Sir Isaac.

G.H. Armstrong, The Origin And Meaning of Place Names In Canada.

GEORGE IV

Sir George Prevost protested the publication of this finding [of the court-martial of the surviving officers of the Battle of Lake Champlain] in a letter to the Commander-in-Chief, HRH Frederick, Duke of York, and requested a court-martial so that he might have a public opportunity of justifying his conduct. A General Court-Martial was summoned for January 12, 1816, which would allow time for witnesses to travel from Canada. Sir George Prevost was in ill health, however, as a consequence of his recent strenuous duties and worries, and died a week before the court-martial was due to Assemble. Nothing could now be done legally to clear Sir George Prevost's reputation, but the Prince Regent did, at the behest of his widow, confer upon her and succeeding baronets a lasting memorial in the form of supporters for the Prevost coat-of-arms, holding banners inscribed "West Indies" and "Canada" respectively, and a motto *Aservatum cineri.*

A.J. Mackay Hitsman, The Incredible War of 1812.

♛ ♛ ♛

The royal charter establishing what is now the University of Toronto, 15 March 1827.

Whereas the establishment of a College within our Province of Upper Canada in North America . . . would greatly conduce to the welfare of our said Province . . . We . . . have of our special grace, certain knowledge, and mere motion, ordained and granted . . . that there shall be established at or near our Town of York, in our said Province of Upper Canada, from this time one College, with the style and privileges of an University . . . for the education and instruction of youth in arts and faculties.

WILLIAM IV

[see also "Chapter 2, Stumping the Dominion," for William IV as Prince William]

On peut s'imaginer avec quelle satisfaction mon excellent et infatigable père put contempler un matin sur sa table de travail, dans une reliure provisoire, un exemplaire complet des *British Dominions in North America* et du *Topographical Dictionary of Lower Canada*. Je partageais sa joie. Une série complète des cartes était déjà tirée, de sorte que nous nous trouvions en possession du résultat complet de nos deux années de travail ardu. Nous éprouvions quelque chose des sensations du marin qui après un long et périlleux voyage rentre enfin sain et sauf au port.

Un exemplaire de l'ouvrage, convenablement relié, fut présenté au roi Guillaume IV, dans une audience spéciale, à Brighton.

"Robert Bouchette ardent Patriote et fervent Royaliste", extracts from the Mémoires of Robert Shore Milnes Bouchette, edited by Elinor Senior, Monarchy Canada.

♛ ♛ ♛

I was busy in the storehouse one afternoon, when Mr Prior entered with a newspaper in his hand, which he had just received from the old country.

"I see by this paper, Strickland, that George IV is dead; and that his Majesty King William IV has been proclaimed. Now, I think, we must give the workmen a holiday on this memorable occasion."

"In what manner do you intend to celebrate the day?" was my rejoinder.

"I have been thinking", he replied, "of making a little fête, and inviting all the settlers within reach to assemble on the Button-wood Flats [at Goderich in the Huron Tract]. We will have some refreshments served round; and if the day is fine, I have no doubt we shall enjoy ourselves much."

Due notice having been given, upon the appointed day everyone within ten miles assembled on the Flats, dressed in their best attire; and ready to show their loyalty in any way Mr Prior might think proper to recommend.

As soon as the squire made his appearance, he ascended a large stump; and, in a patriotic and loyal speech, informed us "that he had called this meeting to hear him proclaim his most gracious Majesty King William IV".

He then read the proclamation, which was received with nine rounds of British cheers. Our party then formed a large circle by joining hands; and sang the national anthem [God Save the King], accompanied by the Goderich band, which was composed of two fiddles and a tambourine. "Rule Britannia" for our sailor-king was also played and sung - I was going to say in good style, but at all events with great loyalty and enthusiasm.

As soon as this ceremony was over, a pail of whisky, with a tea-cup floating on the surface, was handed round, followed by another pail containing spring-water. Every person present drank his Majesty's health; even the fair sex, on this propitious occasion, did not disdain to moisten their pretty lips with the beverage.

The eating and drinking part of the festival now commenced in earnest. We had seated ourselves on the grass, under the shade of four or five immense button-wood trees, which effectually sheltered us from the scorching rays of the sun ... As soon as we had eaten and drunk to our satisfaction, a dance was proposed and acceded to by the party. The band struck up "The Wind Shakes the Barley"; country dances, Scotch reels, and "French fours", were kept up with great spirit on the level turf - "All under the greenwood tree" ... Those of our party who did not patronize the dance, amused themselves with ball-playing and a variety of old English games ...

I was much amused by a Yankee mill-wright, who had contracted to build a large grist-mill for the [Canada] Company, both in Guelph and Goderich. He appeared enchanted with the whole day's proceedings.

"I do declare", he said, "if this don't almost put me in mind of the 4th of July. Why, you Britishers make as much fuss proclaiming your king as we do celebrating our anniversary of Independence. Well, it does me good to look at you. I vow if I don't feel quite loyal. Come, let us drink the old gentleman's health agin. I guess, I feel as dry as a sand-bank after so much hollering".

The setting sun warned us to discontinue our pastime and prepare for a move. Before doing so, however, the squire again came forward, and after thanking us for our attendance, loyalty, &c., he proposed "we should give three cheers more for the King, and three for Queen Adelaide", which were given with all the power of our lungs, not a little aided by sultry potations imbibed by the loyal in drinking their Majesties' healths during the day's proceedings.

Three cheers were then given for the Canada Company, three for the Commissioners, and three for the old Doctor. Thus terminated the proclamation of our sovereign in the Bush.

Samuel Strickland, Twenty-Seven Years In Canada West Or The Experience Of An Early Settler.

VICTORIA

[see Chapter 1, Mother of Confederation]

EDWARD VII

[see also "Chapter 2, Stumping the Dominion," for Edward VII as Prince of Wales]

♛ ♛ ♛

On 8 March 1907 this message was telegraphed to the Governor General, the Earl Grey by Queen Alexandra:

The Queen has learned with great regret of the disastrous fire which has occurred at the Protestant children's school at Montreal. Her Majesty desires me to convey to you her great admiration of the heroic conduct of Miss Maxwell, who gave up her life in a gallant attempt to rescue the little children entrusted to her care, as well as Her Majesty's deep sympathy with the bereaved relations of this brave woman.

The Times, 9 March 1908.

♛ ♛ ♛

Donald Smith, Baron Strathcona and Mount Royal, the man who drove in the last spike of the Canadian Pacific Railway in 1885, was a close friend of King Edward VII.

King Edward VII was, among his other royal qualities, an infallible judge of men, and had the greatest esteem and even affection for Lord Strathcona. He called him "Uncle Donald". He had found him in time of difficulty a real *Pater Patriae* and therefore the right sort not only of "King's Cousin" but even of King's Uncle. For during the trouble in South Africa six years before Baron Strathcona and Mount Royal had for the first time in many hundred years – from the spring of rejuvenation beyond the Atlantic – revived the best feudal traditions of the British House of Peers, and, as a free-will offering to the Empire which he had long served with all his heart and strength, had entirely at his own costs raised and equipped a splendid regiment of Canadian cavalry. That was the kind of man whom the King delighted to honour.

John Macnaughton, Lord Strathcona.

♛ ♛ ♛

A few weeks later King Edward [VII] died. "The loss", wrote Lord Strathcona on the day of the King's death, "sustained by the Empire by the death of His Majesty would have been heavy in any circumstances, but, coming as it does at this juncture of affairs, it is indeed a great calamity". For Edward VII he had always a great personal regard, and this was reciprocated by the Sovereign, who had long been deeply interested in the career of "Dear old Uncle Donald", as he affectionately spoke of him.

"Here comes Uncle Donald", His Majesty once exclaimed, seeing the [Canadian] High Commissioner approach at a garden party, but without his wife, "but where is 'Our Lady of the Snows?'"

Beckles Willson, The Life of Lord Strathcona and Mount Royal.

GEORGE V

[see also "Chapter 2, Stumping the Dominion," for George V as Duke of Cornwall and York]

♛ ♛ ♛

An exchange between King George V and a subject:

Man: I am thinking, sir, of sending my son to Canada. Is life there really hard?
King: It is, but it's a man's life. If your son is a man, he will like it.

♛ ♛ ♛

During dinner [with King George V at Windsor in 1923] the King talked most of the time with [Field Marshal Lord] Ironside; afterwards he came up to Georges [Vanier] and spoke with him for about five minutes. The conversation went as follows:

K: How did you get on as A.D.C. with your [artificial] leg?
G.V. Quite well, Your Majesty.
K: Do you ride?
G.V. Not very well, Sir.
K: That's right, don't try to ride. It's dangerous – you can't get your balance. Is Lord Byng popular?
G.V. Nobody can be more popular. He was appointed at the psychological moment.
K: Yes, yes. Is Lady Byng popular?
G.V. Yes, sir. One of her great assets is her knowledge of French.
K: Does she speak it well?
G.V. Like a Parisienne.
K: Ah yes, I remember. Have you much unemployment?
G.V. No, Your Majesty.
K: Ah yes, unfortunately we have that great trouble – one million unemployed – very sad. There is no work for them. In spite of the War there are 150,000 more people in England than in 1914. No wonder we have unemployment. We must send Englishmen to Canada. But you have too many Americans, you mustn't let them in. Some people tell me Canadians talk of separation from the Empire. I don't believe it. I know the Canadians too well.

The conversation also turned on Baldwin's appointment as prime minister. The King then told Georges to sit down and a chair was brought, while the Queen was asking Pauline whether she pronounced her name Vani*Aer* or Van*Aié* and observing – with a somersault of royal diplomacy – that she 'loved the Canadian climate'. Then the King came up and found Georges disregarding the chair which had been brought for him.

K: I've told your husband to sit down, but he won't even listen to the King . . . Have you been to Toronto? Aha! French-Canadian, you have never been to Toronto. You don't like Toronto. Aha! the rivalry between the two cities.
G.V. I hope you don't think we're so narrow-minded.
K: No, I was only teasing you. I hope you know Ottawa?
G.V. Yes, we were there sometime with Lord Byng.
K: Of course you had to go there, but you didn't like it?
G.V. Oh yes, we loved it.
K: I'm only ragging you. The first time I went to Canada you weren't born – that was in 1883. But you never can tell (with a sly glance at Pauline) women know how to hide their age. But you're not forty.

He then asked where and when Georges had lost his leg, and hearing it was in August 1918 observed what a 'terrible show' that had been.

Robert Speaight, Vanier: Soldier, Diplomat and Governor General.

♛ ♛ ♛

Opening Canada House in London, 29 June 1925.

The Queen and I are very glad to take part in today's ceremony, and to see the new home of Canadian London.

Canada is a great country, alike in the literal sense of vast extent from "sea to sea" and great in achievement and in promise; and it is right and necessary that its official representatives here should be housed in a manner worthy of the Dominion and adequate to the discharge of their ever-growing and important duties.

F.A. Mackenzie, King George V In His Own Words.

♛ ♛ ♛

In 1928 [Mackenzie] King's government re-introduced penny postage throughout the Empire. You could send a letter with two cents on it anywhere in the British Empire after 1928. Those were the days! What's more, the letter probably got there. And King, writing about this episode of the penny postage, said in his diary, "I plan to make it an expression of rejoicing at the King's recovery". [King George V had had a serious illness and was just getting over it.] "I plan to make it an expression of rejoicing at the King's recovery and to make the announcement to the public in the form of a communication from me to the King". There was the ego coming out: "Your Majesty, this is your friend Willie talking". "I believe I can do something in this", he says, "which will touch the King's heart and the heart of the Empire and the heart of our people".

C.P. Stacey, "Mackenzie King and The Monarchy" in Monarchy Canada.

♛ ♛ ♛

The King has a very practical knowledge of what concerns his people in the Overseas Dominions. When Mr Ferguson, the Premier of Ontario, came to England some years ago, he said that the King was the best-informed man on Canadian affairs that he had met in England. He added: "His Majesty has the peculiar problems and features of each province well in mind. Just think of the King knowing about power-developments in Ontario and Quebec, and being able to compare them with the costs of development here, where they have to burn coal to generate electricity! His Majesty talked of South African, New Zealand, and Australian affairs; he showed an intense knowledge of every part of the Empire, and it is quite obvious that he is a close student of world affairs, especially of Empire affairs".

M.C. Carey and Dorothy Margaret Stuart,
The King's Service.

♛ ♛ ♛

Certainly among the happier celebrants [of the Silver Jubilee of George V's reign] were 700 prisoners of Canadian penal institutions, 30 of them at the Manitoba Penitentiary at Stony Mountain, who were freed to mark the occasion by a special amnesty from the King.

Royal Visits, a Manitoba album / Visites royales, un album–souvenir du Manitoba.

EDWARD VIII

[see also "Chapter 2, Stumping the Dominion," for Edward VIII as Prince of Wales]

As Prince of Wales he was always a booster of Canadian interests.
Speech in Washington, 11 November 1919.

As you know, I have recently been travelling in Canada, and I am the richer, since that three months' journey, by a wonderful experience. I come here, therefore, not only as an Englishman and as a representative of the British Empire, but also as a Canadian who is intimately and personally concerned as you yourselves in the life of this North American Continent. The British Empire is held together by the common aims and united sentiment of five sister-nations, all devoted to the same cause of democratic self-government.

♛ ♛ ♛

Speech by the Prince of Wales (Edward VIII) to the Canadian Club of the United Kingdom, 10 November 1922.

I always feel that my small ranch in Alberta is to me a great link with Canada . . . It is only a small ranch. I cannot claim to be raking in the dollars, but I have recently had satisfactory reports . . . I am getting on well with my stock, and people say that the quality and appearance of the Shorthorns bred there has come up to expectations.

♛ ♛ ♛

Speech to the Canadian Club in London, 1927

I want to urge the young business men of this country, who are blessed with imagination and opportunities, to study Canada, her present needs and future possibilities, as I have tried to do.

I recommend not only the study of Canada to my contemporaries, but also that they should step right over and see Canada for themselves – whenever the opportunity happens, step over. To me – and I am not alone in this opinion – Canada and Canadians are a real tonic. They sharpen one up, and they provide, on the serious side, a widened outlook in business ideas which will compensate for any apparent loss of time in work over here.

♛ ♛ ♛

On 26 July 1936 the King unveiled the Vimy Memorial in France. This was the only major external engagement of his short reign.

We raise this memorial to Canadian warriors. It is an inspired expression in stone, chiselled by a skilful Canadian hand, of Canada's salute to her fallen sons. It marks the scene of feats of arms which history will long remember, and Canada can never forget. And the ground it covers is the gift of France to Canada.

THE ABDICATION

The abdication was of direct and great importance to the dominions, constitutionally and politically. The Canadian government was consulted, or at least the Prime Minister was, in all its stages. The King was King of Canada and, unless we wished to keep Edward VIII on his own terms, or to become a republic, the formalities of abdication had to be agreed with London and the accession of the new king timed to synchronise exactly in both capitals so that there would be no interregnum. Certainly Mr King did not wish to make Canada a republic. But he also did not wish to keep Edward as King of Canada, with Mrs Simpson as Queen. He had made it clear, as had the other dominions, that abdication was the only possible course. He saw eye-to-eye with Prime Minister Baldwin, both personally and constitutionally, on what had to be done.

He also must have realised that, while a divided crown was for Canada a constitutional necessity if we were to be an independent part of the Empire and Commonwealth, this division could produce its own complications when action had not only to be taken, but to be taken simultaneously by six governments, and in situations with which only one government, that of the United Kingdom, was in immediate, direct contact and for which it had primary responsibility.

When the moment arrived for the abdication to take effect legally by formal action in the House of Lords in London, it was essential that similar action at the same moment take place in Ottawa and other overseas capitals. Otherwise there would be a constitutional vacuum. We worked out an elaborate system of communications, a 'count-down' which in its precision would have been adequate to launch a moon-rocket. I was to be stationed at Westminster Hall and a telephone line was kept open to Canada House. I could tell the High Commissioner the very second the formal change had been made. He could then talk immediately to Ottawa on a line kept open, so that the necessary action could be taken there without the slightest delay. It was beautifully accomplished in all capitals except Dublin. The slip-up there did not take a form, as one might have expected, which would have eliminated the monarchy from the Irish Free State, if only for a short but symbolic time. The mistake in Dublin led to the very unexpected result of giving that state for some hours *two* British Kings. In the timing, one had ascended before the other abdicated.

Lester Pearson, Mike: Vol 1.

♛ ♛ ♛

A bit of banter remembered from the schoolyard of Toronto's McMurrich Public School at the time of the Abdication in 1936.

Question: Who is the best checker player in the world?
Answer: Wallis Simpson. She got two men and a king.

Ron Stubley, Hamilton.

♛ ♛ ♛

Also told in Toronto, was a more adult Abdication joke.

Question: What did Mrs Simpson do when Edward VIII proposed to her?
Answer: She fell out of bed.

The late Vivienne Davey, Toronto.

GEORGE VI

[see also "Chapter 2, Stumping the Dominion," for George VI as Prince Albert and "Chapter 3, A People's King," for the 1939 tour of Canada by George VI as King]

The Canadian representation at the Coronation of King George VI.

The Government of Canada sent over a contingent from the Royal Canadian Mounted Police to take part in the Coronation ceremonies. They were received with vast enthusiasm in the great procession . . .. The contingent presented its own set of problems. Were the horses of the RCMP to arrive in time to be trained to stand the noise of London streets? Some apprehension was expressed in England as to how the horses would react to the smell of the Guards' bearskins; the fur of a bear normally frightens them. Official correspondence took place on this subject, and the answer from Ottawa was reassuring and, of course, decorously worded. An unofficial communication came more light-hearted in tone. It ran something like this: "Tell them not to worry; we feed the horses bearskins for breakfast every morning".

Vincent Massey, What's Past Is Prologue: The Memoirs of the Right Honourable Vincent Massey.

♛ ♛ ♛

A crisis occurred while the stand [for spectators to view the procession] was being erected at Canada House when the Timber Commissioner from British Columbia informed us that Baltic timber was being used despite undertakings to the contrary. The offending wood had to be ripped out at the contractors' expense and replaced by Canadian lumber.

A special department was set up at Canada House to look after the entertainment of as many as possible of the ten or twelve thousand Canadian visitors at functions of all kinds. Twenty-four Canadian choristers were invited to be members of the Coronation Choir – music had to be sent to them so that they could arrive note-perfect in time for the early rehearsals. Canada was further associated with the music of the Coronation by the presence in the Abbey of the Hart House String Quartet in the orchestra assembled for the occasion.

The rehearsals for the Coronation produced their own amusing touches, as for instance the appearance of a duchess wearing a felt hat and short skirt and a peeress's robe, as one of the four ladies to carry the Queen's canopy, or a page sitting on the floor playing ball with his mother's coronet.

Vincent Massey, What's Past Is Prologue: The Memoirs of the Right Honourable Vincent Massey.

♛ ♛ ♛

On Coronation Day [12 May 1937] Alice and I got to the Abbey very early, for two reasons – we thought there might be traffic jams and also we wanted to drink to the full the glories of the day. We were not worried about getting hungry or thirsty or tired: we wanted to see all we could, like two eager children. I had to be there early to take my place in the procession of those who carried the standards of the Dominions, England, Scotland, and so on. It was a very cold day and the tiny flask of brandy I took along (like, I think, most people) was very useful. In due course our procession was formed and we went down the nave according to the plan finally adopted in the rehearsal. There had been a difference of opinion between the Earl Marshal and Garter King of Arms as to how the standards should be carried. I forget now which won, but the important point was that we all did the same thing. We handed the standards over at the entrance to the choir, to the Mayors of the Cinque Ports and the other associated towns, and then proceeded to our places. As I turned to the left after passing through the choir, my eye rested on a sight I shall not forget – tiers of seats in the north transept occupied by peeresses wearing as many diamonds as I suppose were ever brought together on one occasion, scintillating in a setting of ermine and crimson.

Vincent Massey, What's Past Is Prologue: The Memoirs of the Right Honourable Vincent Massey.

♛ ♛ ♛

Lester Pearson describes his role as a Gold Stick in Waiting at the 1937 Coronation.

I had thought that there would be one major advantage in being an "usher". I would get a perfect view of the historic ceremony. I was soon disillusioned. My post of duty was out of sight of the actual coronation, behind a pillar in an outer aisle. I decided that I would have done far better in the crowds lining the streets. On the great day, only half awake, but in accordance with orders, and in all my sartorial glory, I arrived at 4:30 am at the Abbey, though the first guest didn't come for two or three hours. With nothing to do after my section was filled, I realised that I was going to stand there for hours with no remote possibility of seeing the coronation itself, unless I did something about it. The same idea occurred to a South African friend in charge of the section next to mine. We put our heads together and decided to run the risk of court martial or deportation by deserting our posts, and scout for a spot to see something. We found a door in a tower, opened it, discovered spiralling steps, climbed them as far as we could and found an opening big enough to look out, and down. There we were, right over the Abbey's main transept with a wonderful view of the altar and the whole colourful scene. And there we saw the crowning of the King and Queen; while our charges looked after themselves with no trouble at all.

Lester Pearson, Mike: Vol. 1.

♛ ♛ ♛

Lester Pearson served as a Gold Stick on duty at Buckingham Palace at the first Coronation Ball

The ball itself was not as much fun as the preliminary party or as that which we had later after the ball was over. But it was, for me, unique. The Sultan [of Zanzibar] whom I looked after was undemanding. He was a teetotaller and a non-dancer. So all I had to do was sit beside him as he watched the company dance, or talked to other distinguished guests. My own conversation with him was limited to answering one question, "Where do you live?" My answer "Canada" was greeted with some surprise and only one comment: "Canada, cold." That ended our oral communication. In due course, he was taken away to supper and I was left to my own devices.

So ended, for me, the coronation.

Lester Pearson, Mike: Vol. 1.

♛ ♛ ♛

Coronation Day broadcast by King George VI to the Commonwealth and Empire, 12 May 1937.

It is with a very full heart that I speak to you tonight. Never before has a newly crowned King been able to talk to all his peoples in their own homes on the day of his Coronation . . . To many millions the Crown is the symbol of unity. By the grace of God and by the will of the free people of the British Commonwealth, I have assumed that Crown. In me, as your King, is vested for a time the duty of maintaining its honour and integrity. This is, indeed, a grave and constant responsibility, but it gave me confidence to see your representatives around me in the Abbey and to know that you, too, were enabled to join in that infinitely beautiful ceremonial. Its outward forms come down from distant times, but its inner meaning and message are always new; for the highest of distinctions is the servicc of others, and to the Ministry of Kingship I have in your hearing dedicated myself, with the Queen at my side, in words of deepest solemnity. We will, God helping us, faithfully discharge our trust.

♛ ♛ ♛

Lester Pearson who was serving at the Canadian High Commission in London in September 1939 recalled that there were difficulties over Canada's first declaration of war.

We had no experience in declaring war. I was told that the expert to see was Mr Dunbar, whom I knew personally, and he told me how the document should be drafted. I went back to my office and wrote out the proper words on a plain sheet of paper. Then I telephoned my friend, Tommy Lascelles [Sir Alan Lascelles, Private Secretary to King George VI], at the Palace to ask whether I could show him the draft document for approval or amendment. He told me to come along, and in a few minutes I was in his office. He said that it looked all right to him but, since the King was in the office next door, he would "pop in" and get royal confirmation. He returned in a few minutes to say that His Majesty had not only approved the text but had indicated this by signing it. This was satisfactory, but somewhat startling as it was only a draft for consideration. I was not sure what the King's signature did to it. When I told Mr [Vincent] Massey [Canadian High Commissioner in London], he expressed great interest in the now royally authenticated draft. I had my own designs on it as a very special souvenir. But I knew that in this competition, I would lose to seniority. And so it turned out. I never saw the draft again, even after it was replaced later by other more formal documents.

Lester B. Pearson, Mike Vol 1.

♛ ♛ ♛

The state opening of Parliament on October 26 [1948] was... a profoundly moving spectacle. My instant feeling was, this is *my* King. After Their Majesties had retired and joined the procession to Westminster we could hear the crowds cheering from far away. Londoners do love a pageant, and they saw one that day that warmed their hearts.

The supreme event was the reception at Buckingham Palace by Their Majesties that afternoon at six o'clock. I recorded it in my diary as follows:

We were received by the King and Queen in a medium-sized reception room, then passed through a second into a third where we were received by Queen Mary, and the Duke and Duchess of Gloucester . . . When the receiving was completed the King and Queen took up positions in the large drawingroom where we were. From then until they retired at 7.30 they chatted with delegates who were presented. I record with grateful satisfaction that I had individual chats with the King, the Queen, Queen Mary, the Duke of Gloucester, Princess Alice (Countess of Athlone), and several peeresses. The King was much interested in the Canadian National Exhibition, asked about this year's attendance, and how it all started in the first place. I was able to recall the part his great-uncle, the Marquis of Lorne, played in helping the Exhibition get on its feet. When I referred admiringly to the state opening of Parliament, His Majesty said to me with no attempt at reserve, "Attlee didn't want a state opening, but I insisted. I thought the people needed a lift". They got it, and so did I.

The Queen recalled her visit to Toronto and the reception in front of City Hall, and commented on how well it was done. They were both exceedingly pleasant. They are the most natural people in the world. The King speaks with great readiness in conversation, and without any trace of stuttering. The Queen is beautiful beyond all description, and much of her beauty is in her expression. It is pleasant, sympathetic, and good.

I had quite a lengthy chat with Princess Alice about Canada. She told me she and the earl would have come to Toronto oftener, but there was no place to stay. She didn't think very highly of Premier Hepburn's closing of Government House.

Donald Fleming, So Very Near: The Political Memoirs Of The Honourable Donald M. Fleming.

♛ ♛ ♛

Before dinner on my first evening [at Windsor Castle in the spring of 1951], I happened to meet the King in the great curving corridor in which are placed the cases containing the royal collection of orders and medals . . . The King, who had only recently recovered from the serious operation on his leg, drove an electric invalid chair for much of the time, but managed to walk for short periods – surprisingly well, but probably feeling less comfortable than he looked.

The following afternoon we had another walk. This time the King did not use his chair at all and insisted on walking all the way. One of my fellow guests and I drove the chair alternately. As we approached the castle, I found myself seated in the vehicle the King walking beside me. I thought this inappropriate and suggested to the King that he should drive for the last lap. I said, "There may be people on the terrace looking down on us who will see you walking, sir, and one of your guests seated. This would look very odd". He laughed and continued to walk, quite pleased with the accomplishment.

Vincent Massey, What's Past Is Prologue: The Memoirs of the Right Honourable Vincent Massey.

ELIZABETH II

[see "Chapter 4, Elizabeth II of Canada"]

7

THE FAMILY FIRM

The concept of family is a very strong one in the philosophy and practice of kingship. There is the national family, the extended international family of monarchs, the Commonwealth family and the military regimental family. Not surprisingly the Sovereign's immediate Royal Family plays a vital role in the story of the monarchy in Canada.

To say that the Royal Family is important to the functioning of the monarchy is not to say that there have not been tensions and discord within that family. Our Hanoverian monarchs and their heirs were notorious for not getting along with each other and the gulf of misunderstanding between Queen Victoria and King George V and their respective heirs King Edwards VII and VIII is also a matter of record. But far from being extraordinary these tensions are the tensions of all families and reinforce the monarchy's claim to being the natural structure of society.

For Canada the place of the Royal Family, what the present Duke of Edinburgh calls "the family firm", has if anything been even more important than in Britain. Until the present reign, the monarch was only able to come to Canada in person on one occasion, 1939. It was therefore the role of the Royal Family to travel in Canada and make the monarchy a living reality. Six monarchs themselves came as princes or princesses. But while most members of the Royal Family came on tours [see "Chapter 2, Stumping the Dominion"] others served as governors general, with their regiments, or in other capacities, such as in the most recent case, Prince Andrew, Duke of York who attended school in Canada. In addition members of other Royal Families have lived in or come to Canada. In this way members of the Royal Family developed special ties with and insights into Canada.

Prince Rupert, first cousin of King Charles II

In his capacity of historian of Canada, Stephen Leacock could be expected to take a lighter view of the royal origins of the Hudson's Bay Company.

When the officials of New France cheated Radisson and Groseillers out of their furs, they went to France and appealed to the Crown. This proving vain, they decided to offer their services to England. By a stroke of good fortune they were put into touch with Prince Rupert, the cousin of King Charles II, who became thereby the patron saint of our North-West Territory . . . Born to arms and to adversity as one of the thirteen children of the exiled King of Bohemia, he served as a youth in the Thirty Years' War, was the chief military leader of the King's party of the English Civil War and admiral at sea against the Commonwealth; and in his riper age, a commanding figure at his cousin's court. Prince Rupert was not only a soldier but an art connoisseur, a scholar, an inventor and a scientist, one of the founders of the Royal Society of London . . . Prince Rupert could do everything but spell, a thing no doubt to which he was quite indifferent . . .

The Prince's capable intellect perceived at once the value of Radisson's discovery that the fur country could be reached by sea. The sea route was ice-bound and arduous but shorter than even the voyage to Montreal, the mere starting point of the trade. It substituted a summer voyage for a year in the wilderness.

Rupert and seventeen associates obtained from the King their incorporation as The Governor and Company of Adventurers of England trading into Hudson's Bay. The charter thus granted to these "undertakers" as it calls them, is a lengthy document, containing some six thousand, five hundred words. It has all the relentless repetition of the language of the law. Where literary English would speak of "waters", it says, "havens, bays, creeks, rivers, lakes and seas" . . . But it is worth all its words . . .

The whole of this magnificent territory is christened by the charter "Rupert's Land" . . . The name has been ungratefully edged off our map bit by bit, by the provinces and the territories. It has now been reduced – or elevated – to a purely spiritual meaning as a diocese of the Episcopal Church.

Where their own government ended the company were to have the sole right of trade in all the "havens, bays, creeks, rivers, lakes and seas" into which they could find passage from their own area. This was later to mean that the company could trade over the still unknown Rocky Mountains and into the still unsuspected British Columbia. This access to such "havens, bays and creeks" was to stand us in good stead – it was our first grasp on the Pacific.

Stephen Leacock, Canada, The Foundations of its Future.

Prince Edward, Duke of Kent, son of King George III

I therefore presume to hope that your Majesty, actuated partly by consideration of the unfortunate state of my health in this climate, as well as the infinite advantage of which my removal to a colder one will be to me, will not refuse my request when I petition that if it does not interfere with your commands for other Regiments in your service, youwill allow me to be sent in the Spring with mine to any part of North America which you may chuse to appoint; allowing me, if it meets with your approbation, to prefer Canada.

Prince Edward [later Duke of Kent] to his father, from Gibraltar, 13 December 1790, The Later Correspondence of George III.

♛ ♛ ♛

Prince Edward, later father of Queen Victoria, arrived in Quebec City on 11 August 1791 for what was to be a Canadian residence of nearly nine years. Replying to the address of welcome from the citizens, he spoke of "the pleasure it would give me if I should be fortunate enough to find the opportunity of being personally serviceable to you."

♛ ♛ ♛

The Duke of Kent was highly respected by the settlers of British North America.

Army officials stationed at Niagara had come to the rescue of the settlers and had issued food and other stores to them, but they had charged the settlers for the things they had received, and when hard times were over army officials made an effort to collect the debts incurred by the settlers. Prince Edward was deeply interested in the affairs of these people, who had remained loyal to his father; he had visited Niagara in 1792, and while he was there the settlers had presented him with petitions asking him to prevent the army commissariat from collecting debts incurred by them during the hungry years. He had ordered the officers to cancel all such debts, and to withdraw any lawsuits which had been started.

"My Father", he said, "is not a merchant to deal in bread and ask payment for food granted for the relief of his loyal subjects".

This action earned him the affection of the settlers. When the Prince left Niagara after his visit with the Simcoes, the whole town was illuminated by candles in his honour. Elizabeth [Simcoe] knew this was a sincere tribute because in many homes candles were scarce.

Florence McLaughlin, First Lady of Upper Canada.

♛ ♛ ♛

Like all famous actors, the Marseilles [founders and operators of the marionette theatre in Quebec City] had their night of great triumph, to be remembered all their lives. His Royal Highness the Duke of Kent, father of our gracious sovereign, was kind enough to honour their theatre one evening with his presence. Something new had to be thought of for so great a personage, and the Marseilles genius was not found wanting on this solemn occasion. As the prince had rented the theatre for himself and his guests several days in advance, the players had time to prepare everything for the surprise they had in store.

The curtain falls. The puppeteers have already succeeded in making the prince laugh, but are determined to melt his heart as well, and must needs follow comedy with moving drama. Madame Marseille is seated at the foot of the stage as partner to her worthy husband, as is usual during the performance. Near her is the orchestra, which has been enlarged for the occasion by the addition of a fife to the customary lone violin and drum. Madame Marseille rises, curtseys deeply to the Duke of Kent, and says:

"My Prince, there are no more marionettes: the devil has carried them all off." Effectively, His Satanic Majesty, in the guise of a prairie chicken, has just swept the stage clear of Punchinello and his company in the midst of a whirling dance, and Mother Marseille has drawn the curtain.

"However", she adds, "to make up to Your Principality for so great a loss, we shall present for your entertainment the siege of Quebec by the Americans in 1775, and show you the proper beating that the English and Canadians gave them so they'd learn to treat their neighbours with respect". Having delivered herself of this bellicose speech, Mother Marseille probably amuses the prince by singing "Malbrouk s'en va-t-en guerre, mirliton, mirlitaine", from the first verse to the last.

The curtain rises and the spectators view with astonishment the city of Quebec. True, the miniature town is made of cardboard, but there is no mistaking it. Atop the high citadel floats the British flag. Soldiers and citizens line the ramparts, and cannoneers are at their posts, wick alight. The American battalions begin the assault, the cannon roars, the sound of rapid firing is heard, the besiegers take flight, and the city is saved.

The orchestra plays "God Save the King", at which the entire English royal family parades on stage: King George III leads the way, mounted on a thoroughbred with Queen Charlotte riding pillion on its wide rump. The two sovereigns, wearing crowns, are followed by their large family of princes and princesses seated on high-stepping steeds. But let Mother Marseille, be it only to console her shade, describe this scene so gratifying to her self-esteem.

"When the prince recognised his dear father and mother whom he hadn't seen for so long, he could barely control his feelings, but when he saw his little brother, Rodolph, he broke down completely and hid his face in his handkerchief." Mother Marseille's eyes become misty at the memfory of this, and she takes a strong sniff of tobacco to clear her vision.

A Man of Sentiment, The Memoirs of Philippe-Joseph Aubert de Gaspé 1786-1871.

As Commander-in-Chief of the garrison [at Halifax], Prince Edward kept his finger on the pulse of every aspect of military life, from the construction of major new fortifications to the minutiae of the soldiers' daily routines. He readily admitted: "I never consider anything that happens within my command and that is connected with the King's service, as below my notice or attention" ... He demanded perfect punctuality, though he was greatly hampered by the lack of a garrison clock. But like everything else he tackled, he remedied the situation on a grand scale. In 1798, during a sojourn in London, he ordered "a large clock" from the royal clockmakers, the Swiss Vulliamy family.

The logistics of shipping the mammoth 1000 pound clock mechanism were handled by Sir Brook Watson who had spent some of his formative years in Halifax ... By the spring of 1802, the total cost of manufacturing and shipping the clock, £351.16.5, was paid. By the following year, the heavy, hand-wrought iron clock frame with its myriad of brass cogs and wheels and 12-foot pendulum was installed in the suitably elegant baroque turret designed by William Fenwick. Sergeant Alexander Troop of the 29th Regiment, a Scottish-born watchmaker, set the works in motion.

The perfect precision of the parts and slowness of the movement are remarkable now, in an age when clocks run on a microchip and a battery. The Royal Clock has ticked away the minutes and hours for almost two centuries, and regardless of modern inventions, ticks on.

Elizabeth Pacey, Historic Halifax.

Halifax has always celebrated the presence of royalty with enthusiastic entertainment. In 1787, when Prince William's frigate *Pegasus* put into port at Halifax, citizens lit candles in their windows as a sign of welcome, and a grand ball was held in his honour. Seven years later, William's younger brother Edward arrived to command the garrison. The fact that Edward had a beautiful French mistress heightened the excitement ... they became the darlings of the town's social life, attending balls, levees and plays ... And since there was no official residence for the commander of the garrison, [Sir John] Wentworth [Governor of Nova Scotia] loaned the couple his own property on the Bedford Basin.

There Prince Edward and Julie, as she was known privately, created a romantic country estate with winding paths that spelled her name, a heart-shaped pond and ornamental Chinese and classical garden temples among the trees. One classical temple remains, the Rotunda, a stunning architectural jewel with its circular colonnade supporting the broad dome and large rooftop ball. Sometimes referred to as the music pavilion, the Rotunda was likely the setting for glittering musical soirees where the Prince's band played and Madame delighted the guests with her fine singing.

There was an ending to this idyllic life. Prince Edward eventually gave up his beloved mistress to father Queen Victoria. But maybe it would have pleased the Prince to known that half a century later, his Prince's Lodge grounds were the scene of a grand Civic Picnic in honour of another visiting prince, his grandson Prince Arthur. Maybe it would also please him to know that the Rotunda still reminds us of his lady and their love affair.

Elizabeth Pacey, Historic Halifax.

♛ ♛ ♛

In the Duke of Kent the Nova Scotians lost a kind patron and generous friend. The loyalty of the people, which, when all America was revolting, remained firm and unshaken, and the numerous proofs he received of their attachment to their King and to himself, made an impression upon his mind that was neither effaced nor weakened by time or distance. Should these pages happily meet the eye of a Colonial minister, who has other objects in view than the security of place and the interest of a party, may they remind him of a duty that has never been performed but by the illustrious individual, whose former residence among us gave us rise to these reflections! This work is designed for the cottage, and not for the palace; and the author has not the presumption even to hope it can ever be honoured by the perusal of his Sovereign. Had he any ground for anticipating such a distinction for it, he would avail himself of this opportunity of mentioning that in addition to the dutiful affection the Nova Scotians have always borne to their Monarch, they feel a more lively interest in, and a a more devoted attachment to, the present occupant of the throne [i.e. Queen Victoria], from the circumstance of the long and close connexion that subsisted between them and her illustrious parent. He was their patron, benefactor, and friend. To be a Nova Scotian was of itself a sufficient passport to his notice, and to possess merit a sufficient guarantee for his favour. Her Majesty reigns, therefore, in this little province in the hearts of her subjects, has a dominion of love inherited from her father. Great as their loss was in being thus deprived of their only protector, her faithful people of Nova Scotia still cling to the hope that Providence has vouchsafed to raise up one more powerful and equally kind in Her Majesty, who, following this paternal example, will be graciously pleased to extend to them a patronage that courtiers cannot, and statesmen will not give. While, therefore, as *protégés* of her royal house, they claim the right to honour and serve the sovereign of the empire as "*their own Queen*", they flatter themselves Her Majesty, for a similar reason, will condescend to regard them as "*the Queen's own* ".

Sam Slick, quoted in Rev'd Erskine Neale,
The Life of Field-Marshal His Royal Highness Edward, Duke of Kent.

♛ ♛ ♛

Journal of the House of Assembly of Nova Scotia, June 30, 1798: Resolved, - That an humble address be presented to His Royal Highness Prince Edward, to beg that he will be pleased to accept from the province of Nova Scotia a Star, as a testimony of the high respect which the province has for His Royal Highness's person, as *well as the grateful sense it entertains of the very essential services* which His Royal Highness has rendered to this province...

Address to Lieutenant-General His Royal Highness Prince Edward, commanding His Majesty's forces in the province of Nova Scotia, the Islands of St John [Prince Edward Island], Cape Breton and Newfoundland, Knight of the most noble Order of the Garter, and of the most illustrious Order of St Patrick, &c. &c. &c ... The Lieutenant-Governor, Council, and Assembly, *in the name and behalf of the province of Nova Scotia*, humbly beg leave to approach your Royal Highness, to repeat the unfeigned assurance of their inviolable fidelity, attachment, and affection to the sacred person of our beloved Sovereign, his family and government.

His Majesty's paternal solicitude for the safety and happiness of his subjects in this province, is particularly manifested by his committing the care of protecting and defending them to your Royal Highness in so critical a conjuncture as the present ...

THE ESSENTIAL SERVICES *which your Royal Highness has rendered to this province* will be remembered with gratitude by us, and cannot fail to interest His Majesty's subjects most sincerely in your future glory and happiness; and while we take pleasure in doing justice to your Royal Highness's exemplary conduct and virtues, we shall rejoice in the satisfaction they will afford to our good and gracious Sovereign, whose piety, justice, wisdom, and magnanimity, have riveted to his throne the hearts and affections of all his people...

Reply of Prince Edward: ... I feel infinite satisfaction in expressing to your Excellency, to the Member's of His Majesty's Council, and to the Gentlemen of the House of Assembly of this province, my grateful thanks for the distinguished and flattering mark of your attachment and good-will which is so handsomely conveyed in your address.

Nothing could afford me higher gratification than to receive so unequivocal a proof of your approbation of my conduct during the time His Majesty has been pleased to honour me with the command of his troops in this province. My utmost endeavours have always been exerted to obtain your good-will, by pursuing that line of conduct which I thought would be most acceptable to the King, and most beneficial to his service, as well as best calculated for the protection of the province. To have succeeded therefore in this object, of which circumstance your address of to-day affords me so honourable a testimony, is the more gratifying to my feelings, as I flatter myself when His Majesty is informed of it, he will not hear it with indifference.

After having said this much, it will be almost needless to add, how ready and how happy I shall be to accept of the present you intend me, which I shall ever esteem and highly prize, as the mark of your attachment to my person, and of your acknowledgment of my feeble exertions for your security and protection.

Permit me to take leave of you, Gentlemen, by expressing towards all my best wishes, both for your individual happiness and the general welfare of the province at large.

Rev'd Erskine Neale, The Life of Field-Marshal His Royal Highness Edward, Duke of Kent.

The Marquis of Lorne and Princess Louise, daughter of Queen Victoria.

The Marquis of Lorne, appointed Governor General of Canada in 1878, was the son of the Chief of Clan Campbell, a fact which did not go unnoticed by the many Canadians of Scots origin or descent. A traditional song was reworked to express their joy.

The Campbells are comin' Hurrah, Hurrah!
The Campbells are comin' Hurrah, Hurrah!
The Marquis of Lorne, the Princess an' a'.
The Campbells are comin' Hurrah, Hurrah!

They come to a land that has won some renown,
A people most loyal to Queen and the Crown.
They come to hold court at fair Ottawa,
The Campbells are comin' Hurrah, Hurrah!

The Campbells are comin' Hurrah, Hurrah!
The Campbells are comin' Hurrah, Hurrah!
The Marquis of Lorne, the Princess an' a'.
The Campbells are comin' Hurrah, Hurrah!

♛ ♛ ♛

I think it possible you may come here one day. Canada is so loyal, so interesting, and with such a marvellous future that it really seems as if the Governor Generalship should always be filled by a member of our family.

Princess Louise writing to her brother Prince Arthur, Duke of Connaught, with a prophecy that came true, from Canada in 1878.

♛ ♛ ♛

Lines on the occasion of the Marquis of Lorne and the Princess Louise visiting Kingston:

Of a Royal Princess we now can boast,
And drink a health and loyal toast
To QUEEN VICTORIA, whom God may spare,
Who honoured Canada with her daughter fair.

From deceitful enemies or their foes,
May God the Royal couple keep in sweet repose;
And let nations see that this fair land
Can uphold Royalty with heart and hand.

Kingston, fair city of the thousand isles,
Where the noble St Lawrence so gently smiles;
With its Royal Military College of much renown,
And the grand old buildings of this ancient town.

Though this city much of limestone smells,
There are British hearts that ever swell,
To respond to Royalty and one so fair,
And to the Princess Louise who visited there.

Was e'er such honour paid to Kingston before,
As a Princess and Marquis inside their door?
The honour paid her was much deserved,
For she stood true and loyal when others swerved.

With the noble Marquis and the fair Louise,
The loyal Kingstonians were much pleased;
At their reception Mayor Gildersleeve did preside,
With the city aldermen on either side.

To give a loyal welcome to those we love so dear,
And show our loyalty in old Kingston here,
For that we Kingstonians all are sworn
To stand together - aye, for Lorne!

Thomas Faughnan, Stirring Incidents In The Life Of A British Soldier, An Autobiography.

♛ ♛ ♛

Reply by Princess Louise to the Ladies Educational Association of Montreal when asked to become their patron in 1878.

The fruits of education are so attractive that we are often tempted to force them prematurely, without sufficient tillage, and thus loose sight of the true objects of education, which consist much more in the development of the intellect than in the mere putting in of superficial knowledge and of 'cramming'. Hence our necessity of grounding in the rudiments of knowledge, and thoroughness in all that is done. Knowledge thus got never dies. Knowledge got otherwise never lives.

J.E. Collins, Canada under the Administration of Lorne.

♛ ♛ ♛

The balance between stuffiness and informality proved hard to strike. In preparation for the first Drawing Room at Montreal, held shortly after their arrival there in November 1878, Colonel Littleton had issued orders that ladies should appear in low-cut, evening dresses, as they did in England on such occasions. Canadians did not wish to have to incur extra expense of dress for them. The only drawback to Lorne's appointment had been the prospect of the establishment of a royal Court in Canada. When Colonel Littleton's instructions were made known, it seemed to ordinary Canadians as if their worst fears had been realised.

Papers representing the whole political spectrum in Canada reported that a terrible mistake had been made and "it caused a great row". Lorne was not unnaturally annoyed, since Littleton had purposely been left behind to guide and advise him about the customs of the country. He ensured that, in future, only "Evening Dress" should be stipulated in the official announcement of evening receptions: "and then let people come as they like", he told Lord Lansdowne, "I shdn't care if they came in blankets!"

Jehanne Wake, Princess Louise: Queen Victoria's Unconventional Daughter.

♛ ♛ ♛

The new Governor General of Canada and his wife Princess Louise gave their first state ball on 19 February 1879 at Rideau Hall.

Although the supper and dancing were a success, Princess Louise's first official ball was marred by various mishaps. A fire nearly broke out while she was at supper, caused by a half tipsy bandsman pulling a curtain over a gas lamp. Then some of the guests were obviously drunk. Neither Lorne nor the Princess were used to seeing their guests, six according to Lorne, literally carried out by footmen and put into sleighs.

Jehanne Wake, Princess Louise: Queen Victoria's Unconventional Daughter.

♛ ♛ ♛

The antics of Torontonians at viceregal presentations [on the first visit by the Marquis of Lorne and Princess Louise to the Ontario capital] made even the dour Alexander Mackenzie smile. "Lady Howland went through in grand style curtseying so low that every one wondered how the whole of that 300 pound woman ever got up again" Mackenzie wrote his daughter. "Another stupendous woman a head taller than me and three times as thick went through with the preliminary movement to a curtsey. The officer immediately behind stepped back hurriedly, evidently seized with a sudden apprehension of what might become of his family if the curtsey should fail in the recover. Someone whispered, 'is that whole woman to be presented at once?'"

Robert Stamp, Royal Rebels: Princess Louise and the Marquis of Lorne.

♛ ♛ ♛

The Princess's own artistic endeavours had been prodigious. She had invited her friends, Clara and Henrietta Montalba, to spend three months painting and sculpting with her in Canada. She used to pass many an hour sitting at an upstairs window with Clara Montalba to sketch what continues to be called "the Princess's Vista", a view of the Ottawa River. Reid, the carpenter, was asked to build her a sketching-box on wheels, which could be moved about the grounds. One side of it was a sheet of glass so she and Clara Montalba could sit inside and sketch away, regardless of the weather. The Princess also painted on to the doors of her boudoir "charmingly placed" boughs of crab apple trees in leaf, laden with fruit. One of these extremely pretty painted doors still survives at Rideau Hall, a record of her attempt to beautify the house. She also began working on two oil portraits, one of Clara as the Dark Lady, and one of Russell Stephenson.

Jehanne Wake, Princess Louise: Queen Victoria's Unconventional Daughter.

♛ ♛ ♛

Before going home [to the United Kingdom] for Christmas [in 1879], Princess Louise had drawn up some designs for the decoration of the interior of the Houses of Parliament which had been accepted by the Canadian Ministry of Works. Since the decorations remained unfinished, the Princess had to superintend the stencilling of her designs to ensure their completion by the opening of Parliament on the 12th. Her aim was to "take off the bare cold look" of the interiors, which were in such contrast to the picturesque exterior of these fine buildings.

Jehanne Wake, Princess Louise: Queen Victoria's Unconventional Daughter.

♛ ♛ ♛

A serious accident at Government House, Ottawa.

The winter of 1880 had been an unusually treacherous one. On the evening of St Valentine's Day, three sleighs left the front entrance of Rideau Hall for the Houses of Parliament, where the Princess was to hold a Drawing Room. Princess Louise was seated in the last covered sleigh with Mrs Langham on her right, opposite Colonel McNeill and Lorne. Turning left into the main road, the horses took the corner too quickly, so that the sleigh skidded violently out to the right, over a bank of snow, and was turned over on to its right side. The coachman and footman were thrown out and the frightened horses bolted, dragging the overturned sleigh behind them.

The Princess was tossed head-first sideways against one of the iron bars supporting the roof; she was knocked unconscious for a second by the blow and her head slipped on to the ground. Mrs Langham being on the right side to begin with, was dragged along with her body only partially protected from the ground by the leather roof. Remaining conscious throughout, she remembered for ever after "that horrible night" with the "horrid broken glass rushing past my face".

It was the Princess who saved her from much worse injury. "If it had not been for Princess Louise's wonderful presence of mind my face must have been cut to ribbons", she told her Aunt Cecy, "but directly the sleigh overturned she seized me around the neck and held my head back" from the ground. The Princess's body lay across Lorne, who was trapped underneath her, unable to move, expecting "the sides of the carriage to give way every moment", which would have killed them. Colonel McNeill was able to steady himself and push his left hand under the Princess's head, in order to support it. He could feel his hand and arm becoming damp and then wet, as they bumped along.

What was extraordinary about this scene was that it took place in complete silence. Not a sound escaped the lips of the four occupants as they rattled through the darkness. Gradually, the horses began to grow calmer and slacken their pace, as they overtook the sleigh ahead. One of the ADCs, Mr Bagot, jumped from his sleigh with a groom, and managed to run beside and clutch at the horses' heads. The alarm was raised at the lodge and an empty sleigh was sent to convey the injured back to Government House. On arrival there, Princess Louise and Mrs Langham were helped inside and supported as they slowly climbed the stairs to their bedrooms.

Dr Grant arrived shortly afterwards. He found that Princess Louise was severely concussed and in shock; it was judged "a wonder that her skull was not fractured". If she had been hit directly, Dr Grant declared, she would have been lucky to remain alive. The dampness, Colonel McNeill had felt, was caused by Princess Louise's injured right ear, which bled so profusely that it saturated his whole sleeve. One of her earrings had caught in the side of the sleigh and, as her head was thrown forward, the earring was pulled out of her ear, tearing her lobe in two.

The Princess suffered the most serious injuries, although Mrs Langham's shoulder and side were badly bruised and her nerves remained fragile for some months after. Lorne had only a few bruises, whilst Colonel McNeill escaped injury entirely. Mr. Bagot, who pulled up the horses, was hurt about his knees and legs. Writing about him five years later, Queen Victoria was much grieved "to think he should continue lame from the dreadful accident in Canada when he contributed to save dear Louise's life".

Jehanne Wake, Princess Louise: Queen Victoria's Unconventional Daughter.

Princess of Wales, (Queen Mary)

Letter from the Right Honourable Earl Grey, Governor General of Canada, to Sir Robert Falconer, President of the University of Toronto, dated Ottawa, 20 November 1908.

It is my duty to be allowed to forward to you, by command of the Princess of Wales [later Queen Mary], a Banner, for presentation to the University of Toronto.

The Princess of Wales hopes that the students of the University of Toronto will welcome this Banner as an abiding proof of her interest in their well-being.

On one side of the Banner is the original flag of England, the time-honoured emblem of St George, suggesting at once the chivalry of the Crusades, the Charity of the Ambulance, and the self-sacrifice of the Cross.

On the other side is a beautifully embroidered picture suggesting the duty and dignity of reverence and service. King Edward III is here represented on the battlefield of Crécy, pointing to his son, the Black Prince, the flag of the dead King of Bohemia.

The King authorises his victorious son to adopt as his own, the motto and device of the fallen monarch, and exhorts him to pledge his life to the service of mankind. The reverential acceptance by the Prince of Wales of the King's appeal is beautifully depicted.

Her Royal Highness hopes that her Banner may inspire successive generations of Undergraduates to adopt for the guidance of their lives the motto "I serve" which from the days of the Black Prince has been the stimulating motto of every Prince of Wales.

University of Toronto Archives.

Prince Arthur, Duke of Connaught, son of Queen Victoria

Reply to the address of welcome presented to him on his arrival in Canada in 1869.

Most anxious am I to consider for the time being Montreal as my home, and to lose no opportunity of becoming fully acquainted with its institutions, its people, and its commerce. The selection of Montreal as my residence is sufficient proof of the confidence Her Majesty places in the devotion of the city to her Throne.

Major-General Sir George Aston, His Royal Highness The Duke of Connaught and Strathearn.

♛ ♛ ♛

Queen Victoria's third son Prince Arthur was stationed in Montreal with his unit, the King's Royal Rifle Regiment.

From Montreal the Prince journeyed to Ottawa, where he met with an equally enthusiastic reception. There he paid a visit to the lumber mills, and, to the huge delight of the workers, "ran a slide" in a "crib", or, in words more readily understood by the average reader, he took a trip on a log raft down the narrow channels through which the logs are sent. From one of these rafts the lumbermen sent to the Prince and his party some plates of the pea soup off which they were dining, and, much to their amused gratification, the young Prince demolished his plateful with obvious enjoyment.

Major-General Sir George Aston, His Royal Highness The Duke of Connaught and Strathearn.

♛ ♛ ♛

The Duke of Connaught was preparing to leave Canada in 1914 when war broke out after serving as Governor General since 1911. He was to have been replaced as Governor General by Queen Mary's brother Prince

Alexander of Teck (later Earl of Athlone). A series of farewell tours had been arranged by the Connaughts.

At the Lake of the Woods, Kenora, a farewell regatta was arranged in honour of the Royal visitors. Over 400 motor-boats took part, and it was a very gay function. The Royal party were as usual taking a full share in the festivities when an accident occurred that might easily have had fatal results. The motor-boats in which they were travelling struck some floating logs with such force that large holes were knocked in them, and they began rapidly to sink. Luckily there were other boats near enough to go to the rescue in time, and the Duke and his party were rescued from their boats just as they were sinking. It was a narrow escape, but the Royal party, not wanting the mishap to interfere with the festivities, made light of the danger.

Major-General Sir George Aston, His Royal Highness The Duke of Connaught and Strathearn.

♛ ♛ ♛

His farewell visit to the Canadian National Exhibition, Toronto, 5 September 1916.

I have the Canadian Fenian Medal for Services in 1870 and I spent a year with my regiment at Montreal. My first visit to Toronto was when I accompanied the then Governor General, Lord Lisgar, who paid his first visit to Toronto as Governor General, and I was with him in the carriage. I can remember the splendid reception we received. I merely mention this as I should not like you to think that I am a relatively new Canadian. In coming back I came to a country which I knew fairly well and which had already shown to me the greatest kindness.

John Cowan, Canada's Governors General: Lord Monck To General Vanier.

♛ ♛ ♛

Princess Patricia of Connaught [Lady Patricia Ramsay], daughter of the Duke of Connaught.

Princess Patricia, who, as may be imagined, was by this time idolized in Canada, entered into all these [winter] amusements with much zest. She was an expert skater. Often, too, with a party of young people, she would don snowshoes and go for long expeditions over the snow-clad country.

She soon accustomed herself to the cold, and when writing home to her friends she sometimes quoted the limerick ascribed to Kipling:

> There was a small boy of Quebec
> Who was buried in snow to his neck.
> When asked "Are you friz?"

He replied "Yes, I is;
But we don't call this cold in Quebec".

A photograph of her clad in furs was sold in thousands to the admiring Canadians.

Major-General Sir George Aston, His Royal Highness The Duke of Connaught and Strathearn.

♛ ♛ ♛

The Canadians liked Princess Patricia's high spirits, lack of conventionality, and great interest in sport of all sorts. Like her mother, she was a good horsewoman and whip, and she was always ready for any adventure that offered itself. During one of their tours through the Rockies she rode on the cowcatcher of the engine, as Queen Mary did when she visited Canada as Duchess of Cornwall and York.

Major-General Sir George Aston, His Royal Highness The Duke of Connaught and Strathearn.

Gustavus V of Sweden

As one of the thousands of penniless emigres fleeing revolutionary Russia, my uncle, Prince Nicholas Troubetzkoy, eventually found himself in the New World with no professional training or preparation for the realities of the business world. Among other occupations, Uncle Kolya developed into a reasonably expert bridge master and soon came to be much in demand not only to teach the game but to be wined and dined by the high society bridge fraternity. He had a delicious sense of humour and a gregarious personality.

It happened one day that while in Europe Uncle Kolya found himself partner with Sweden's King Gustavus V, a monarch who took his bridge as seriously as he did his tennis. For whatever reason my uncle uncharacteristically, and in the true sense of the word, goofed by leading with the wrong card. His Majesty was unamused by the careless opening and unhesitatingly made known his irritation.

"Good Lord! exclaimed the King, "how could you possibly have led with the clubs?"

Uncle Kolya fumbled, paused but quickly regained composure. "Forgive me, Your Majesty, that was silly", he smiled in reply. "But, Your Majesty, this is the first time I'm playing with five kings!"

Prince Alexis Troubetzkoy, Toronto.

King George II of Greece's visit to Ottawa.

We were giving quite a large and formal dinner. The guests were assembled. Their Excellencies were ready to make their rounds of welcome. King George was very conspicuous by his absence.

I went to seek him out upstairs.

"Come in! Come in!" he called, in answer to my knock. "I'm late. I'm sorry. I'm a fool."

"Something wrong, sir?" I broke in on his agitation.

"My bath, man, my bath! I can't understand your so-highly civilised plumbing. The water won't stay in the tub. I've been trying for an hour."

So I practically gave the King his bath, dressed him and rushed down to dinner.

H. Willis-O'Connor and Madge Macbeth,
Inside Government House.

Queen Wilhelmina of the Netherlands was in wartime Ottawa.

When Her Majesty Queen Wilhelmina came to Canada, everyone noticed the difference between her manner and that of her popular daughter. One of the Queen's retinue told me that if anyone spoke first to Her Majesty, she would say:

"We did not ask you a question."

This lady-in-waiting also said that smoking was not encouraged. "We smoke", she admitted, "behind a screen".

H. Willis-O'Connor and Madge Macbeth,
Inside Government House.

♛ ♛ ♛

One day, when the Princess [Juliana of the Netherlands] had come to swim with us in MacKay's Lake at the foot of our garden, a dusty jeep drove up and a dusty chap in an Air Force uniform got out.

I strolled over to him and asked what he wanted, thinking he had a message for me.

"I'm looking for my wife", he said.

"Well, I'm afraid she's not here", I told him. "Perhaps you've come to the wrong house."

"I don't think so." It may have been my imagination but I thought he seemed embarrassed. "They said – er – are you Colonel O'Connor?"

"Yes, but we have no extra wives here. There's just a friend with us swimming."

"Maybe it's the friend I'm looking for", said the stranger. "Her name is Juliana, and I'm Bernhard, her husband."

H. Willis-O'Connor and Madge Macbeth,
Inside Government House.

♛ ♛ ♛

A story about Queen Wilhelmina's granddaughter, the present Queen Beatrix of the Netherlands.

Princess Beatrix . . . with her sister, Irene, went to the Rockcliffe public school. Beatrix was strongly attracted to a little boy in her class. She made several friendly approaches, but the young lad resisted them with a coldness that puzzled her.

Finally, one day she caught him on the recreation field and asked:

"Why don't you play with me? I want you to play with me. Why won't you?"

The little boy answered with the engaging if uncompromising frankness of childhood:

"My Mummie's awfully particular about the children I play with. I don't know you, and maybe my Mummie doesn't know your Mummie. So I'll have to ask her. What's your name besides Beatrix?"

H. Willis-O'Connor and Madge Macbeth,
Inside Government House.

Earl of Athlone (brother of Queen Mary), Governor General of Canada and his wife Princess Alice, granddaughter of Queen Victoria

Edson Sherwood, an A.D.C., E.H. Coleman, Under Secretary of State, and I travelled to Halifax in the private car to meet our new Governor General and the Princess. The journey was unusually dreary and we enlivened the hours by dipping into our supply of Scotch. That would not have been so bad except that Their Excellencies' ship was many hours late. By that time, the supply of Scotch in the private car was completely exhausted. So were we.

It would never have done to impose on Lord Athlone a completely dry journey from Halifax to Ottawa, so we scrounged about Halifax to pick up a fresh supply. It was war time and good liquor was scarce, but we found a few bottles of very indifferent whiskey and stowed them away in the private car.

Our new Governor General sampled a drink and then observed:

"Well, I don't think much of the Scotch we use at Government House".

Avoiding the eyes of my two guilty companions, I replied:

"It's awful sir! We're thoroughly ashamed of it, but it's the last of the old stock and I promise you won't get any more of that stuff!"

H. Willis-O'Connor and Madge Macbeth,
Inside Government House.

♛ ♛ ♛

I approached His Excellency rather hesitantly when Jack Benny came to Ottawa with his company. Although Lord Athlone liked having the screen stars around, I feared he, too, might draw the line on this occasion.

"Shall we invite the entire company?" I enquired of him.

"Certainly."

"Do you realise, sir, that Rochester is a coloured man?"

"Of course, I realise it", said His Excellency quite testily. "Don't I listen to the programme every Sunday night at 8 o'clock? And anyway", he added, giving me a stern look, "I didn't know that Government House went in for any of that Nordic nonsense!"

H. Willis-O'Connor and Madge Macbeth,
Inside Government House.

♛ ♛ ♛

Anna Neagle was one of our most interesting guests [at Government House, Ottawa]. Remember her *Victoria the Great*? Her contract was a rigid affair. Everything was definitely laid down, even to the number of interviews she could or should give. Tired or not, she had to go through her heavy day's routine wearing her queenly role, as a sort of propaganda stunt.

A small party was given for her at the Chateau Laurier after her "personal appearance" in the theatre, and most of us felt that we were actually in the royal presence. When she was leaving Government House, the Princess said:

"I hope you will come back"; and His Excellency added, "when you can just be yourself and natural".

H. Willis-O'Connor and Madge Macbeth,
Inside Government House.

♛ ♛ ♛

The Earl of Athlone had no interest in bargains. He wanted to do his shopping in a big way, grandly . . . The first time I accompanied him on one of these expeditions we dismissed the car at the Chateau Laurier and strolled toward Sparks Street. We strolled along Sparks Street, twice, I believe. I led him to windows displaying men's shirts, shoes, ties, underwear. I paused at windows showing women's garments, some of the variety described by the wag as being "dressless evening straps".

He showed a greater interest in jewellery.

"Let's buy something", he suggested.

I felt embarrassed. We aides were supposed to carry a minimum of $10.00 on our persons, enough to cover any ordinary emergency. I had forgotten to supply myself with the regulation amount of cash.

"Sir", I said, "you've put me in a jam. I'm awfully sorry to confess I have only about $5.00 in my wallet".

"No matter", returned His Excellency. "I have $200.00." He spoke with undisguised satisfaction.

Showing my surprise, I ventured:

"Isn't that a good deal of money to carry round, sir?"

"Of course! Of course!" he agreed. "But I do it. You see, I never was able to get my hands on that much money until I became Governor General, and I like the feeling of it in my pockets."

H. Willis-O'Connor and Madge Macbeth,
Inside Government House.

♛ ♛ ♛

The Princess Royal's son Gerald Lascelles, now Earl of Harewood, was an A.D.C. at Government House during the time the Earl of Athlone and Princess Alice were there.

There were still [1945 to 1946] a fair number of smaller official functions, and people came constantly to see the Governor General. He had a marvellous memory but hardly ever attached a name to the person or place he had in mind. Most people were referred to as 'he' or 'she'; 'there' was the place they came from, and all the time one had to remembered that 'she' could be either his sister Queen Mary, or else Princess Alice. Ministers who knew him well referred to the visits as 'playing Dumb Crambo', because, unless they by luck caught on immediately to what was being referred to, they could skate dangerously and anonymously from one confidence to another, agreeing with the Governor General at every turn only to be asked a penetrating question which brooked no evasion.

There was a story of the lady on H.E.'s left at a luncheon party who came from the provinces of Canada, and, not having been to Government House for two or three years, was understandably nervous. He didn't speak to her for half an hour, which helped her nerves not at all, and then suddenly turned and asked, 'How are they?' She searched for the right kind of answer and produced, 'Oh, very well, Your Excellency', and he said, 'Yes, yes, no trouble with them at all?, which she took to be a reference to her family, who were grown up and in the services. 'Never sir.' But when he followed up with, 'I had some difficulties at first', she knew she was out of her depth. Finally he asked, 'Do you never have any trouble keeping them in in the morning?', and she realised that on the only other occasion they had met they had each got a new set of false teeth, and were going through what you could only in the circumstances call teething troubles. But it would have taken a Sherlock Holmes to have deduced at the start of the conversation that 'they' were teeth.

Once, while I was there, he sent for Neville Ussher who was A.D.C. in waiting. "This fellow Edwards, I think we should ask him to lunch". "When, sir?" H.E. said: "Tomorrow, there's nobody coming, I see". So Neville asked, "Will I be able to get hold of him easily?" and got the reply,"Oh yes, just ask Edson" (the Canadian Naval Commander who was in charge of the A.D.C.s). Sure enough, a Major Edwards, known to be a friend of H.E.'s, was located and invited to lunch. Neville told the Governor General who smiled and shook his head. "No, no, no, not that Edwards at all. The other one..." So, rather nervous by now, Neville went off, consulted Edson, and together they decided it must be Colonel Edwards, one of the honorary A.D.C.s, who lived with his wife in Ottawa. They turned out to be wrong too. The right Edwards was actually Adjutant-General, just returned from Europe. We got him, and next day at lunch the three pairs of Edwardses were all lined up, wives next to husbands in order of seniority, and presented. We never made out if they thought it a quirk or a practical joke, but none of them could have known it was a variant of Government House Dumb Crambo.

7th Earl of Harewood, The Tongs And The Bones:
The Memoirs of Lord Harewood.

♛ ♛ ♛

One had as an A.D.C. to announce the names of visitors clearly and audibly, and on big occasions this was important. Neville [Ussher] knew far more of the visitors than I did, and the great thing was to make quite sure that you teamed up husbands and wives, who were liable to stray even while waiting in a presentation line. On one occasion I distinguished myself by insisting on announcing, "The Archbishop of Quebec and Mrs ...", not realising that he was the Catholic archbishop.

7th Earl of Harewood, The Tongs and The Bones:
The Memoirs of Lord Harewood.

♛ ♛ ♛

The Athlones always managed – no matter how tired – to show convincing interest and to find a pleasant thing to say. Here is where His Excellency showed to best advantage. He would stop beside a workman, watch him and then compliment him in just the right terms, speaking French or English as the occasion demanded. He left a trail of good fellowship and stimulation.

H. Willis-O'Connor and Madge Mabceth,
Inside Government House.

♛ ♛ ♛

The Viceregal party was going once by train across the prairies, sitting in absolute silence before lunch and sipping pink gins. The Governor General was looking out of the window as the train crossed miles of nothing until a solitary house came in sight, and he asked: "Who lives there"' The Comptroller looked up and rang the bell. A black attendant came in and the question was put to him by the Comptroller. "I don't know, Your Excellency. Some son of a gun." The Governor General was perfectly satisfied with the answer, and the story goes that when about six months later he met a man called Gunn who came from that part of the world, he said, "I know where you live".

7th Earl of Harewood, The Tongs and The Bones: The Memoirs of Lord Harewood.

♛ ♛ ♛

[Lord Athlone] wasn't an especially learned man, and yet he made a success wherever he went – I believe as Governor General of South Africa, certainly in Canada, where they asked him to prolong his stay. His success was not least because he was the kindest and most generous of men and because, whenever there was any problem towards whose solution he could contribute, he invariably made the right contribution.

I was on duty at the great farewell dinner given by the Government at the Country Club the night before the Athlones left Canada, and it was an emotional occasion, distinguished by an eloquent (but forty-minute) speech by the Prime Minister, Mackenzie King. When the Prime Minister, who was a sentimental old man, went to see them off next day, he made his little bow, blew his nose and stammered out to them, "We do love you", and it was of course perfectly true.

7th Earl of Harewood, The Tongs and The Bones: The Memoirs of Lord Harewood.

♛ ♛ ♛

One of our aides was Alastair, the young Duke of Connaught, son of Prince Arthur [of Connaught] and grandson of a former Governor General.

Alastair was a likeable fellow but very much one who walked alone. He wasn't suited temperamentally for his work. He would slip away just at the time he was needed, and we would find him in some remote corner thoughtfully doing nothing. He was a dreamer and his thoughts seemed to be fixed on far-away places. He never shirked his duty. He just didn't see it coming.

One bitterly cold night, he returned to Government House from a party in town and we suppose he must have had some sort of seizure when opening his window, for the following morning he was found lying beneath it covered with snow and all but frozen. He died before he reached hospital.

H. Willis-O'Connor and Madge Macbeth, Inside Government House.

♛ ♛ ♛

We often invited groups of Air Force Cadets to informal dances [at Government House] in the afternoon. One youngster devoted himself assiduously to the Princess throughout the party. He really was quite firm in trying to prevent her from dancing with other boys. She didn't seem to mind, and so I did nothing about it.

When the young lad was making his farewells, he asked me: "Who was the precious white-haired lamb I've been rushing all afternoon? I've fallen for her in a big way. To hell with these young moderns we're supposed to find attractive!"

H. Willis-O'Connor and Madge Macbeth,
Inside Government House.

Dowager Queen Mary

We had the immense privilege during these war years of getting to know Queen Mary, and of being able to appreciate the fine combination of warmth, intelligence, and dignity that made her so dearly loved a figure in the Commonwealth. When the Beaver Club was about to close in February 1946, I was very anxious that she should appear on the final day. She gladly consented. The club was full, and the hundreds of service men and women, probably few of whom had ever seen Queen Mary, greeted her with affection. There were numerous cautionary measures in connection with the visit. No flash-bulbs, no cameras too close, not too long a time in the club. All of this she swept to one side and she entered into the spirit of the occasion with the zest of a girl, conveying by her own subtle means her real pleasure at being where she was. Thus the Beaver Club finished its time with a fitting climax.

Vincent Massey, What's Past Is Prologue: The Memoirs of the Right Honourable Vincent Massey.

Grand Duchess Olga of Russia

The Grand Duchess Olga, younger daughter of Emperor Alexandra III of Russia and niece of Queen Alexandra, lived in Canada from 1948 until her death in 1960.

Having once settled down at Campbellville, [Ontario] Olga hoped for a more or less complete retirement, but hostesses in Toronto sought her out. There came invitations to luncheons, dinners, and cocktail parties . . . At one such gathering . . . she met the late Mazo de la Roche. The name meant nothing to Olga and, with her accustomed forthrightness, she admitted that she had never read any of the author's novels. "But they have been translated into seventeen languages", said Miss de la Roche, and, turning to the hostess, remarked that the Grand Duchess did not appear to be very well read.

If Olga was blunt, the other was rude. None the less, the incident was smoothed over, and the two became friendly.

Alan Vorres, The Last Grand Duchess: Her Imperial Highness Grand Duchess Olga Alexandrovna.

♛ ♛ ♛

[The Grand Duchess] kept in touch with the [Russian] *émigrés* to the very end. Members of her old Akhtyrsky Hussar Regiment, scattered all over the world, were not forgotten by her. Olga had a phenomenal memory and remembered most officers and even some of the men by their name and surname. Once Colonel Odintzov came to Cooksville to accompany the Grand Duchess to a regimental memorial service at the Russian Cathedral in Toronto. He brought with him a list of all the men fallen in the First World War. Olga read it through carefully. Then she said:

"Oh, you have forgotten to put in Vassily... Oh, what was the man's surname? Never mind, it is certain to come back to me, and of course I shall pray for him just the same."

Colonel Odintzov replied that he did not think there had been a single Vassily among the officers.

"He was not an officer", the Grand Duchess said quickly, "but a sergeant and I was very fond of him. Now, I have remembered his surname – Bazdyrev, Vassily Grigorievich."

Colonel Odintzov later checked the regimental records. There had been a sergeant – Vassily Bazdyrev. He joined the Akhtyrsky Hussars in 1898 and was killed in action in 1915.

Alan Vorres, The Last Grand Duchess: Her Imperial Highness Grand Duchess Olga Alexandrovna.

♛ ♛ ♛

[Grand Duchess Olga] had lent me some of her most precious icons for the Byzantine Art Exhibition in Toronto, and I was naturally anxious that she should come to its opening. She promised she would. It proved a brilliant occasion, the female society of Toronto, richly gowned and bejewelled, turning up in strength. Into that hall, crowded with men in uniforms and women in the latest "creations", came the little Grand Duchess wearing an old grey cotton dress and worn down brogues. Anyone else would have cut a grotesque figure at such a gathering. Not so Olga. Her poise was the true Romanov poise. The simplicity of her manner enchanted everybody. As she walked down the hall everybody's eyes followed her in admiration. She looked what she was born. And more than that. There was something in the carriage of her head that spoke of an undefeatable will.

Alan Vorres, The Last Grand Duchess: Her Imperial Highness Grand Duchess Olga Alexandrovna.

♛ ♛ ♛

"I've seen you laughing so often", [Ian Vorres] remarked [to the Grand Duchess Olga]. " have yet to see you cry!"

"If I ever start crying", the Grand Duchess replied, her face suddenly grave, "I might never be able to stop. So I laugh instead".

Alan Vorres, The Last Grand Duchess: Her Imperial Highness Grand Duchess Olga Alexandrovna.

♛ ♛ ♛

As a young, newly-commissioned officer with the Royal Canadian Navy (Reserve), I spent the sultry summer of 1959 in Hamilton, Ontario.

Before leaving Montreal to take my post, my parents prepped me on the Grand Duchess Olga, daughter of Emperor Alexander III of Russia and sister of Nicholas II, who then lived in Cooksville, Ontario, within a short distance of Hamilton. Whatever might happen, under no circumstances was I to permit much time to pass without formally calling on the Grand Duchess. The prospect, quite frankly, appalled me and filled me with awe. If I were to visit her, how would I greet her? What would we talk about? Could I handle the situation?

The days came and went as I put off the inevitable. Telephone conversations with home turned from parental vexation to anger, but eventually I mustered my courage to telephone the Grand Duchess. The conversation was crisp and business-like: yes, my parents had forewarned her of my possible visit, and I would be welcome on Saturday afternoon for tea.

Throughout the morning of the appointed day and during the previous night, I sweated out all the possible scenarios of my initial encounter with the grand lady. As I walked up the driveway to her charming but modest bungalow, perspiring hands clutching a bouquet of rapidly-wilting roses, I felt claustrophobic. Undefined fears and rampant imagination had blown things out of all proportion, like they do to a child entering a dentist's office. I knocked on the door and after what seemed an interminable wait a little, old lady dressed in a scruffy, unpretentious dress, answered. Obviously the maid.

"Is the Grand Duchess home?" I asked in Russian.

"And what do you want with the Grand Duchess?" came the somewhat flighty reply.

"I have an appointment with her", I replied with a touch of irritation.

"Well", said the woman gravely, looking at me with feigned suspicion, "I don't know ...". She paused, flashed the warmest smile possible, and throwing her arms about me, exclaimed with delight, "I'm she!" Everything melted; I was at home.

Prince Alexis Troubetzkoy, Toronto.

♛ ♛ ♛

I visited the Grand Duchess on a number of occasions that summer. It was the year of the opening of the St Lawrence Seaway and Queen

Elizabeth II and President Eisenhower shared the honours. The Royal Yacht *Britannia* brought Her Majesty to Toronto for a few days, a visit which was between a couple of my visits with Grand Duchess Olga.

Great excitement: the Grand Duchess, together with her son, Tikhon, were invited to the *Britannia* for a private dinner with the Queen and Prince Philip. Olga was, after all, King George V's first cousin and thus a cousin to Elizabeth and Margaret. She knew both sisters well when they were small children.

The day following the notable dinner, I called on the Grand Duchess and lost no time in asking how things went and what her impressions were.

"Ah", she said, "it was a cosy evening, and it was great fun to have seen Elizabeth once again after these many, many years". Eyes glistening and bubbling with excitement, the Grand Duchess went on to tell the details of the evening and to give impressions of the now grown-up Elizabeth. She spoke of the two sisters as small girls and she carried vivid memories of them, one of whom she found "considerably less serious and playful" and the other "pensive and perhaps a bit less warm". The Grand Duchess commented on a table which stood in one of the salons; it was taken from the Russian Imperial Yacht *Standard* and presented to King George V for the Royal Yacht. She remembered it.

What impressed me most of all was that the Grand Duchess had not been forgotten by the Queen. At the time of the Revolution, Olga together with her mother, the Empress, and sister, Xenia, found themselves safe in Denmark. The Empress died there in 1928 and Xenia settled in England at Hampton Court, living under the protection of King George V in a "grace and favour" residence. Olga's life, however, evolved considerably less comfortably. She was married to a commoner and the couple made their way to Canada to begin life afresh as farmers. At the time of my visits, Olga had been recently widowed. In the decades which lapsed between Olga's visits with the child Elizabeth, no substantive contact had been maintained between the Court and the exiled Grand Duchess. But, despite the many years which had lapsed, it was family once more.

Prince Alexis Troubetzkoy, Toronto.

Emperor Haile Selassie of Ethiopia

The Emperor of Ethiopia [Haile Selassie] was one of my guests, and a very welcome one. Everyone knows about his courage and patience over a terrible period in the history of his country; he, as a person, is most impressive. He has a dignity that befits his ancient kingdom, and at the same time an entirely natural bearing. He combines a deep sense of the traditions of his country with a determination to modernise its institutions. The Emperor is not without a sense of humour. I asked where he had stayed when he was in London during the war. He said, "At Brown's Hotel". I asked him why this choice and he said, 'Because Brown's was the one hotel in London which didn't employ Italians!'

Vincent Massey, What's Past Is Prologue: The Memoirs of the Right Honourable Vincent Massey.

Queen Giovanna of Bulgaria

Queen Giovanna is the widow of King Boris III of Bulgaria and the daughter of King Victor Emmanuel III of Italy. One September she arrived at Oakville, Ontario, to visit her daughter, Princess Marie Louise, a neighbour of ours living close to the grounds of Appleby College. One evening Her Majesty came to our home for drinks, following which we were to drive to Toronto for a formal dinner. Somewhat late in leaving the house, we eventually hurried to our car, the Queen taking her place in the front seat. Marie Louise dawdled unduly and Her Majesty became visibly irritated. "Maria", she exclaimed sharply, "hurry up! We shall be late".

"Yes, mummy", replied the Princess, getting into the back seat with my wife, "but really, they can wait. You are, after all, the Queen".

"All the more reason to be on time!" grumbled Giovanna.

Prince Alexis Troubetzkoy, Toronto.

Prince Andrew

In 1976, as Headmaster of an independent boys' school in Montreal, I undertook a tour of half a dozen similar such schools in Ontario and one of them was Lakefield College, where my friend and former colleague, Terry Guest, was Headmaster. It was a Saturday and I was instructed to appear in time for an informal soup-'n-sandwich lunch in the kitchen with Terry and his wife, Sue. I arrived at the appointed hour and found the school unusually quiet; the students were at lunch.

Leisurely preparations for our own lunch proceeded well as we chatted and caught up on old times. Eventually we were ready to sit down and dig into the mountain of mouth-watering sandwiches that awaited us, when there was a knock at the front door. Terry answered it and returned to explain that it was one of the students. The boy had waited for well over an hour at the College's front entrance for the arrival of his date from Kingston for that evening's school dance. The poor fellow had missed his meal, was starved and his date hadn't eaten either. Both youngsters were invited to join us and they would be with us shortly, as soon as the girl had unpacked her dress.

In due course the two arrived into the kitchen and I immediately recognised the boy as Prince Andrew. Introductions, drinks poured - beer for the adults, milk for the youngsters and the five of us started in on the copious lunch. We were having a cold and rainy day. "It's not much better at home", commented Andrew, "I just phoned home and mum says it's raining cats-and-dogs".

"This is excellent cold milk", commented Andrew's friend.
"Humm, it is", agreed the Prince, "but you should taste the thick milk from Charles's herd in Cornwall; a real treat".

"What a peculiar way of lacing your boots", observed the girl, nodding to Terry's heavy work boots.

"That's the naval manner of doing them up", quickly explained Andrew. "Dad always laces his shoes the same way." And so lunch went and with it a fun and light conversation of no real consequence. Particularly striking was Andrew's simple and easy manner, his charm and total lack of pretence and his sparkling blue eyes which for a sixteen-year-old boy were indecently beautiful. Above all, however, I was struck by the sense of family which obviously prevailed in Andrew's household. The interpersonal relationships within Andrew's family, I thought, despite the unique circumstances, probably functioned not much differently from those of my own family. That particular lunch was a special treat.

Prince Alexis Troubetzkoy, Toronto.

8

THE MAPLE CROWN

One of, if not the most, important section of the Constitution Act 1867 is Section 9 which states, "The Executive Government and Authority of and over Canada is hereby declared to continue and be vested in the Queen". This conveys three essential truths about the Canadian state. Authority rests with the Queen. Her authority was not newly constituted in 1867 but was a continuation of her authority as it already existed, being manifested in the new structures of Canadian federalism. And the Constitution derives from the Queen's authority, the Queen's authority does not derive from the Constitution.

Section 9 sets the framework for the legitimate evolution of the monarchy in its Canadian context and the evolution of Canada from a colonial monarchy to an independent one sharing its monarch with other independent countries. This is both an old and a new idea. Old, because many countries have shared monarchs throughout history. New, because most of the precedents were of distinct countries acquiring a shared monarch through dynastic marriages or conquests whereas Canada evolved its distinctiveness under a common Crown.

The evolution of a distinctive Canadian perception of kingship is perhaps an unappreciated achievement of Canada. Living next door to the most dynamic, even if usually benevolent, republic in the world has forced Canadians to think about the value and role of monarchy in society in a way that most other monarchical people have not had to. The result has been a relatively exceptional contribution to the understanding of kingship by Canadians.

By royal proclamation the King [George III] promises representative government to the Canadian possessions over which he has just obtained sovereignty:

Whereas We have taken into Our Royal Consideration the extensive and valuable Acquisitions in America, secured to our Crown by the late Definitive Treaty of Peace, concluded at Paris, the 10th Day of February [1763] . . . We have thought fit to publish and declare . . . that as soon as the state and circumstances of the said Colonies will admit thereof, they shall, with the Advice and Consent of the Members of our Council, summon and call General Assemblies within the said Governments respectively, in such Manner and Form as is used and directed in those Colonies and Provinces in America which are under our immediate Government . . .

In 1783 the King in a speech to Parliament asked it to aid the Loyalists who were settling Ontario.

I have ordered enquiry to be made into the application of the sum to be voted in support of the American sufferers, and I trust you will agree with me that a due and generous attention ought to be shown to those who have relinquished their properties or progressions from motives of loyalty to me or attachment to the Mother Country.

Canada's largest city had a royal beginning

Very few Canadian cities have had the distinction of receiving their names accompanied by a royal salute. Such was the case for Toronto. It was 24 August 1793 and the site, protected from lake-borne gales by Toronto Island, had for inhabitants a few friendly Indians and a small garrison. It was at this time that Lieutenant-governor John Graves Simcoe learned of the Duke of York's victory at Famars earlier in the year. To celebrate the victory and to mark the naming of the new station, York, Simcoe soon marshalled his resources. Drawn up on the sandy beach at the edge of the pine forest were twelve- and eighteen-pounders brought earlier from Oswegatchie and Carleton Island, and a detachment of the Queen's Rangers. Offshore lay HM schooners *Mississauga* and *Onondaga*. All the forces that day participated in the royal salute which simultaneously gave thanks for success against the enemy in Europe and marked the beginning of a great city which would rise out of the wilderness of the New World.

E.C. Russell, Customs and Traditions of the Canadian Armed Forces.

♛ ♛ ♛

In 1814 the Duke of Kent (son of King George III) proposed a greater union of the provinces of British North America in a letter to Chief Justice John Sewell of Upper Canada. This letter was later quoted by Lord Durham in his famous Report and foreshadowed Confederation.

Kensington Palace,
3rd November, 1814.

My Dear Sewell,

I have this day the pleasure of receiving your note of yesterday with its interesting inclosure . . .

Allow me to . . . suggest whether you would not think two Lieutenant-Governors, with two Executive Councils, sufficient for an Executive Government of the whole, viz.: – one for the two Canadas, and one for Nova Scotia and New Brunswick, comprehending the small dependencies of Cape Breton and Prince Edward Islands; the former to reside at Montreal, and the latter at whichever of the two stations may be considered most central for the two Provinces, whether Annapolis Royal or Windsor.

Believe me ever to remain with the most friendly regard, my dear Sewell,

Yours faithfully,
Edward.

♛ ♛ ♛

American views of nineteenth century Canada's royal character

Ther ain't nothin very wonderful to be seed gwine down seven miles on the Niagary to Lake Ontario, except it is the Old Fort Niagary, what's been tuck and re-tuck, and capitilated and surrendered so often, 'mong the French, the Ingins, the British, and the Americans, that it ain't very easy to make out who is got the best rite to it now . . .

It was a bright sunshiny day, and the water of the lake as if it wanted to show us how well it could behave itself, after its frollick among the rocks of the Niagary, was as still and quiet as a mill-pond. Our splendid steamer, with its British flag flynin – jest as natural as if it was the banner of a sovereign peeple and had a right to wave "over the land of the free and the home of the brave", – went spankin along, on its way across the lake to Toronto, where the passengers amused themselves accordin to ther likin . . .

We wasn't long gwine to Toronto, whar we only stopped long enuff to git into another bote, and in a fe minits we was under way agin in the steambote "Sovereign" of the "Royal Mail Line", as they called it, on our way down the lake to Kingston.

The names of things begun to sound monstrous queer to my republican ears, and the red and gold crowns what was painted on the cabin dores, and was sticken about in different places on the bote whar the eagle ought to be, looked odd enuff; but I didn't find that they made the bote go any faster, or that my clothes got any tighter for me, because I was on a British *Sovereign* on the *royal line* gwine to *Kingston.*

William Tappan Thompson, Major Jones's Sketches of Travel: Comprising the Scenes, Incidents, and Adventures, in his Tour from Georgia to Canada, quoted in Yankees in Canada: A Collection of Nineteenth-Century Travel Narratives.

♛ ♛ ♛

The booksellers' [in Montreal] were full of Canadian editions of our authors, and English copies of English works, instead of our pirated editions; the dry-goods stores were gay with fabrics in the London taste and garments of the London shape; here was the sign of a photographer to the Queen, there of a hatter to HRH the Prince of Wales; a barber was "under the patronage of" HRH the Prince of Wales, H.E. [sic] the Duke of Cambridge, and the gentry of Montreal. *Ich dien* was the motto of a restaurateur; a hosier had gallantly labelled his stock in trade with *Honi soit qui mal y pense*.

William Dean Howells, "Their Wedding Journey", quoted in Yankees in Canada: A Collection of Nineteenth-Century Travel Narratives.

♛ ♛ ♛

But let me not impugn royalty, for the Provinces [New Brunswick and Nova Scotia] are loyal to their sovereign. King streets, and Queen streets, and Prince streets abound, and everywhere the sign of the crown over lintel and doorpost indicates a living faith in monarchical institutions. Otherwise the casual observer might say that the social fabric here lacketh somewhat the fire and fibre which distinguishes the adjacent republic.

Mary Abigail Dodge, "A Neighborly Call", quoted in Yankees in Canada: A Collection of Nineteenth-Century Travel Narratives.

♔ ♔ ♔

At the Quebec Conference the principles on which the Canadian state was constituted were hammered out. On Thursday, 20 October 1864,

Mr John A. Macdonald moved:–

That the Executive authority or Government shall be vested in the Sovereignty of the United Kingdom of Great Britain and Ireland, and be administered according to the well understood principles of the British Constitution by the Sovereign personally or by representative duly authorised.

Mr Tupper – Is it meant to leave it to the Queen or to make any suggestions as to the appointment of a Viceroy?

Mr John A. Macdonald – I think it advisable not to make any suggestion. At least it should not be a constitutional suggestion. Hereafter the Parliament of the Federation may represent a desire for one of the Royal Family as Viceroy.

G.P. Browne, Documents On The Confederation Of British North America.

♔ ♔ ♔

There exists in Canada a very strong desire that Her Majesty would be graciously pleased to designate the Union a "Kingdom", and so give her representative the title of "Viceroy". The wish is based on ... the natural yearning of a growing people to emerge ... from the provincial phase of existence.

Charles, Baron Monck, Governor-General of Canada, writing to Lord Carnarvon in 1867, quoted in Elizabeth Batt, Monck - Governor-General 1861-1868.

♔ ♔ ♔

Sir John A. Macdonald and The Kingdom of Canada

My dear Lord Knutsford:

A great opportunity was lost in 1867, when the Dominion was formed out of the several provinces . . . had United Canada been declared to be an auxiliary kingdom, as it was in the Canadian draft of the bill, I feel sure (almost) that the Australian colonies would, ere this, have been applying to be placed in the same rank as "The Kingdom of Canada".

P.S. On reading the above over, I see that it will convey the impression that the change of title from Kingdom to Dominion was caused by the Duke of Buckingham. This is not so. It was made at the instance of Lord Derby, then foreign minister, who feared the name would wound the sensibilities of the Yankees.

Chief among popular verse inspired by the union of the provinces of British North America under Queen Victoria in 1867 was 'The Maple Leaf Forever'.

In days of yore from Britain's shore
Wolfe the dauntless hero came
And planted firm Britannia's flag
On Canada's fair domain.

Here may it wave our boast our pride
And join in love together
The lily, thistle, shamrock, rose
The Maple Leaf forever

The Maple Leaf, our emblem dear
The Maple Leaf forever
God save our Queen and Heaven bless
The Maple Leaf forever.

In 1905 Earl Grey, the Governor General of Canada inaugurated the two new provinces of Saskatchewan and Alberta, and in his report to King Edward VII coined a new expression for the Canadian Monarchy.

[Each province is] a new leaf to Your Majesty's Maple Crown.

In all his major speeches [on his 1919 tour of Canada], the Prince [of Wales] hammered home his creed that he was not primarily a Briton and only secondarily a Canadian: "On the contrary, I regard myself as belonging to Great Britain and to Canada in exactly the same way". This was not just rhetoric reserved for public consumption. He told the Queen that the royal family must keep closely in touch with Canada and pay regular visits." *We* belong to Canada and the other dominions just as much as we do to the UK". The King warned him that if he called himself a Canadian in Canada then he would have to be an Australian in Australia and a New Zealander in New Zealand. "And why not?" asked the Prince.

Philip Ziegler, King Edward VIII: The Official Biography.

George V and Canada's coat-of-arms.

Had a meeting of the Arms Committee today at which we definitely decided to proceed with the adoption of the new Canadian Arms despite the opposition of the Heralds' College. This attitude - a most unusual one for me - is justified by the fact that the King had approved our draft, and that this approval was officially communicated to us by His Majesty's responsible Minister, the Secretary of State for the Colonies. This is enough for me. The Heralds raise all sorts of objections, some puerile as I think, so supported by H[is]. M[ajesty].'s sanction we are going ahead. Our Arms are very handsome, loyal, British, Monarchical with due recognition of Canada, in fact everything that can be desired. The motto "A Mari usque ad Mare", which is an original suggestion of my own, I regard as very appropriate.

Maurice Pope, Public Servant -
The Memoirs Of Sir Joseph Pope.

♛ ♛ ♛

King George V to the people of Canada on the sixtieth anniversary of Confederation, 1 July 1927.

To-day my people of Canada unite to celebrate the Diamond Jubilee of the Federation: and on such a day they may well look with a just pride on the achievements of the past and with a confidant hope to the promise of the future.

In sixty years the boundaries of the Federation have been extended tenfold, and its Governments are now responsible for the welfare of nearly ten million inhabitants. By the labours of peace and the sacrifices of war Canada has become a mighty nation.

Aims as lofty and labours as strenuous await her in the future. Within her own bounds her people have before them the task of developing the heritage which their fathers have left them. In a yet wider sphere she has to take an ever-increasing share in guiding the counsels and solving the problems of the great Commonwealth in which she is a part, conscious that within it there is perfect freedom and that the unity of the nations of the British Empire is the surest guarantee of the peace of the world to-day.

With all my heart I join in the prayers and hopes of my peoples throughout the world for the peace and prosperity of Canada.

The King To His People: Being the Speeches and
Messages of His Majesty King George the Fifth
delivered between July 1911 and May 1935.

♛ ♛ ♛

Canada and the coronation of King George VI

When the coronation date was fixed for 1 May 1937 and the complicated and detailed preparations began, the High Commissioner [Vincent

Massey] thought, as he so often did in such situations, that the Commonwealth significance of the occasion should be emphasised. One way to do this was to have the High Commissioner carry the Standard of Canada up the aisle of Westminster Abbey in the coronation procession, alongside the great Standard of England, borne by the Earl of Derby. The other dominions, of course, would also have their standard bearers. Indeed, the South African High Commissioner claimed the right to carry two standards because the British had three: one each for England, Scotland, and Northern Ireland. Why then only one for South Africa? This knotty problem was left to the Duke of Norfolk, the Earl Marshal, to settle. He was the unchallenged autocrat over all ceremonial rules and procedures, and resolved this issue by decreeing that a single banner for each dominion was acceptable.

Lester Pearson, Mike: Vol. 1.

♛ ♛ ♛

King George VI gave the Royal Assent in person only once during his reign in any of his realms (including the United Kingdom) and that was in Parliament in Ottawa on 19 May 1939.

A message from His Majesty the King was delivered by Major A.R. Thompson, Gentleman Usher of the Black Rod, the House standing: "Mr Speaker, the King commands this honourable House to attend His Majesty immediately in the chamber of the honourable the Senate."

Accordingly Mr Speaker, with the house, went up to the senate chamber to attend His Majesty.

And being returned, Mr Speaker reported that when the house did attend His Majesty in the senate chamber, His Majesty was graciously pleased to give his royal assent to the following bills: An Act respecting a certain Trade Agreement between Canada and the United States of America. [Seven other Acts are then listed.]

To these bills [with the traditional nod from the King] the royal assent was pronounced by the Clerk of the Senate in the following words:"His Majesty the King doth assent to these bills."

Then the honourable the Speaker of the House of Commons addressed His Majesty the King as follows: "May it please Your Majesty:

"The Commons of Canada have voted supplies required to enable the government to defray certain expenses of the public service.

"In the name of the Commons I present to Your Majesty the following bill: an act for granting His Majesty certain sums of money for the public service of the financial years ending the 31st March, 1939, and the 31st March, 1940, respectively.

"To which bill I humbly request Your Majesty's assent."

To this bill the Clerk of the Senate [with another nod from the

King], by command of His Majesty the King, did thereupon say: "His Majesty the King thanks his loyal subjects, accepts their benevolence, and assents to this bill."

After which His Majesty was pleased to make a most gracious speech from the throne to both houses of parliament, as followeth: [the text of the speech is then given].

Hansard, 22 May, 1939.

♛ ♛ ♛

In 1953, a year after coming to the Throne, the Queen by Act of her Canadian Parliament adopted a new royal style and title as Queen of Canada. It ran: "Elizabeth II, by the Grace of God, of the United Kingdom, Canada and Her Other Realms and Territories Queen, Head of the Commonwealth, Defender of the Faith". Not only was this the realisation of the dream of 'the Kingdom of Canada' that the Fathers of Confederation had had, it was also a very real concept to Canadians, as the Montrealer John Farthing pointed out.

The Crown is not merely a far-off institution, having vaguely to do with the Commonwealth of which we are a member, but holds a place of primary significance in our own established order of democratic government. In other words, when we speak of the Queen as the Queen of Canada it is no mere empty formality but a simple affirmation of the fact that we have a royal and not a republican form of democratic government . . .

It is not a new idea. It is as old as human civilisation itself, and for that very reason provides the surest available means of preserving, not only our civilisation as such, but all true humanity as well. Being British or being loyal to the Throne is no mere matter of sentiment; it has to do with a basic ideal of social life, and with a fully enlightened attachment to the highest ideal of democracy that the life of man has ever known. Nor has that ideal essentially to do with any single land or language or class. It is an ideal of universal significance relating to man as such. That we and others should find it enshrined in the British Monarchy we share is due, not to any claim that the ideal itself is the monopoly of the British, but to the historical fact that it is in the British monarchical order that a certain universal ideal has been preserved and most highly developed.

John Farthing, Freedom Wears A Crown.

♛ ♛ ♛

Queen Elizabeth II assumes the official title "Queen of Canada".

Another stirring scene occurred a few days later [January 1953] when [Rt Hon. Louis] St Laurent [Prime Minister of Canada] submitted to the House of Commons the proposed changes in the Queen's title. Her

Majesty was the Queen of Canada, not as holder of a separate office, he declared, but "because the people of Canada are happy to recognise as their sovereign the person who is the sovereign of the United Kingdom". The words "by the grace of God" implied a recognition by Canadians that worldly affairs were not determined exclusively by human will, but "by men and women as agents for a supreme authority". Similarly, the expression "defender of the faith" did not refer to a particular church, constituting rather a proclamation by the civil authorities of their "continued belief in a supreme power that orders the affairs of mere men" and recognition of the sovereign as "a believer in and a defender of the faith in a supreme ruler". The new royal title, "head of the Commonwealth", he went on, reflected "the realistic genius of the British people" to "accommodate itself to the requirements of new situations in the lives of men and . . . conserve the essential without having to conserve forms that to some appear to have become so outmoded that they can no longer be accepted". He stressed particularly the importance of having found a title acceptable to both Western and Asian member countries of the Commonwealth. "I think it is a magnificent thing that the peoples of India and the peoples of the Occident can look upon each other as human beings equal in every respect", he declared; just as the founders of the Canadian state realised that equality must be recognised and practised within a single country, so the founders of the modern Commonwealth realised that true equality must be recognised in international affairs . . . "It was a most moving address", replied John Diefenbaker for the official opposition. ". . . As we listened to the Prime Minister without regard to party considerations, this Parliament became a cathedral in devotion to our history, to our heritage, and to our common pursuit of freedom".

Dale C. Thomson, Louis St Laurent: Canadian.

♛ ♛ ♛

On 14 October 1957 Elizabeth II became the first Sovereign to open the Canadian Parliament in person.

I greet you as your Queen. Together, we constitute the Parliament of Canada.

♛ ♛ ♛

When the Queen, on 14 October 1957, for the first time in history opened Canada's Parliament, I wanted all Canadians to share this event. In consequence, television cameras appeared for the first time in the House and the Senate. Across the land, people were able to watch the Gentleman Usher of the Black Rod approach the door of the Commons, to see it slam in his face, and to hear him knock three times with his ebony staff and answer, "Black Rod", to the challenge, "Who is there?" The ceremony exactly as my father had seen it in 1891, and as I saw it from the benches to the left of the Speaker on 16 May 1940, and as those yet unborn will see it in their day and generation.

John G. Diefenbaker, One Canada, Vol. One.

♛ ♛ ♛

It is quite inadequate to speak of the idea of a king or of a kingdom; neither is a single idea. Each is a word as pregnant with meaning as any in human speech. Indeed, the supremest wisdom that was ever spoken could find no higher means of expression than to say: 'the kingdom ... is ... like unto ...' The word itself is like a seed, a single word in which all is involved, from which all may therefore be evolved until there grows a tree with branches sheltering the life of man. The ideal of the king and the kingly, the queen and the queenly, is inherent and ineradicable in the human heart. In it may be found all that is truly innate in the moral life of man.

John Farthing, Freedom Wears A Crown.

♛ ♛ ♛

A king is the personal centre of an order rooted in freedom and one that defies all possibility of mechanical or mathematical explanation. A king involves an ideal of life at once social and personal. Indeed it can be said that it expresses not simply an ideal of human life, but the ideal; the truly human ideal of life. Deny its true expression and one is then under compulsion to set up a hydra-headed array of substitutes.

Kingship is innate in human life precisely because all life is essentially organic in form and functioning. It follows that the British tradition of order of life is not a mere compromise or *via media*. Its middle position is in fact a third position, eschewing absolutist assumptions right and left. It affirms, not the supremacy of law, but the idea of law and order. Nor does order here mean only that which results from law. It means rather that law is but an ingredient in a social order.

John Farthing, Freedom Wears A Crown.

♛ ♛ ♛

Much of the terminology of our courts suggests that the courts are the King's courts dispensing the King's justice. Is such terminology a mere formality? The justice dispensed derives from the law and the judges who apply and interpret that law act quite independently of the will of the sovereign. The royal reference would therefore seem to be a mere matter of form.

But form is not in fact so mere and the royal form here appears to be a formality only if we assume that a king to be a king must make his individual will the law of the land. Hence the next mistaken assumption;

that when the law of the land is independent of the will of the monarch any royal reference must be a relic of the days when the king possessed all power.

But kings were not initially men who ruled according to their individual wills. Power was centred in the kingly person only because all authority was vested there. Such a centring of authority was not mere form; nor yet a cloak to conceal the absolute self-will that lurked within. It expressed rather the idea that a king was a man whose life was so completely dedicated to his people that he had no will of his own whatever.

Precisely because the royal authority expressed a certain ideal of order a king was able to delegate his judicial powers to others; men entrusted with seeing that all social conflicts were resolved in accordance with the monarchical order of life, and the principle inherent in that order. Hence the fact that courts act in independence of the individual will of the King does nothing to make our traditional terminology a formality.

John Farthing, Freedom Wears A Crown.

♛ ♛ ♛

Lester Pearson addressed the Queen at Expo in Centennial Year, 1967.

The new Canada is as modern as the day after tomorrow. But it appreciates, I hope and believe, what the heritage of our past means to our future, in the depth of our roots and the stability that comes from institutions that have proven their enduring value. One of these is the Monarchy which symbolises the political and parliamentary freedom we have inherited, broadening down throughout the ages and giving to our political life the cohesiveness which comes from continuity. It is a continuity that goes back unbroken from the budget of 1967, approved by Parliament in Ottawa, to the clerk of the exchequer in the thirteenth century making in French a report on the state of his treasury to a French-speaking king, who then tried to persuade a French-speaking council to grant him more money by raising taxes, from the people of course, particularly the wealthy ones.

La monarchie, en tant qu'institution, présente un attrait particulier quand notre Reine et son époux et sa famille symbolisent si bien et de façon si réelle tout ce qui nous est cher dans la vie familiale et dans les services désintéressés et dévoué aux autres.

Lester B. Pearson, Words & Occasions.

♛ ♛ ♛

"Canada's centennial gift to the Queen should have been her own Canadian Crown."

Jean-François Pouliot, Liberal Senator.

A Royal Wedding celebration.

On the last night of my tour of the Soviet Union in the summer of 1981, our group gave a party for our Intourist guide, Natasha. It was held in a kind of roof garden on the top floor of the Hotel Leningrad, from which we could see the battleship *Aurora* that had fired the first shot of the Bolshevik Revolution... My friend Bessie Webb and I had been sitting at the bar for a few minutes when two or three personable looking young men came and sat next to Bessie. They were Finns. It was the practice for people from Finland to go via Estonia to Leningrand to drink, because it was cheaper there. The men could speak English and they asked us if we were Canadians. We said we were and they immediately began to tell us that they had just watched the wedding of the Prince and Princess of Wales on television. They knew the exact length of the Princess' train and so many other details of the ceremony that it was obvious they had paid close attention. All of us then joined in toasting the royal couple. As Canadians we were most impressed that people from such a far away country would immediately connect Canada and the Royal Family.

Rosemary Campbell, Toronto.

The strength of Canada's constitution lies not in the words it contains but in the foundation upon which it rests, the desire of the people of Canada that their country remain strong and united.

Queen Elizabeth II, Ottawa, 17 April 1982.

A letter from the President of the United States to the Queen of Canada on the occasion of the proclamation of the Constitution Act 1982.

Your Majesty,
On the occasion of the proclamation of the Constitution Act, 1982, it gives me great pleasure to extend to Canada and to all Canadians the congratulations and best wishes of the American people.

Canada and the United States have a common dedication to the principles of individual liberty and representative government which are embodied in the Constitution that Canada celebrates today. An occasion such as this reminds us of our shared heritage and values, and the close ties of friendship that link us and have made us allies in pursuing common purposes in the world.

It is with great happiness and satisfaction that all Americans join me in saluting the kindred nation and people of Canada on this historic occasion and in assuring all Canadians of our deep and lasting goodwill.

Ronald Reagan

Dear Mr President,
Today in Ottawa I have brought into force by proclamation the Constitution Act, 1982 and I greatly appreciated your message of congratulations and best wishes.

This has indeed been an historic day for me as Queen of Canada and for my Government and people of Canada. We are delighted to know that our celebrations are shared by our close friend and neighbour.

As Canada starts another chapter in her history, we look forward to the continuation of the friendly relations with the Government and people of the United States which are so important to both countries. We extend to you and to them our warmest thanks and greetings.

Your good friend
Elizabeth R.

♛ ♛ ♛

In proposing a very gracious toast to the Prince and Princess of Wales at the Government dinner [in Vancouver in 1986], the Prime Minister reasserted his own faith in the Crown. Noting the presence of the leaders of the Progressive Conservative, Liberal, New Democratic and Social Credit Parties, Mr Mulroney quipped, "Only royalty, Sir, could bring unity out of the political diversity represented by the four of us".

Monarchy Canada.

♛ ♛ ♛

[Joseph Piccininni] still chuckles when he tells the story of the 83-year-old man he [as Citizenship Court Judge] granted citizenship to , who bowed deeply and said "Thank you, Your Majesty".

Toronto Sun, 1 May 1990.

♛ ♛ ♛

Our ceremony today brings together Sovereign, Parliament and people —the three parts of Consititutional Monarchy. That is a system in which those who represent the community come together and remain together, rather than dwelling on differences which might further divide them.

Queen Elizabeth II, Ottawa, 1 July 1990.

9

THE FEATHER, THE LILY AND THE ROSE

The relations between the French and the English (or perhaps more properly, the British) in Canada and those between both these groups and the aboriginal or first nations have been discussed, analysed and debated so much they have almost buried other equally valid aspects of Canadian existence. One cannot deny however that the relationship between these three founding peoples in Canada is the hinge upon which the fate of the Canadian state swings.

The Monarchy's historic role has been to provide the common ground or parameters within which the tensions, differences and even eruptions in those relationships can be worked out. The Monarchy has been well-placed to do that because as an institution and concept it is as much a French idea as it is a British one. The Royal Family of Canada in its traditions and ancestry is itself almost as French as it is English. And building on its natural attributes the Royal Family has for over two hundred years made a conscious effort to be a bridge and a reconciler in their Canadian realm. The Royal Family was fluently bilingual before it became fashionable in Canada but more than that its members have displayed an instinct for understanding the culture and dreams, not merely the language, of English and French in Canada.

Similarly the Monarchy is derived from tribal societies in Europe which were similar to those it found in North America. Native leaders were perceived as "kings" no different in kind from the great kings and queens in France or Britain and the native peoples of North America became the Crown's most loyal allies and subjects and developed a distinctive relationship with the Sovereign.

The Royal Family has provided true leadership, by establishing a standard of tolerance and understanding for Canadians to aspire to and actively supporting those who were willing to make an effort to reach that standard.

The *Grâce-de-Dieu* reached Port Royal towards mid-summer, on the 17th June [1609] . . . within a few days a small band of Indians arrived at the Habitation. The two captains, tall Membertou and the taller Poutrincourt, embraced like long-lost brothers . . . It was then put to Membertou that he and his family should renounce the devil and accept the Christian God and the loving Jesus whom they could see on the crucifix. Jessé Fleché would make the sign of the cross with some water on their foreheads, and give them a French name. They would then be Christians like the French. After this ceremony Poutrincourt would hold a tabagie for them to celebrate their deliverance from the devil. Membertou listened and decided that he and his group would all become Christians ...

And so Membertou became the first Indian to receive the sacrament of baptism on the shores of New France. As sagamo he was named after the King [Henri IV], who was considered to be his real godfather while Poutrincourt was only his sponsor by proxy. For this gentleman had no means of knowing that in May an assassin's knife had ended Henri's eventful life and that now all France was mourning his death.

Then came the turn of the other twenty Indians, all members of Membertou's family. His wife was baptised Marie after the Queen, his daughter Marguerite after Henri's first wife, both Queens of course being regarded as the real godmothers. Another instant convert was Membertou's oldest son. Three years before some of the French used to tease him by calling him Judas, a name he knew meant something dishonourable. On this occasion he was graced with the name of Henri's eldest son, Louis [XIII].

Elizabeth Jones, Gentlemen and Jesuits:
Quests for Glory and Adventure in the Early Days of New France.

Most of the Acadians were quiet, hard-working farmers devoted to their families and their church. The faith and courage that inspired them to build new homes on the shores of a distant sea are suggested by their national hymn.

"Ave, maris stella" has been sung in Acadia for well over three hundred years. When the early settlers were leaving the shores of France for the New World, King Louis XIII (1610-1643) suggested that they adopt a special hymn for the colony, and the one he named was this ancient Latin cantique. The Acadians still regard it as their national hymn and sing it at all their festivals, thus providing an abiding link with those first pioneers who braved the wilderness so long ago.

Edith Fowke and Alan Mills, Canada's Story In Song.

♛ ♛ ♛

Anne of Austria, the Consort of Louis XIII represented as patron to the Indians.

Other canvases scattered throughout Quebec are suggested as by this artist [Frère Luc] but they lack signatures or precise documentation and are inconsistent stylistically with those already mentioned. Their subject-matter is Canadian. *La France apportant la Foi aux Indiens de la Nouvelle-France* in the Ursuline Convent, Quebec, is one such canvas and here again there is a certain didactic pomposity of execution. It was partially repainted in the early nineteenth century, and guide-books of a hundred years ago declare that it was the work of a Franciscan in 1700. France, symbolised by the Queen Mother, Anne of Austria, shows a painting of New France's spiritual patrons to an Indian kneeling on the shore of the broad St Lawrence, while a little mission station in the distance is strangely reminiscent of that in Pommier's *Martyre*.

J Russell Harper, Painting in Canada — A history.

♛ ♛ ♛

The birth of the future Louis XIV was celebrated in North America in 1638.

In the log cabins of New France, Indians decided that "our good King has given us clothes, we will now send a gift in return", and there arrived at Saint-Germain for the heir apparent the beaded outfit of a Redskin papoose.

Vincent Cronin, Louis XIV.

♛ ♛ ♛

On the occasion of the marriage of King George III to Princess Charlotte of Mecklenburg–Strelitz in September 1761, the Indian tribes of North America took the opportunity of sending their loyal congratulations, to which the King replied by having a special medal struck which was duly sent out for presentation either at the end of 1761 or the beginning of 1762.

Melville Allan Jamieson, Medals Awarded to North American Indian Chiefs.

♛ ♛ ♛

For in those days the fields of New France produced crops of the finest wheat - a gift which Providence has since witheld. "The wheat went away with the Bourbon lilies, and never grew afterwards", said the old *habitants.*

William Kirby, The Golden Dog: A Romance of Old Quebec.

♛ ♛ ♛

King George III To Madame Chaussegros de Léry, who was the first French-Canadian lady presented at Court after the transfer of Canada to the British Crown:

Madame, si les dames canadiennes vous rassemblent, j'ai vraiment fait une conquête. [Madame, if all Canadian women resemble you, I have indeed made a fine conquest.]

♛ ♛ ♛

King George III supports the Quebec Act

The corporation of London having resolved to petition the King to refuse his sanction [to the Quebec Act], the Lord Mayor, with several aldermen, the Recorder, and a great many members of the common-council, attending at St James's just as the King was going to the house, was informed that as the petition related to a bill agreed on by the two houses of Parliament, of which his Majesty could not take notice until it was presented for his consent, they were not to expect any answer . . .

In terminating the session [in 1774], the King applauded the Quebec Act, as founded on the clearest principles of humanity and justice, and calculated to produce the best effects in quieting the minds and promoting the happiness of the Canadians.

John Adolphus, History of England, From The Accession To The Death Of King George The Third.

♛ ♛ ♛

The American rebels try to win over Jospeh Brant.

During the early part of the year 1775, while it was yet considered doubtful which side the Mohawks would espouse, and when it was of course very desirable to ascertain the views of [Joseph] Brant upon the subject, President Wheelock was applied to as a medium of communication with his former pupil. The doctor, according to the tradition, wrote him a long epistle upon the aspect of the times, and urged upon Brant those considerations which appeared most likely to win him over, or rather to secure his neutrality, if not his friendship, to the Colonists.

Brant replied very ingeniously. Among other things, he referred to his former residence with the Doctor – recalled the happy hours he had passed under his roof – and referred especially to his prayers and the family devotions, to which he had listened. He said he could never forget those prayers; and one passage, in particular, was so often repeated, that it could never be effaced from his mind. It was, among other of his good preceptor's petitions, "that they might be able to live as good *subjects* – to fear God, and HONOUR THE KING".

William L. Stone, Life of Joseph Brant – Thayendanega.

♛ ♛ ♛

When the American attack on Quebec in 1776 failed, the existence of a separate Canadian state became likely.

Le 8 mai [1776]...A la réception du succès des royalistes, les Dames Ursulines ont chanté ce matin un *Te Deum*, pendant la messe.

Invasion Du Canada Par Les Americains en 1775.

♛ ♛ ♛

When I joined the English in the beginning of the war, it was purely on account of my forefathers' engagements with the King. I always looked upon these engagements, or covenants between the King and the Indian nations, as a sacred thing: therefore I was not to be frightened by the threats of the rebels at that time; I assure you I had no other view in it, and this was my real cause from the beginning.

Joseph Brant to Sir Evan Nepean, Under Secretary of State, 1783, quoted in William L Stone, Life of Joseph Brant – Thayendanega.

♛ ♛ ♛

During his residence in London [in 1785-6, Joseph] Brant found time to supervise a new edition of the Prayer Book and Psalms in the Mohawk language, to which was added the Gospel of St Mark translated by himself. The edition was published for the S.P.G. [Society for the Propagation of the Gospel] under the immediate patronage of the King, who took a personal interest in the production. The book is printed in alternate pages of English and Mohawk; it contains several engravings of scriptural subjects, and a frontispiece representing the interior of a chapel with groups of Indians receiving copies of the volume from the hands of the King and Queen, a bishop standing on either side of the throne.

John Wolfe Lydekker, The Faithful Mohawks.

♛ ♛ ♛

With the King and royal family [Joseph Brant] was a great favourite - not the less so on his part of his Majesty, for having proudly refused to kiss his hand on his presentation. [Brant was regarded and frequently referred to as an Indian 'King' by contemporaries.] The dusky Chief, however, in declining that ceremony, with equal gallantry and address remarked that he would gladly kiss the hand of the Queen. George the Third was a man of too much sterling sense not to appreciate the feelings of his brother chief, and he loved his Queen too well not to be gratified with the turning of a compliment in her Majesty's favour, in a manner that would have done no discredit to the most accomplished cavalier of the Court of Elizabeth [I] - Sir Walter Raleigh.

William L. Stone, Life of Joseph Brant – Thayendanega.

♛ ♛ ♛

Near Mon[t]real the Indians begin to inhabit. Lord Dorchester assembled them to the amount of four hundred, & from what I experienced at first seeing these barbarians, it is not difficult to conceive that the troops under General Braddock were panick struck & cut up by them. The sensations they expressed at my visit were too strong not to be natural; their language was peculiarly pointed in saying they then saw one in whose veins flowed the same blood as in the body of their Great Father in the East, meaning your Majesty; that in the late rebellion the evil spirit had done them harm in the eyes of their loving father, but that he has sent his own son to examine them & trust that they were convinced that now they were again received as favoured children by their Great Father in the East. The Indians not only love your Majesty but they go further in adoring, their respect being so wonderfully great for every thing that relates to your Majesty. The evil spirit is General Burgoyne, for whom they have a most singular aversion.

Prince William to his father, from H.M.S. Pegasus at Quebec, 9 October 1787, The Later Correspondence of George III.

♛ ♛ ♛

The [French-] Canadians are likewise very well attached, & feel those proper sentiments of loyalty & affection for their Sovereign; in my opinion they are the happiest of your Majesty's subjects & will ever continue so till a House of Assembly will of course set them by the ears. They are very sensible of your Majesty's paternal affection in having appointed Lord Dorchester, in whose discretion they totally rely ... The universal marks of respect, love & attention that have been shown to me by all ranks of your Majesty's Canadian subjects have been invariably marked: in short, Sir, I am pleased & delighted at their attachment & respect for your Majesty. In this country a perfect harmony consists in uniting this happy people to defend their rights & privileges they can only enjoy under your Majesty. I hope to be pardoned, but as the inhabitants have all wished me to make known these sentiments, I have done it with peculiar satisfaction, as I do really believe me [sic] they are dictated by their hearts.

Prince William to his father, from H.M.S. Pegasus at Quebec, 9 October 1787, The Later Correspondence of George III.

♛ ♛ ♛

Prince Edward, later Duke of Kent and father of Queen Victoria, arrived in North America just as the Constitutional Act of 1791 separating Quebec into Upper and Lower Canada was being put into effect. This act gave Quebec its first assembly and the elections held to choose the members resulted in a riot in Quebec City which the Prince personally quelled. He exhorted the mob to

Part then in peace. I urge you to unanimity and accord. Let me hear no more of the odious distinction of English and French. You are all His Britannick Majesty's beloved Canadian subjects.

♛ ♛ ♛

The famous 'Tiger' Dunlop arrived in Canada as assistant surgeon to his regiment in 1813, at the moment an American invasion of Lower Canada threatened.

The news had arrived that the long threatened invasion had at last taken place, and every available man was hurrying [to Montreal] to meet it. We came up with several regiments of militia on their line of march. They had all a serviceable effective appearance - had been pretty well drilled, and their arms being direct from the tower, were in perfectly good order, nor had they the mobbish appearance that such a levy in any other country would have had. Their capots and trowsers of home-spun stuff, and their blue *tuques* (night caps) were all of the same cut and colour, which gave them an air of uniformity that added much to their military look... They marched merrily along to the music of their voyageur songs, and as they perceived our uniform as we came up, they set up the Indian War-whoop, followed by a shout of *Vive le Roi* along the whole line.

William Dunlop, Recollections Of The American War 1812-1814.

♛ ♛ ♛

I found myself along with my friend, Mautass, a Soc Chief, and his Indians ... These Socs or Sacs were the only genuine unadulterated Indians I ever saw. They were very fine men, few of them under six feet high, and their symmetry perfectly faultless ... Their features, too, had not the rounded form or stolid expression of many Indian tribes, particularly those towards the North. They had European features, or, more properly, those of the Asiatic. Their Chief had so strong a resemblance to George the Third that even the tribe called the head on the half penny Mautass, and he certainly might have passed for a bronze statue of that worthy and estimable Monarch.

William Dunlop, Recollections Of The American War 1812-1814.

♛ ♛ ♛

Louis-Joseph Papineau on the death of King George III in 1820.

[His Majesty] was a Sovereign respected for his moral qualities and his devotion to duty. Under his rule, religious tolerance, trial by jury - equal protection guaranteed by law to the person, honour and property of citizens, the right to obey only laws made by us and adopted by our representatives - all these advantages have become our birthright. In order to conserve them, we should act like British subjects and free men.

Speech delivered in Montreal.

♛ ♛ ♛

Victoria receives an Ojibway petition, 14 September 1838.

A court official opened the black doors. Before them stood an attractive young woman about twenty years of age, near the centre of the reception room below the crystal chandelier. To Her Majesty and the half-dozen lords and ladies in attendance Lord Glenelg announced, "Kahkewaquonaby, or Sacred Feathers, a chief of the Chippewa Indians of Upper Canada".

Sacred Feathers approached, bowing several times. The Queen returned his bows, then walked toward him, extending her hand for him to kiss. The Indian knew the exact etiquette to follow. When they met, he immediately knelt on his right knee and held up his right arm. As Victoria placed her hand on his hand he lifted and kissed it, then rose to present the petition. What a physical contrast they presented: the tall, muscular Indian and his delicate Queen, just under five feet tall.

The Indian began by explaining the Christian Indians' prayer that "Her most Gracious Majesty's Government may be pleased to secure to them and their posterity for ever all their lands on which they have located themselves". Lord Glenelg, he added, had already accepted the

Indians' request for title deeds to their reserves, documents that would prevent their removal.

Glenelg immediately bowed to the Queen, who bowed in return, acknowledging her minister's wise judgement. Thinking she might wish to keep it as a curiosity, Sacred Feathers then offered her the document, to which he had attached white and black wampum. Victoria smiled and replied; "I thank you, sir, I am much obliged to you" . . .

The Indian chief informed the Queen that the white beads represented peace and prosperity but that the black wampum at the end of the long white strings symbolised danger, suspicion, and fear. Yet when the Lieutenant-governor of Upper Canada carried out Lord Glenelg's instructions and granted title deeds it would sweep the path clean, removing all obstacles to friendship. Then the Indians would take out the black beads.

Some discussion followed of Sacred Feathers' year-long visit to Britain to raise money for the mission work in Canada, then the interview drew to a close. The Queen was engaged to join Lord Melbourne, her prime minister, Lord John Russell, and Lord and Lady Portman on a riding party. The Queen bowed, indicating that the interview had ended. The Indian did the same, stepping backward until the Queen turned her back. Lord Glenelg and the lords-in-waiting then escorted the Indian chief and the Reverend Robert Alder to an adjoining room, where the two guests were served a substantial meal before they left for London.

The visit impressed the Queen greatly, for that evening she recorded in her diary: "Soon after the Council I went into the White drawing room, attended by Lady Portman, and my Lord, Groom and Equerry, etc., and Lord Glenelg introduced an Indian Chippewa Chief – who is a Xtian [Christian] and came with a Petition. He is a tall, youngish man, with a yellowish complexion and black hair; he was in his National dress, which is entirely of leather; leather leggins, etc. He kissed my hand; he speaks English very well, and expressed himself very well".

Donald B. Smith, Sacred Feathers.

♛ ♛ ♛

The following abridged anecdote from Catlin's North American Indians *indicates how highly the Indian Chiefs regarded the medals which had been conferred upon them. George Catlin was an American painter who in 1851 published a book containing the portraits of two hundred Chiefs and warriors, together with the fullest descriptions of their history which he had collected during the previous twenty years whilst visiting forty-eight tribes in their native haunts.*

During the early years of Queen Victoria's reign, while gathering material for his book and making sketches of Indians in the United States, Catlin found several Chiefs of the Sioux and Dahcotas tribes, though living several hundred miles south of the Canadian border, wearing the medals bearing the effigy of George III and still cherishing a lasting friendship for the English. These medals had been presented to them as rewards for their services to the British during the war of 1812–1814. One of the Chiefs, learning that Catlin was soon to return to England, shook him cordially by the hand and then brought forth, with great pride, a large George III medal, which, from being worn next to his naked breast, had become very highly polished. Exhibiting the obverse of the medal and pointing to the face of His Majesty, the Chief made this singular and significant speech. "When you cross the Big Salt Lake, tell my Great Father that you saw his face, and it was bright." To this Catlin replied, "I can never see your Great Father, he is dead". After a long silence the Indian asked if there was no Great Chief in England, and on being told that a young and beautiful woman was now Queen of Great Britain, he again withdrew the medal and with much solemnity said, "Tell my Great Mother that you saw our Great Father, and that we keep his face bright".

Melville Allan Jamieson, Medals Awarded to North American Indian Chiefs.

♛ ♛ ♛

We are in our customs, by our laws, by our religion, monarchists and conservatives ... if this country ever ceases to be British, the last cannon shot fired for the maintenance of English power in America will be fired by the hand of a Canadien.

Sir Etienne Pascal Taché, Pre-Confederation Prime Minister of Canada.

♛ ♛ ♛

Eugène Tâché's famous evocation of the historic relationship of French Canada and the Crown gave Quebec its motto Je Me souviens

I remember that born under the lily I have prospered under the rose.

Je me souviens que né sous le lys je crûs sous la rose.

♛ ♛ ♛

Lord Dufferin on unveiling the statue of Queen Victoria at Montreal, 21 November 1872:

Le spectacle de deux peuples composées des nationalités si diverse s'efforçant; à l'envi l'un de l'autre de prouver leur loyauté à la Reine et au gouvernement, et travaillant de concert et dans une harmonie parfaite au bien de leur commune patrie, restera l'un des faites les plus remarquables et les plus heureux de l'histoire du monde, en même temps qu'il témoingera de la sagesse politique et des sentiments magnanimes dont sont pénétrés tous les membres de la grande famille canadienne.

Canada's Governors General, John Cowan.

♛ ♛ ♛

O Canada was written for the first visit of Queen Victoria's son-in-law the Marquis of Lorne, Governor General of Canada, to Quebec City in 1880. This is the concluding verse.

Amour sacré du trône et de l'autel
Remplis nos coeurs de ton souffl' immortel.
Parmi les races étrangères
Notre guide est la loi;
Sachons être un peuple de frères
Sous le joug de la foi;
Et répétons comme nos pères
Le cri vainqueur - Pour le Christ et le Roi!
Le cri vainqueur - Pour le Christ et le Roi!

♛ ♛ ♛

Sometimes the Indian subjects of the Queen, loyal as they were, could be exasperated by the Queen's officials. A story, perhaps apocryphal, relates a North West Mounted Police constable's account of a meeting on the plains.

The superintendent wished to express to the Chiefs the extent of the Empire and the many peoples included in it. He remarked that "the Great White Mother has many children. She has white children and brown children and yellow children and red children". Two braves were standing near me and I overheard one say, loosely translated, "It seems the morals of the Great White Mother are not what they should be".

♛ ♛ ♛

We will be loyal to the Queen whatever happens.

Crowfoot, Chief of the Blackfoot, 1885.

♛ ♛ ♛

Mr Justice Loranger . . . related at some length what the French-Canadian societies were doing towards making the celebration [of Queen Victoria's Diamond Jubilee] a success, going on to say that with a view of heartily combining with the people of all classes in the city they had decided to abandon the usual St-Jean-Baptiste procession on June 24, and join with all the citizens of all nationalities in doing honour to Her Majesty Queen Victoria ... "The parade", added the Judge, "was not one of any particular nationality, but of the subjects of Her Majesty, who had no more loyal or devoted citizens than the French-Canadians in this province".

The Montreal Gazette, 5 May 1897.

♛ ♛ ♛

The picture of the French Canadian Emma Lajeunesse, Madame Albani, singing at the funeral of Queen Victoria, inspired French Canadian poet Louis Féchette.

Albani
Au chevet funéraire de la reine Victoria
Froide, et couronne au front, la morte bien-aimée
Reposait sur un lit de rose et de jasmin;
Sombre, et debout devant la forme inanimée,
Pleurait le fils d'hier, monarque de demain.
Non loin se prosternait une autre renommé,
Artiste dont la gloire a doré le chemin,
Diva cent et cent fois des foules acclamée...
Le roi s'approcha d'elle, et la prit par la main:
"Chantez!" dit-il. Alors une voix chaude et tendre
Vibra dans le silence auguste, et fit entendre
Comme un long chant de deuil doucement sangloté...
Emotion suprême! ineffable harmonie!
C'étaient la Royauté, la Mort, et le Génie
Qui mélaient devant Dieu leur triple Majesté!

Emma Lajeunesse, Madame Albani,
Forty Years Of Song.

♛ ♛ ♛

The Duke of Cornwall and York, (later King George V) replies to the address by the Archbishop of Quebec, 1901.

I am glad to acknowledge the noble part which the Catholic Church in Canada has played throughout its history.

The hallowed memories of its martyred missionaries are a priceless heritage, and in the great and beneficent work of education and in implanting and fostering a spirit of patriotism and loyalty it has rendered signal service to Canada and the Empire ...

If the Crown has faithfully and honourably fulfilled its engagement to protect and respect your faith, the Catholic Church has amply fulfilled its obligation, not only to teach reverence for law and order, but to instil a sentiment of loyalty and devotion into the minds of those to whom its ministers.

Joseph Pope, The Tour Of Their Royal Highnesses The Duke and Duchess of York Through The Dominion Of Canada In The Year 1901.

♛ ♛ ♛

The Duke's speech on Parliament Hill, Ottawa, 20 September 1901.

The federation of Canada stands pre-eminent among the political events of the century just closed for its fruitful and beneficent results on the life of the people concerned. As in ancient times, by the union of Norman and Saxon, the English nation was produced, so by the federation of Canada the two great nations which form its population have been welded into a harmonious people, and afforded free play and opportunity to contribute each its best service to the public well-being. Creditable as this achievement is to the practical wisdom and patriotism of the statesmen who founded the union and who have since guided its destinies, it is no less honourable to the people upon whose support they had to rely, and who have, in the spirit of mutual toleration and sympathy, sustained them in the great work of union. This spirit is no less necessary than it was in the past, and I am confident that the two races will continue, each according to its special genius and opportunity, to aid and co-operate in building up the great edifice of which the foundations have been so well and truly laid.

F.A. Mackenzie, King George V In His Own Words.

♛ ♛ ♛

Reply to addresses of loyalty from the Indian tribes of south Alberta, 28 September 1901

An Indian is a true man. His words are true words; he never breaks faith; and he knows, too, that it is the same with the Great King, my Father, and with those whom He sends to carry out His wishes. His promises last as long as sun shall shine and waters shall flow, and care will ever be taken that nothing shall come between the love there is between the King and you, His faithful children.

Joseph Pope, The Tour Of Their Royal Highnesses The Duke and Duchess Of Cornwall And York Through The Dominion Of Canada In The Year 1901.

♛ ♛ ♛

As Prince of Wales, George V presided at the Tercentenary Celebrations of the founding of Quebec City in July 1908.

And here, in Quebec, I recall with much pleasure the no uncertain proofs which I have received on my several visits to Canada of the loyalty of the King's French Canadian subjects. Their proved fidelity in time of difficulty and danger, happily long passed, is one of the greatest tributes to the political genius of England's rule, and the knowledge that they and their fellow-Canadians of British origin are working hand in hand in the upbringing of the Dominion is a source of deep satisfaction to the King, as well as to all those who take pride in British institutions.

F.A. Mackenzie, King George V In His Own Words.

♛ ♛ ♛

Message sent by the King to his Inuit subjects and delivered to them in the Inuit language, 19 July 1934.

King George, who rules the British Empire, and Queen Mary, his wife, to the Inuit –

The Queen and I send our loyal Inuit subjects who dwell throughout Northern Canada and on the shores of Labrador a message of greeting from our home in the great encampment of London.

In every part of the Empire, be it ever so many sleeps from our encampment, the happiness of our subjects deeply affects the personal happiness of the Queen and myself.

You should know that we have often heard that no people are merrier or more thoughtful of their families than the Inuit.

In the same way as parents are proud of their children, the Queen and I take especial pride in our faithful and hardy Inuit.

May each Inuit family thrive, and may your children and grandchildren learn in their turn to do honour alike to their parents and to the British Empire.

The King To His People: Being the Speeches and Messages of His Majesty King George the Fifth between July 1911 and May 1935.

♛ ♛ ♛

[King George V] gave me wise advice. One thing he impressed upon me was to be sympathetic to the French people in Canada, and jealously to respect their traditions and their language.

John Buchan [Baron Tweedsmuir,
Governor General of Canada],
Memory Hold-The-Door.

♛ ♛ ♛

Two Canadian regiments [serving in the United Kingdom during World War Two] of which the King and Queen were colonels-in-chief respectively, the Royal 22nd and the Toronto Scottish, were given the honour of providing the King's Guard at the Royal Palaces for a tour of duty. The

Guard Commander on each occasion kindly asked me to dine in the Mess at St James's Palace. When the Royal 22nd was on duty, the sentry's orders were printed in both French and English, and French was used at the Mess dinner when the King's health was proposed by the junior officer – 'Messieurs, le Roi!' To anybody with any historical feeling, that was very moving. I wondered when French had last been officially used in the precincts of the Palace – certainly not since medieval times. That, of course, was Norman French and here was a link, for the young officer on this occasion, like nearly all French-speaking Canadians, probably had a Norman background.

Vincent Massey, What's Past Is Prologue: The Memoirs of the Right Honourable Vincent Massey.

♔ ♔ ♔

From an address by Queen Elizabeth II to the Quebec Legislature, 1964, delivered while separatists rioted outside.

The role of a constitutional monarchy is to personify the democratic state, to sanction legitimate authority, to assure the legality of its measures, and to guarantee the execution of the popular will. In accomplishing this task, it protects the people against disorder.

♔ ♔ ♔

The French language newspaper L'Action wrote of the Queen's presence with a sense of history. [translation]

Long before Ottawa was seized, as it is now, of the bilingual and bicultural ferment, the Crown was establishing the fact, in all its interventions in Canada, of equality of the two languages beyond the letter of the Constitution. The Queen as an ally of Quebec nationalism? And why not? In a sense she always has been.

L'Action, Quebec City, 7 August 1964.

♔ ♔ ♔

It is agreeable to me to think that there exists in our Commonwealth a country where I can express myself officially in French.

Queen Elizabeth II , St. Pierre, Manitoba, 1970.

10

GOVERNOR GENERALITIES

An obviously vital link in the functioning of the Monarchy in Canada is the viceregal one, which comprises the Governors General of Canada and the provincial Lieutenant-governors since Confederation and the Governors, Governors-In-Chief and Governors-General of British North America and New France and provincial Lieutenant-governors before Confederation.

The essential role of a viceroy is to be a conduit or channel between the Sovereign, when not present, and the people. Their success is a measure of how well they have performed this task. In fulfilling their role they have wide scope for means and emphasis and as they have been drawn from such a wide spectrum of backgrounds and interests this diversity in the Crown has been given full play in Canada.

It is inevitable that a few, such as Vincent Massey, have been exceptional in their understanding of kingship and in the written and oral legacy they have left us. As well Col. H. Willis-O'Connor, who served as Principal Aide-de-Camp to Governors General for a quarter century (when appointed in 1921 he was the first Canadian to hold the post since Charles de Salaberry in 1821), left a treasure chest of reminiscences. Thus, there follows no attempt to provide a geographical or chronological balance in anecdotes or comments on the Monarchy involving viceroys but rather to select those which best convey its essence and offer the most interesting or significant expressions of the Crown.

Religious Canada prays each Sunday that [the governor general] may govern well, on the understanding that Heaven will never be so unconstitutional as to grant her prayer.

Goldwin Smith.

COUNT LOUIS DE FRONTENAC

When a New England army under Sir William Phipps besieged Quebec City in 1690, an emissary of Phipps called on Frontenac in the name of King William III and Queen Mary to surrender, concluding with the admonition that he must have a reply within an hour. Frontenac replied:

"I will not keep you waiting so long. Tell your general that I do not recognise King William, and that the Prince of Orange, who so styles himself, is a usurper, who has violated the most sacred laws of blood in attempting to dethrone his father-in-law [King James II]. I know no King of England but King James. Your general ought not to be surprised at the hostilities which he says that the French have carried on in the colony of Massachusetts; for, as the King my master, has taken the King of England under his protection, and is about to replace him on his throne by force of arms, he might have expected that His Majesty would order me to wage war on a people who have rebelled against their lawful prince."

The emissary, taken aback, asked if the governor would give him his answer in writing. Frontenac replied

"No, I will answer your general only by the mouths of my cannon."

Francis Parkman, Count Frontenac and New France under Louis XIV.

SIR JOHN WENTWORTH

On his journeys as surveyor general, [Sir John] Wentworth had visited the black settlements at Shelburne, Annapolis and Digby and was aware of the discontent among the Black Loyalists. He attributed their difficulties to their sudden emancipation from masters who had suppressed any sense of their ability to provide for themselves; he blamed the government for not paying enough attention to their settlement in the confusion surrounding the Loyalist migration. Once he was governor, Wentworth made a point of visiting those blacks who remained, assuring them of his interest and protection. A number were recruited into the Nova Scotia Regiment as pioneers (infantry labourers) and a black company was formed and attached to the 1st Battalion of the Halifax militia. Under Wentworth's administration the blacks received more considerate treatment from government and had reason to put some trust in it. Wentworth was proud of the fact that during his governorship slavery virtually died out in Nova Scotia.

Brian C. Cuthbertson, The Loyalist Governor: Biography of Sir John Wentworth.

♛ ♛ ♛

On Seeing His Excellency Sir John Wentworth [Governor of Nova Scotia] Passing Through Granville, On His Way To Annapolis

When Tyrants travel, though in Pompous State,
Each Eye beholds them with indignant Hate;
Destroying Angels thus are said to move
The objects more of Terror than of Love;
For Grandeur can't, unless with Goodness join'd
Afford true pleasure to the virtuous Mind.

But when our loyal WENTWORTH deigns to ride,
(The Sovereign's fav'rite and the Subject's Pride,)
Around his Chariot crowding Numbers throng,
And hail his Virtues as he moves along:
Such high Respect shall be conferr'd on HIM
The King delights to honour and esteem;
Whose LOYALTY unshaken, spotless Fame,
And social Virtues shall endear his Name
In ev'ry loyal Bosom long to live,
As our lov'd MONARCH'S REPRESENTATIVE.

Brian C. Cuthbertson, The Loyalist Governor: Biography of Sir John Wentworth, quoting an anonymous poet.

VISCOUNT MONCK
an American view

I'm at present existin' under a monikal form of Gov'ment. In other words I'm travelin' among the crowned heds of Canady. They ain't pretty bad people. On the cont'ry, they air exceedin' good people.

Troo, they air deprived of many blessins. They don't enjoy, for instans, the priceless boon of a war. They haven't any American Egil to onchain, and they hain't got a Fourth of July to their backs.

Altho' this is a monikal form of Gov'ment, I am onable to perceeve much moniky. I tried to git a piece in Toronto, but failed to succeed.

Mrs. VICTORIA, who is Queen of England, and has all the luxuries of the markets, incloodin' game in its season, don't bother herself much about Canady, but lets her do 'bout as she's mighter. She, however, gin'rally keeps her supplied with a lord, who's called a Gov'ner Gin'ral. Sometimes the politicians of Canady make it lively for this lord – for Canady has politicians, and I expect they don't differ from our politicians, some of em bein' gifted and talented liars, no doubt.

The present Gov'ner Gin'ral of Canady is Lord MONK. I saw him review some volunteers at Montreal. He was accompanied by some other lords and dukes and generals and those sort of things. He rode a little bay horse, and his close wasn't any better than mine. You'll always notiss, by the way, that the higher up in the world a man is, the less good harness he puts on. Hence Gin'ral HALLECK walks the streets in plain citizen's dress, while the second lieutenant of a volunteer regiment piles all the brass things he can find onto his back, and drags a forty-pound sword after him.

MONK has been in the lord bisniss some time, and I understand it pays, tho' I don't know what a lord's wages is. The wages of sin is death and postage stamps. But this has nothing to do with MONK.

Passage by dialect humourist Charles F. Browne from Artemus in Canada, quoted in Yankees in Canada: A Collection of Nineteenth-Century Travel Narratives.

EARL OF DUFFERIN

Lord Dufferin was keenly interested in the debates that took place in the House of Commons and suggested to Sir John A. that a place might be found for him in the House where he could follow the proceedings, and suggested that a secret closet be arranged for him. However this could not be done as under the British Constitution, the King cannot attend the session of Parliament, and this applied also to the Governor General as his personal representative. In a letter dated 30 September 1873, His Excellency wrote to Sir John A. as follows: "You half promised to arrange for some little closet for me in the House of Commons from whence I could hear what was going on. I hope you will be able to see your way to gratifying my wishes in this respect. Considering how untrustworthy are the newspaper reports, it is a matter of some importance that I should be able to hear with my own ears what passes".

The reply of Sir John is an indication of his shrewdness. He said that he would be only too glad to comply with His Excellency's request but doubted the prudence of [it] himself... "I do not suppose the Opposition leaders would use any unsavoury phrases, but there are several truculent blackguards in the House – annexationists and the like – who would like nothing better than snubbing the Sovereign. I shall send for Scott this week and see if a plan can be devised whereby you can be present without being known. I doubt his being able to manage this, and, if not, I would advise you to forgo the advantage which a hearing of the debate would certainly be to you". Of course the arrangement could not be carried out, but, by a piece of diplomacy the problem was solved – Lady Dufferin could be present in the House, which she was, and was able to tell her husband all about the debates and the agility displayed by Sir John during the debate.

John Cowan, Canada's Governors General.

♛ ♛ ♛

From Lord Dufferin's speech to the National Club, Toronto.

"The head of the State in a constitutional régime is the depository of what, though undoubtedly a very great, is a latent power – a power which, under the auspices of wise parliamentary statesmanship, is never suffered to become active, and his ordinary duties are very similar to those of the humble functionary we see superintending the working of some complicated mass of steam-driven machinery. This personage merely walks about with a little tin vessel of oil in his hand and he pours in a drop here and a drop there, as occasion or the creaking of the joint may require, while his utmost vigilance is directed to no higher aim than the preservation of his wheels and cogs from the intrusion of dust, grits or other foreign bodies. (Roars of laughter.) There, gentlemen, what was I saying? See how easily an unguarded tongue can slip into an ambiguous expression – (uproarious laughter) – an expression which I need not assure you is on this occasion entirely innocent of all political significance." When it is remembered that "Grits" was then the popular name for Liberals, the humour of these remarks will be appreciated.

John Cowan, Canada's Governors General.

♛ ♛ ♛

Lord Dufferin's address to the St Jean-Baptiste Society of Quebec:

Your past has refused to die. Its vitality was too exuberant, too rich with splendid achievements, too resonant, too replete with the daring and gallantry of stately seigneurs – the creations of able statesmen – the martyrdoms of holy men and women, to be smothered by the dust of ages, or overwhelmed by the uproar of subsequent events . . . I can truly say that whenever I pace the frowning platform of your Citadel, or make the circuit of your ramparts, or wander through your gabled streets, I instinctively regard myself as much the direct successor of those brave and courtly Viceroys who presided over your early destiny, as I am the successor of Lord Lisgar, Lord Monck or Lord Elgin.

John Cowan, Canada's Governors General.

♛ ♛ ♛

Lord Dufferin told me himself . . . that on the occasion of his official visit to British Columbia . . . as Governor General, he was expected to drive under a triumphal arch which had been erected at Victoria, Vancouver Island. This arch was inscribed on both sides with the word "Separation". I remember perfectly Lord Dufferin's actual words in describing the incident: "I sent for the Mayor of Victoria, and told him that I must have a small – a very small – alteration made in the inscription, before I could consent to drive under it; an alteration of one letter only. The initial "S" must be replaced with an "R", and then I would pledge my word that I would do my best to see that "Reparation" was made to the Province". This is so eminently characteristic of Lord Dufferin's method that it is worth recording. The suggested alteration in the inscription was duly made, and Lord Dufferin drove under the arch.

Lord Frederic Hamilton, The Days Before Yesterday.

EARL OF MINTO

A spell of bad weather was responsible for an untoward contretemps when the Governor General and Lady Minto came West. They had been invited by Mr Elliot Galt, president of the Coal Company, to pay him a visit, and to go out to a new settlement named Magrath, about twenty-two miles from Lethbridge. It was settled by Mormons, who had announced their intention of making the country blossom like the rose. Their Excellencies were coming to us from the Pacific Coast, and Mr Commissioner Perry and I met their train at Fernie, which had been known as "Coal Creek" when I had spent a night or two there in the "tote" road days. The new name was given to it after that of the original settler. Our first objective was Lethbridge, where rain was threatening. The programme for the morrow was this: eighteen miles out from Lethbridge on the south-bound railway was the village of Stirling, which was the name of the first Mormon bishop, and there we had placed a temporary camp of half-a-dozen men, with saddle horses for the family and suite of the viceregal party who might wish to ride, and light spring wagons for the convenience of others. It came on to rain heavily that night, and the next morning was so wet that I went to ask Mr Galt what the programme was to be. He replied, "Oh! I think you'll find they'll go", and so it was. We all took the special train which had been provided as far as Stirling, and there we naturally found everything sopping wet. It only remained to pack the ladies into a spring wagon with oil sheets, etc.; the gentlemen elected to ride, and we galloped over the twenty-mile prairie road to Magrath. We duly arrived at our destination in good spirits and with good appetites, but a little later than we had intended.

It was, therefore, somewhat disconcerting to find that the Magrath people had come to the conclusion that even English men and women would not be crazy enough to travel in such weather, and had *eaten the luncheon* provided for their guests. Their Excellencies, as might be expected of English nobility, took the whole matter so good-naturedly and unconcernedly that the situation was in no way uncomfortable. It was not long, however, before a very nice, satisfying mid-day meal was served to make up for our long fast. In the unsatisfactory state of the weather there was little else to be done but to talk and speechify, and that came quite easy to Mormon apostles, so that as soon as the weather cleared a little we started on our twenty-two mile run to Lethbridge.

We had ahead of us a similar jaunt on the following day to the Blood Reserve from Macleod, and to facilitate this operation we loaded our horses into a box-car and attached it to the viceregal train. We then went out to the Blood Reserve, and had luncheon, and we saw what was to be seen, being guests there of Mr W. Wilson, the Indian Agent. Lady Minto told the Indians that she was descended from a famous Indian princess, Pocahontas. They were not at all impressed by the circumstance, and as a matter of fact did not believe the story.

Captain R. Burton Deane, Mounted Police Life in Canada, A Record of Thirty-one Years' Service.

VISCOUNT BYNG

The other tour which has lived clearly in my memory was made the following year [1923]. Everything had been planned for a visit to the Maritimes but between the planning and the tour, a bad strike broke out in Sydney, N.S., and the Ottawa Government – getting the wind up, after the fashion of Governments, decreed that we must cut out that part of our tour. They hadn't realised that my husband had a mind of his own and, once he had undertaken to do a thing, or keep a promise, he never reneged "come hell and high water". So he turned down their objections with the plain statement that he was going to Sydney. Then they suggested, perhaps with an idea of still stopping him, that, of course "Her Excellency couldn't go". He answered that it depended entirely on what I decided. Naturally I said I was going – why not? There was much head-shaking in political circles and they disapproved still more when Julian announced that he wished to have no police protection during our stay there. To them this seemed rank madness. But my husband was wiser than they, so we went.

Having visited the other places on the schedule we reached Sydney on a hot summer's day, to find a seething mob milling on the platform onto which we stepped, as cheers rang out. Everybody crowded round us laughing, shouting, welcoming us warm-heartedly till a way was cleared to the waiting cars by the leaders of the strike, and we drove off to the town hall for the usual reception, speeches and lunch – just as we should have done in any other town when on tour. After the meal we were taken round by the managers of the works – who didn't seem much pleased at doing so, to judge by their rather gloomy faces as crowds mustered everywhere, friendly crowds. Before returning to the train the workers asked if we would be their guests at a reception in the public gardens that night and we accepted. More horror from the officials! But it was, they decided, our funeral, not theirs – if there was to be a funeral at all. I shall never forget that reception of thousands, mostly ex-soldiers and their wives and families, of whom not one of them would have allowed anything to harm us. How many handshakes we gave and received that night I never knew – but our hands and arms ached by the time we were escorted back to the train, to find a bodyguard of the strikers – because they knew there were no police.

How right my husband had been in his judgement! Had we allowed the presence of police it would have looked as though we didn't trust the people in Sydney, and they were quick to respond to the trust placed in them. When we left next day it was from the same seething crowd, singing "Will ye no come back again?" From what little I glimpsed of conditions there, in those days, my sympathy was entirely with the men, for I never saw a more wretched lot of hovels or a more complete lack of any attempt at social service for the employees, though I believe all that has changed since those long-ago days.

(Evelyn) Viscountess Byng of Vimy,
Up The Stream Of Time.

♛ ♛ ♛

Another episode occurred when visiting two small and remote towns within a mile of one another. Nothing would induce them to make it a joint affair, so we had to pass from one to the other, and how we were able to do this had evidently been a bone of contention. Town A had a fire engine and two white horses; town B had a hearse and two black horses plus an antiquated landau, the only horse-drawn vehicle available. That led to more discussion – to put it mildly! – till they decided to pool their resources. The hearse horses, rather rusty blacks, were put between traces of the landau, the white fire-engine horses in the lead, and to satisfy the two Jehus they were both put on the box, each driving his own team. Away we went, a long snake-like procession in the summer sunshine, headed by the local band, the ex-Servicemen, and so forth, while behind the carriage came Boy Scouts, Girl Guides, the "City Fathers" in cars, and the rest of the outfit. All went well till we realised there was a violent argument raging between our drivers, which terminated in the abrupt halting of the carriage, so that everybody behind us telescoped with everybody else, while the band and ex-Servicemen got a good start. Then we saw the cause of the trouble. One of the coachmen had been chewing tobacco and the time had come for him to spit, and had he not stopped we should have had it full in the face. However, he did stop, spat vigorously and harmlessly over the side, then whipped the horses into a smart trot in order to overtake the advance guard; which meant that those behind us had to come along breathlessly at the double in order not to lose touch. I often wonder who said what to who, when we had left the district!

(Evelyn) Viscountess Byng of Vimy,
Up The Stream Of Time.

♛ ♛ ♛

An episode of a different type happened to us on, I think, the Arrow Lakes. We were scheduled to do a show at a very small place there and, as usual dressed in our best, on a dry hot day we foregathered on the deck of the steamer which was our temporary home, rather bemoaning the fact that we couldn't go for a walk in the cool of the evening instead of stewing at a reception. The small settlement for which we were making lay round a wooded promontory jutting into the lake and the Captain sounded a formidable blast on his siren to appraise the inhabitants of our august approach. Round the corner we swung, to find a completely bare stretch of sand, except for an old, old man sitting on a log and smoking a pipe, while a few dogs flew barking furiously to the water's edge at this disturbance of their siesta. It was rather startling, as we had settled long ago – at the request of the local reeve – to visit this spot, so an A.D.C. was sent ashore to tackle the barking dogs and "the oldest inhabitant", who hadn't stirred on our approach, but continued smoking his pipe. Back came the emissary convulsed with laughter and leaving the old man still peacefully smoking. He had simply jerked his pipe towards the distance and said that everybody was fighting a fire up in the forest out of sight! Evidently in the excitement of the fire our visit had been wiped off the tablets of their minds. Anyhow, we were delighted and I don't think any of us ever made a quicker change of clothes from best bib and tucker into "ratcatcher", and we went for a lovely walk, though pestered by flies and mosquitoes. But that was the only complete "flop" in all our trips on thousands of miles. I believe if my memory serves me right we covered by boat and train well over a hundred thousand miles in our five years of office.

(Evelyn) Viscountess Byng of Vimy,
Up The Stream Of Time.

♛ ♛ ♛

There always remained in Julian – as I think in all really great men – something of the mischievousness of a boy. He delighted in escaping from the tutelage and supervision of his staff, and I remember an occasion when he managed to sneak off the train while we were in the West, parked in a remote siding and ready to pull on next morning for a "show" in some neighbouring town. As he strode over the prairie, there wasn't another soul in sight except an elderly farmer in an equally elderly buggy, who stopped, and they began to talk. Gathering that the man on foot was a stranger the farmer said, "Guess you've come in for the Governor General's visit in town tomorrow?"

My husband said he had and the farmer asked whether he knew "Old Byng", to which Julian answered, "Yes".

"Umph", grunted the farmer "What's the — like?"

"Oh, not so bad on the whole."

"High hat?"

"I don't think so. But why not come and see for yourself at the reception?"

A grunt from the old man. Then grudgingly, as he moved on "Well, I guess I may as well go and see the old son of a —. My lad served under him and said he was a damned good fighter".

Next day at the reception he duly appeared, and when he came up, rather taken aback, to shake hands with us, Julian said, "Well, is the old — so bad after all?" They had a good laugh over it and the farmer slapped him hard on the shoulder, for Julian had made a firm friend.

(Evelyn) Viscountess Byng of Vimy,
Up The Stream Of Time.

♛ ♛ ♛

Winter was the busiest time at Rideau Hall, with entertaining, while the House was in session. Soon after our arrival my husband inaugurated small parties for M.P.s, who dined informally with himself and a few other men, and in this way he entertained members, many of whom did not own evening dress, for, as he wisely said, why should they be denied the hospitality of Rideau Hall by such a minor thing as lack of the "wedding garment"? These small dinners, of from twelve to fourteen, were much appreciated by all concerned, and by nobody more than the host, who met his guests informally and gained, at first hand, knowledge of conditions in far-flung corners of the Dominion better than by any other means. I know how keen he was for these dinners to be continued by his successors, but they weren't.

(Evelyn) Viscountess Byng of Vimy,
Up The Stream Of Time.

♛ ♛ ♛

So never let us give up pomp and shows, but let Parliament throughout the Empire open to the noise of guns, the crash of bands and all those attributes which pertain to kingship and its representatives. But once that representative has stepped off his temporary pedestal let him put all this behind him, remember that the honour and glory never belonged to him as an individual, but only as the representative of the Sovereign, and let him slip back into his own niche in life, glad to feel that he has done his best to serve his King and country.

(Evelyn) Viscountess Byng of Vimy,
Up The Stream Of Time.

VISCOUNT WILLINGDON

The Governor General in those days was always surrounded by an English staff, and [the Prime Minister, Mackenzie] King just did not get on with them too well. And I must say, I began to appreciate his feelings just recently when I was down in Ottawa digging in the archives, in the Governor General's records, and I came across some notes made by the Secretary to the Governor General. I am not sure which secretary it was, but the Governor General was Lord Willingdon. The notes were made of tours around Canada by the Governor General and Lady Willingdon. It was not the Governor General talking, it was the secretary . . . the whole thing is a record of a trek through a foreign land. There are the strangest things: Fredericton, although the capital of New Brunswick, is "a small and unimportant place", and then it goes on to say that the people were not really interested in the Governor General, and the local aide de camp drank too much; and there are condescending comments about the Lieutenant-governor and his wife. After reading things of that sort, I rather sympathise with Mackenzie King in his feelings about the enclave at Government House.

C.P. Stacey, "Mackenzie King and The Monarchy",
Monarchy Canada.

♛ ♛ ♛

The best secretary we ever had, beyond any doubt, was Eric Mieville (now Sir Eric). He went to India with the Willingdons and was given a knighthood, which he richly deserved. Later, he was appointed assistant secretary to His Majesty, King George V.

To catalogue Eric's virtues would make him sound like the spotless hero of an early Victorian novel. He was certainly no gilded saint, but he was pure gold. Responsible and dependable in his duties, calm under stress, courteous at all times and broad in his sympathies, he was the embodiment of a Governor General's dream. In social activities his manners were flawless. He gave to an old lady of eighty or a young girl of eighteen the same flattering and courtly attention and his interest was not assumed, it was genuinely warm and spontaneous. He kept his ear to the ground, and was exceedingly well-informed on Canadian affairs.

H. Willis-O'Connor and Madge Macbeth,
Inside Government House.

♛ ♛ ♛

The Willingdons instituted a new routine called Personally Conducted Tours. After luncheon, guests were shown certain parts of Government House.

It was my turn to "guide" when a group of British pressmen came to us. In passing the portraits of George III and his Queen, I said: "This is really George III, but when taking United States visitors through this room I always tell them it is George II, realising that George III doesn't linger in their memory as a very sympathetic person".

An appreciative laugh rewarded this confidence, so I tried out other bits of nonsense. Ushering them into a screened-in verandah, I announced seriously:

"We call this the Meat Safe."

After a moment's puzzlement, a bright lad cried:

"Of course! The sort of thing they have in India to protect food from animals."

Somewhat later, an account of the "tour" was published in an English paper. My foolishness was reported word for word, in all seriousness.

"Her Excellency isn't going to see the funny side of this", I told myself uneasily. So I hid this paper under a pile of junk that no one ever touched.

But she got another copy of the article somewhere, and sent for me.

I approached the viceregal presence with a falsely jaunty air.

"Willis", she said, "have you read this amazing report of the British pressmen's visit to us?" The glint in her eye and flush on her cheek warned me that a spot of innocence was indicated.

"Not yet", I trifled with my conscience. "What does it say?"

She told me in no uncertain terms, and it didn't sound any better in the telling. I thought fast.

"What absurdity!" I cried. "And those fellows seemed so intelligent. I can't think what the British press is coming to, Your Excellency. Soon it'll be worse than the Hearst papers!"

H. Willis-O'Connor and Madge Macbeth,
Inside Government House.

EARL OF BESSBOROUGH

At 10 o'clock each morning Lady Bessborough used to receive us aides in her bedroom, in accordance with a good old French custom. We discussed the programme for the day.

This is not an hour when the majority of women look their best, but I never entered the room without being struck afresh by her loveliness. She wore some kind of a negligée over what I supposed were her night clothes and one day in a bold, bad moment, I said:

"Your Excellency, I feel like Louis XIV visiting Madame de Maintenon."

"Oh, but Colonel", she laughed, "I am completely dressed under this peignoir. I am almost ready for the street".

H. Willis-O'Connor and Madge Macbeth,
Inside Government House.

♛ ♛ ♛

His Excellency's big headache however, was a monthly private letter to the King. He would stew over this for days. In fact, he was always stewing, for he no sooner finished one report than he began another.

I was relaxing in my office one afternoon after a trying day, a cigarette in my mouth, my feet on the desk, when a pattering of steps sounded in the hall, the door opened and Lord Bessborough walked in.

I jumped up, pulled out a chair and mumbled:

"Well, you have certainly caught me, today sir. What can I do for you?"

"Nothing. It's only that I've finished my letter to the King and I had to tell somebody!"

H. Willis-O'Connor and Madge Macbeth,
Inside Government House.

♛ ♛ ♛

We received a magazine which had published a full-page picture of Their Excellencies in Court regalia, a large Coat-of-Arms and a small paragraph featuring the soup. Of course, we were furious, but there wasn't much we could do. Anonymous letters began to arrive, protesting against the indignity of linking the King's representative with vulgar advertising. We knew that Lord Bessborough would be exceedingly annoyed at this exploiting of his name and position, not only on his own account but because of possible unpleasant repercussions at Buckingham Palace, so we decided to prevent the article from coming to his attention. We searched every magazine that came in and cut out the offensive pages.

However, the advertisement *did* reach Buckingham Palace, at about the same time that letters – mostly condemning it – poured in. An official close to His Majesty wrote me:

"What's all this excitement about in Canada? Why shouldn't Bessborough be 'in the soup'? Don't any of you know that the King's head decorates every chocolate bar in England?"

There was an amusing aftermath to this flurry. When Mrs Herridge (Mildred Bennett [sister of Rt Hon. R.B. Bennett, Prime Minister of Canada]) was chatelaine of our Embassy in Washington, her name appeared in a testimonial of Borden's Milk. His Excellency expressed sharp disapproval.

"I think it's shocking", he said one night at dinner, "that Mildred has allowed her name to be used for such a purpose".

H. Willis-O'Connor and Madge Macbeth,
Inside Government House.

BARON TWEEDSMUIR

[The King's] importance is not so much in what he does as what he is. We are a democracy in which the will of the people prevails by means of their elected representatives. But the King represents the people in a deeper sense – the abiding continuity of the nation behind all the mutations and vicissitudes of parties.

Baron Tweedsmuir, Governor General of Canada, quoted in Vincent Massey, Confederation on the March.

♛ ♛ ♛

From a speech by Lord Tweedsmuir at the tenth anniversary of the Canadian Institute of International Affairs, 1937.

Canada is a sovereign nation and cannot take her attitude to the world docilely from Britain or from the United States or from anybody else. A Canadian's first loyalty is not to the British Commonwealth of Nations but to Canada and to Canada's King, and those who deny this are doing a great disservice to the Commonwealth.

Quoted in John Cowan, Canada's Governor-General.

♛ ♛ ♛

From a speech at the Canadian-American Conference, Kingston, Ontario, 17 June 1937.

I like to think of her [Canada], with her English and French peoples, as in a special degree the guardian of the great Mediterranean tradition which descends from Greece and Rome, and which she has to mould to the uses of a new world. I want to see her keep her clear-cut individuality, for that is of inestimable advantage, not only to her, but to her neighbour. There is far more hope of effective co-operation between nations which are not too much alike, but which understand and respect each other's stalwart idiosyncrasies. We, in Canada, get a good deal from the United States, most of it good, some of it, like all borrowings, not so good. I believe that the time will come when the United States will get a good deal from us. Sometimes I hear pessimists here complain of the dangerous influence of the United States on Canada. Some day I hope pessimists on the other side of the border-line will talk of the dangerous influence of Canada on the United States. And then I shall die happy.

John Cowan, Canada's Governors General.

♛ ♛ ♛

Lady Tweedsmuir went to visit an Institute Branch in some small community Behind the Beyond, and because her lady-in-waiting, Mrs Pape, was ill, I was asked to accompany her. We were greeted by *God Save the King* played on an organ of the hand-pumping type and most of the events of the afternoon might be described as period pieces. When it was all over, Her Excellency said to me:

"I have just been asked whether my valet would eat with me or in the kitchen!"

Me a valet? Why, I was dressed in full military uniform including the King's aiguillette which is a solid gold cord with gold tassels worn over the chest.

"What did you say?" I stuttered.

"That it would be better to have you with me; that you might be in the way in the kitchen!"

H. Willis-O'Connor and Madge Macbeth,
Inside Government House.

EARL OF ATHLONE

Speech to the Canadian and Empire Clubs at Toronto, 20 January 1941 by the Earl of Athlone.

We must never forget that the Throne, as we know it and have made it, is far greater than anyone who can ever occupy it. It is the keystone of the way of life and system of government, with all its imperfections, we believe to be the best that has yet been devised.

It is ours and we mean to keep it, and when we say we are going to fight for it, we mean we are going to fight for the cause of freedom of thought and liberty of conscience and for the smaller humble and harmless things that make up daily life.

John Cowan, Canada's Governors General.

VINCENT MASSEY

B.K. Sandwell, publisher of Saturday Night, on hearing of the appointment of Vincent Massey as Governor General, quipped:

Let the Old World, where rank's yet vital,
Part those who have and have not title.

Toronto has no social classes -
Only the Masseys and the masses.

Quoted in William Kilbourn, The Toronto Book: An Anthology of Writings Past and Present.

♛ ♛ ♛

When I first went to Government House, the question arose in the minds of some whether I would abolish some of the existing practices. Why this question was asked I cannot say, except that some people thought that as a Canadian I would introduce, to use a sadly abused word, a more 'democratic' atmosphere. The matter went further than mere gossip. I was under strong pressure from some persons in high places to abolish the practice that ladies have always followed of curtsying to the Governor General. This, I felt, was a matter I had to settle for myself; curtsying, of course, as so many people know, is simply a survival of a practice followed by ladies until very late in the nineteenth century – a form of salutation to anyone, as natural and normal as that of lifting of a man's hat. It survives in relation to the Sovereign, members of his or her family, and the Sovereign's representatives, and is comparable to the bow that marks a man's respect for these offices. I decided without any hesitation to let matters take their course, and the curtsy remained unchanged. It was quite obvious that the ladies preferred to have it so. When an inquiry was made about the matter, which didn't happen often, the answer given from Government House was that it is customary but not obligatory.

Vincent Massey, What's Past Is Prologue.

♛ ♛ ♛

The rights of the Monarch are, in essence, indestructible, and in practice they provide the quality of give-and-take vital to the working of government. Like shock-absorbers, they reduce jolts to the body politic and, in difficult situations, provide the flexibility which is the secret of success.

Vincent Massey, Confederation on the March.

♛ ♛ ♛

There are those who deny the potency of pageantry even when confronted with concrete examples. These people profess to 'see through it all', and because they believe themselves unaffected they think everyone else is as unemotional and, indeed, cynical as they wish to be. But the facts are against them; the vast majority of people are intensely moved by a fine ceremony that has meaning.

And the facts are equally against those who, having no respect for the Crown themselves, believe everyone else to be similarly disposed. Of course, the people's support for it will be influenced by their leaders' respect – or disrespect. Disparagement is catching, and those who would try to make the Crown a cock-shy can do it enormous damage that takes years to repair. The Sovereign can rarely reply except by example, and so the support of the Crown by popular leaders is the more important. Like disparagement, respect is also catching.

This is especially so in the case of the Monarchy, because it is so related to our emotions. It has clearly not been scientifically conceived. While, as I have said, its powers and qualities may sometimes seem unreal, in fact they do exist, and it is for the very reason that they are so entirely human that they are real and perform real functions.

Vincent Massey, Confederation on the March.

♛ ♛ ♛

What is a more understandable complaint is that, by being abroad, the Sovereign is, in some indefinable way, not wholly ours. No doubt this is true – the Queen is ours, but not wholly ours, and therein lies not something less, but something more, for us to cherish.

Vincent Massey, Confederation on the March.

♛ ♛ ♛

In Canada, the roots of monarchy have existed since the earliest times. Canada has always been a monarchy. First, under the French, next, under the English, and now, under our own Queen – for, as a Canadian prime minister pointed out sixty years ago: "The compact which the King makes with his people when he ascends the Throne is a compact which he makes with us as well as with the people of the Mother Country". So said Sir Robert Borden. The doctrine of the divisibility of the Crown is the type of mental gymnastic that delights only the constitutional lawyer. All of it that matters to us is that the Queen is, in fact, as she is known to be: the Queen of Canada. This is not a romantic fiction, but a constitutional truth. A host of usages underline Her Majesty's place in a singularly Canadian institution of monarchy that has claimed and can continue to claim the hearts and allegiance of all Canadians.

Vincent Massey, Confederation on the March.

♛ ♛ ♛

... under our system, the prime minister speaks for the government, the sovereign for the people.

Vincent Massey, Confederation on the March.

♛ ♛ ♛

The Monarchy is essential to us. Without it as a bastion of Canadian nationality, Canadian purpose, and Canadian independence, we could not, in my view, remain a sovereign state. It is to the Crown we can look to encourage the spirit of nationhood and to warn against its neglect. The Sovereign, as has been said in another context, is not "the keeper of a museum, but the tender of a garden".

Vincent Massey, Confederation on the March.

♛ ♛ ♛

Our feeling for the monarchy is marked everywhere by warmth and devotion, but our attitude to Great Britain, naturally, differs with the backgrounds of the Canadians concerned, and their knowledge of the people of the United Kingdom. Persons of British ancestry must think differently from those of other origins and who know nothing of life in the British Isles. These cannot share the strong feeling for Great Britain and the deep sentiment with which the thoughts of so many of us are charged: but that does not keep the newer Canadians from having a deep respect for British traditions. Stephen Leacock in writing of them once observed, "Leave them alone and pretty soon the Ukrainians will think they won the battle of Trafalgar!"

Great Britain is separated from us by an ocean. The Crown is not separated from us at all, because the Crown belongs to us, as it does to the people of England, or Australia, or Nigeria. The words "Queen of Canada" do not come from the world of romance. The phrase stands for conventional reality, and when Her Majesty, in a speech made in Ottawa in 1957, said that she was going to visit the United States as "Queen of Canada", she expressed a truth profoundly important to us and of deep significance to the Commonwealth of which she is Head.

Vincent Massey, Confederation on the March.

♛ ♛ ♛

The Crown gives to government a personal quality that mellows and humanises it. When convicts are released in Canada, under a royal amnesty, there are often expressions from them of gratitude to the Sovereign. Lawyers would tell them that such an act of clemency is a governmental action, but governments under our system, as we know, act in the name of the Sovereign. Our allegiance is not to a document, nor to the design on a piece of bunting, but to a person ... There exists today no human institution whose influence for good surpasses that of the Monarchy we cherish.

Vincent Massey, Confederation on the March.

♛ ♛ ♛

Duke Dimitri Leuchtenberg de Beauharnais was the fourth to hold that title, and was a direct descendant of Eugène de Beauharnais, son of

Josephine, Napoleon's first wife. The first Duke was adopted by the Emperor and eventually made a brilliant career in Bonaparte's Grand Army. Duke Dimitri and the Duchess for many years lived in St Sauveur, Quebec, where they operated a "paying guest" home, welcoming at one time up to forty people who travelled in from all over the world.

One winter evening the discussion turned to the forthcoming visit of Canada's Governor General, Vincent Massey, who was slated to arrive for a four-day weekend in company with a small retinue. As an impressionable high school student, I was much taken by the prospect of such a distinguished visit.

"Uncle Dimitri", I asked, "aren't you awed, anticipating the Governor General in your home? Doesn't it sort of frighten you to look forward to greeting such a great person who holds such an important position?"

"I've met great people before", he replied. "Besides, there is nothing of which to be afraid. A person is a person, despite title, decorations or position. Think of it this way: stripped naked, in the shower, the Governor General will appear remarkably like you and me!"

Years later, as a Headmaster, it was my duty to greet the Governor General. The motorcade drew to a stop in front of the school and out stepped the viceregal presence. As I moved forward to shake his hand, a picture flashed in my mind of a very naked and soapy individual, with the Order of Canada about his neck, under the shower. I giggled inwardly and certainly was neither awed nor frightened.

Prince Alexis Troubetzkoy, Toronto.

GEORGES VANIER

The protocol at Government House [1959-1967] was correct without being fussy and, generally speaking, the Vaniers maintained the traditions they had inherited. If it were suggested that in this democratic day and age ladies should not be expected to curtsey to the Queen's representative – because, after all, they no longer curtsied to the Queen of the Netherlands – Georges Vanier replied that he represented the Queen of Canada, not the Queen of the Netherlands, and that so long as people curtsied to the Queen's representatives in her other Dominions they should continue to do so in Canada. But here, as in everything else, he had a characteristic lightness of touch; when he tried to demonstrate a curtsey to Alice Gadoffre – not easy for a man with only one leg – her laughter, and his, did not assist the experiment. Nor has the subsequent abolition of the curtsey proved so popular as its egalitarian advocates predicted. On State occasions General Vanier and his wife insisted on receiving guests by themselves, leaving the Prime Minister, if he so wished, to receive them in another room. The Royal Toast – "The Queen

–La Reine" – was always drunk when the Governor General was at table, and when three or more persons were present. Etiquette prescribed that he should precede his wife into the dining-room, but Lord Tweedsmuir had noticed that the King always made the Queen go first, and General Vanier followed his example except on the most official occasions. He and Madame Vanier were served before any other guests; and after every formal dinner, when the men remained behind in the dining-room, the ladies curtsied to him before they left. A curious custom dictated that there should be no second helpings, and guests were encouraged to eat their fill while the going round was good.

Robert Speaight, Vanier: Soldier, Diplomat and Governor General.

PROVINCIAL VICEROYS

I can remember once up in the north country [of Ontario], I was with Colonel MacKay (Lieutenant-governor of Ontario 1957–1963), and, as you know, when a Lieutenant-governor gets to his or her place at the table, if it's an official function, the viceregal salute is played. We just got in the room and out boomed the viceregal salute. That was fine, we all stopped and came to attention. We took about four more steps and out it came again. This was a little much and when it started again I kept on going and walked up to the pianist, and I said,

"What are you doing?"

"Oh, I'm just practising."

Interview with Colonel Frank McEachren, Monarchy Canada.

♛ ♛ ♛

In 1967, the Centennial of Confederation, governors and their wives were guests at a dinner aboard the Royal Yacht *Britannia* at Kingston, Ontario. "It was a nice affair and ran into several hours." One exchange of the evening occurred when Phyllis [MacEwan] recounted an experience at the waterfront earlier in the day. She and Grant [MacEwan, Lieutenant-governor of Alberta] were walking along the shore when an American pulled up in a houseboat, and, mistaking the formal Windsor uniform for that of a policeman, inquired as to where he should tie up. Without setting him right, Grant immediately directed him to steer clear of the crowded area and moor his craft further downstream. The man remarked on how friendly the Canadian police were, thanked him, and sailed onward.

Prince Philip laughed boisterously at the account and said, "If you had told that American that you were Lieutenant-governor of Alberta he'd probably have replied 'Ho, ho, ho, I'm Father Christmas'".

The Queen and her representative again met in Calgary in July 1973 at the Stampede. At a state dinner MacEwan sat beside Her Majesty. "Her Majesty is not one to make comments but is tireless in asking questions", he said. "Our conversational exchanges consisted of her questions and my replies as well as I could make them – mostly about Alberta."

R.H. Macdonald, Grant MacEwan: No Ordinary Man.

♛ ♛ ♛

John Black Aird, Lieutenant-governor of Ontario

... a sense of the importance of family endures with most people, and there is still much respect for the sharing of basic values. I do not think the family unit is about to disappear. The Royal Family serves as a symbolic reminder of its value.

When we see that there is an ordered succession, by which Prince Charles will become King of England [sic] and King of Canada, then clearly there is an ongoing process, an identity for families to follow in their own family groups. Furthermore, that Royal identity is an encouragement for all families to take pride in their own group.

John Black Aird, Loyalty in a Changing World.

♛ ♛ ♛

A final word from Col. H. Willis-O'Connor

Ottawa people are humorous folk. They groan "Oh, dear! I've *got* to go to Government House on the 20th. Such a bore! I'd rather take a beating!" But if they are not invited . . . Well, you see what I mean!

H. Willis-O'Connor, Inside Government House.

11

FOR GOD, KING AND COUNTRY

Since time immemorial defence of the realm has been a prime requisite for monarchs, and the legends of warrior kings in fiction and fact, from King Arthur to King Henry V, have come down through the ages to the present day. In modern society the Sovereign no longer leads troops in war (the last of our kings to do so was George II). But the advent of total war in the twentieth century revived the concept in a broader context and King George VI very much led his people in the Second World War.

As kingship is about service, and military service is in so many ways the ultimate degree of service (with an unlimited liability clause), it is only natural that a special bond has evolved over the centuries between monarch and servicemen and women. This has been reinforced by the British-derived regimental system in the Canadian army which reproduces the monarchical concept of the national family as the regimental family, often with a member of the Royal Family at its head as Colonel-in-Chief.

In addition, several members of the Royal Family have actually served in the Canadian forces or served in Canada with the Imperial forces, leaving their mark in our history. The Duke of Kent served with his regiment and ultimately as Commander-in-Chief of British Forces in North America from 1791 to 1800, preparing the defences that defeated the Americans in the War of 1812. Prince Arthur, son of Queen Victoria and later Duke of Connaught, fought the Fenians south of Montreal in 1866. Edward VIII, while Prince of Wales, served with the Canadian Corps in World War I.

I am a Whigg of the old Stamp – No Roundhead – one of King William's Whiggs: for Liberty & the Constitution.

William Smith, a Loyalist and later Chief Justice of Quebec, 2 December 1777, quoted in L.F.S. Upton, The Loyal Whig: William Smith of New York & Quebec.

♛ ♛ ♛

Even though in the course of a mess dinner there may be several toasts, dining in the mess today is the acme of moderation compared to that of our military ancestors. A young subaltern of the 4th Regiment of Foot in garrison at Halifax in 1788 left a record of a mess dinner honouring His Royal Highness Prince William Henry [King William IV], Captain of HMS *Andromeda*:

"We sat down to a very good dinner . . . After the royal toasts, and after we had given the Prince of Wales and the Duke of York, we had three times twenty-one, and two bands playing 'Rule Britannia'. We drank twenty-eight-bumper [brim-full] toasts, by which time, as may be well supposed, we were in pretty good order. At nine o'clock a 'feu de joie' was fired by the garrison from the citadel. Those that could walk attended. I was one of the number that got up the hill."

E.C. Russell, Customs and Traditions of the Canadian Armed Forces.

♛ ♛ ♛

Message of the Prince Regent to the victors of the Battle of Chateauguay, 1813.

His Royal Highness has observed with the greatest satisfaction the skill and gallantry so conspicuously displayed by the officers and men who composed the detachment of troops opposed to General Hampton's army . . . It gives His Royal Highness peculiar pleasure to find, that His Majesty's Canadian subjects have at length had the opportunity (which His Royal Highness has been long anxious should be afforded them) of refuting, by their own brilliant exertions in defence of their country, that calumnious charge of disaffection and disloyalty with which the enemy prefaced his first invasion of the Provinces.

♛ ♛ ♛

The Duke of Kent congratulates Lieutenant-Colonel de Salaberry, Senior, at Beauport, Quebec, on his son's celebrated victory at Chateauguay.

I received your interesting letter of 10th November, in which you give me an account of the advance of the Canadian army on 27 October, and of the brilliant affair which your son gained by his arrangements . . . I do not hesitate to declare my opinion, that you have reason to be proud of the victory gained by my *protégé* over forces so superior in numbers to those which he commanded, but also that he displayed talents and judgements rarely to be found, unless in veterans, both in making his dispositions and during the battle.
15 March 1814.

♛ ♛ ♛

The Prince of Wales [Edward VII] defined civilised patriotism in his speech at the unveiling of the monument to Sir Isaac Brock, the saviour of Upper Canada, at Queenston, 18 September 1860.

I have willingly consented to lay the first stone of this monument. Every nation may, without offence to its neighbours, commemorate its heroes, their deeds of arms and their noble deaths. This is no taunting boast of victory, no revival of long-passed animosities, but a noble tribute to a soldier's fame; the more honourable because we readily acknowledge the bravery and chivalry of that people by whose hands he fell.

I trust that Canada will never want such Volunteers as those who fought in the last war [of 1812], nor her Volunteers be without such a leader; but no less and most fervently I pray that your sons and your grandsons may never be called upon to add other laurels to those which you have so gallantly won.

♛ ♛ ♛

The 2nd Duke of Cambridge[grandson of George III] takes up a Canadian idea

For three weeks [during the Fenian Raid of 1866] we were at Fort Erie doing outpost and patrol duties. We had a camp fire in the middle of our camp every evening and the men not on duty gathered around it, singing songs and telling anecdotes and enjoying themselves. The men got the nickname of "Denison's Guerillas", partly, I think, from the fact that I had got them all supplied with jack-boots into which their trousers were tucked, and we all, both officers and men, wore them. As no mounted officers or men wore these in the army at that time, and those we had were common lumberman's boots, they looked very rough and ready and gave the men an irregular appearance, but they were very serviceable and useful; and when I published my *Modern Cavalry* in 1868 the

Duke of Cambridge took up the suggestion I made in that book in favour of the jack-boot, and now, I believe, every mounted officer and man in the British service wears the long boots instead of the booted overalls in use in 1866.

George Taylor Denison, Soldiering In Canada.

♛ ♛ ♛

Denison's strong hand

Lord Wolseley asked me if I would like to see the Jubilee review in honour of the visiting royalties, which was to take place at Aldershot in a week or so, and offered to provide me with a horse for the purpose. I said I should like very much to see it. We came back to London and nothing more was said about it. I did not hear anything further for some days, and should not have been at all surprised if Lord Wolseley, in the great rush of business which devolved upon him at that particular time, had forgotten all about it. A day or two before the review, however, I received a letter giving me full instructions as to the hour and the station, platform, etc., where I was to meet him on the morning of the day. I never supposed for a moment that I should be able to do more than ride about with the ordinary public outside of the lines, and went down in plain clothes, as I would have gone to ride in the park.

As soon as the train arrived at Farnborough station, Lord Wolseley hurried me out, called for my horse, which a trooper of the Royal Horse Artillery led up at once, and told me to keep with the group of the staff, not to get separated, but to ride up the lines and down with them, and not to get too far away from him. He told the Royal Artillery trooper that he was to act as my orderly, to ride with the other six orderlies who were in attendance on the Royal party, till the field day was over, and then he was to show me the way to the Headquarters mess of the Artillery, where I was to lunch. Then Lord Wolseley left me, to go and help the Duke of Cambridge to look after the Kings and Crown Princes, etc. In a few minutes they were all mounted and ready to start off for Aldershot. I understood there were four Kings, seven Crown Princes, and about ten or fifteen other royalties, and about an equal number of officials and staff. The brother of the King of Siam was there, with a couple of foreign office officials in plain clothes with him, and I fell in with them and rode up and down the lines during the inspection, and kept with the party all day, for there were some very extended manoeuvres after the review, the regular force making an attack upon a position held by a number of militia battalions.

Once, as we were galloping from one point to another, I happened to come near Prince George, the Duke of York. He looked over at me, then looked again, earnestly, as we were galloping along, and waved his hand at me in a very friendly way, saying, "How are you, how are you?" I took off my hat to him in return and was much surprised that he should have remembered me after four or five years had elapsed.

I had been feeling all the time as if I were somewhat of an intruder in such a distinguished gathering, and, naturally, kept as much out of the way as possible, on the outskirts of the group. Towards the end of the day we were all standing upon a hill, commanding a splendid view of the turning movement of one or two brigades of infantry in the valley below. I noticed Lord Wolsely coming through the group looking about, at last he saw me at the edge of it, and beckoned and called to me. I rode over, and he said, "Come with me, the Duke wishes to see you". I had to go to where the Duke of Cambridge was sitting on his horse, with the Prince of Wales, and other Royal personages around them. When I came up, Lord Wolsely introduced me to him. I took off my hat and bowed to him. He spurred his horse towards me, put out his hand and shook hands with me, and said, "How do you do Colonel Denison? You are a very keen cavalry soldier, and I have read your books. I know all about you. What do you think of our cavalry?" I said, "I think they are the finest in Europe, sir; certainly the finest I have seen". "Which regiment do you like best", said he. I replied, "Where they are all so good it is difficult to draw comparisons, but if there is any difference, I think the 5th Lancers the smartest regiment I have seen here today". "I think you are right", he said, "It is a very smart regiment".

I had noticed that the Horse Artillery had only four guns to the battery. I knew they formerly had six. I mentioned this to the Duke. He said: "I do not wonder you noticed it, the Government have cut them down from motives of economy". "But, sir", said I, "I thought we were short of guns in proportion to the other arms, as compared with other armies". "Of course we are", said he. I went on to say I could not understand it, that infantry might be improvised in a short time, cavalry took much longer, artillery longer still, and Horse Artillery the longest of all, and it seemed incomprehensible to me that the economy should strike in the very worst place. This pleased the Duke, and feeling that he had a sympathetic listener he went on for some time to tell me what difficulties he had, until he suddenly remembered the Kings around him, and he said: "I am glad to have met you Colonel Denison. I must just speak to the King of Denmark", and he shook hands with me and said: "Good-bye", and I rode back.

The Duke of Cambridge has a very gruff, blunt way of speaking, and glared at me almost when I came up, as if he were trying to look right through me, and then spoke to me very sternly, but it was only a mannerism. I thought him a straightforward, kind-hearted man, and I do not wonder that he is a great favourite with the army. Telling this anecdote when I came home to a friend of mine his remark was, "that was a strong hand the Duke had when you came up – four kings and a knave. It is very hard to beat".

George Taylor Denison, Soldiering In Canada.

♛ ♛ ♛

The first battalion of Canadians to go overseas in World War One was composed of mostly ex-servicemen privately raised and equipped by Hamilton Gault of Montreal. It was named Princess Patricia's Canadian Light Infantry and became one of Canada's most famous regiments. The Princess who was their Colonel-in-Chief and daughter of the Governor General gave them on 23 August 1914 their colours, the last colours carried into battle by a regiment in the British Empire.

I have great pleasure in presenting you with these colours which I have worked myself; I hope they will be associated with what I believe will be a distinguished corps; I shall follow the fortunes of you all with the deepest interest, and I heartily wish every man good luck and a safe return.

♛ ♛ ♛

Known as the Ric-A-Dam-Doo, the colours presented by Princess Patricia were immortalised in the regimental song.

The Princess Pat's Battalion
They sailed across the Herring Pond,
They sailed across the Channel too,
And landed there with the Ric-A-Dam-Doo, Dam-Doo,Dam-Doo.

Old Ackity-Ack, our Colonel grand,
The leader of this noble band,
He'd go to Hell and charge right through
Before he'd lose the Ric-A-Da-Doo, Dam-Doo, Dam-Doo.

Old Hammy Gault, our first PP,
He led this band across the sea,
He'd lose an arm, or leg or two
Before he'd lose the Ric-A-Dam-Doo, Dam-Doo, Dam-Doo.

The Ric-A-Dam-Doo, pray what is that?
'Twas made at home by Princess Pat.
It's Red and Gold and Royal Blue;
That's what we call the Ric-A-Dam-Doo, Dam-Doo, Dam-Doo.

♛ ♛ ♛

The King's message to the first Canadian troops to arrive overseas 1914.

It gives me great pleasure to have this opportunity of welcoming to the Mother Country so fine a contingent of troops from the Dominion of Canada. Their prompt rally to the Empire's call is of inestimable value, both to the fighting strength of my Army and in the evidence which it gives of the solidarity of the Empire. The general appearance and physical standard of the different units are highly creditable. I am glad to hear of the serious and earnest spirit which pervades all ranks, for it is only by careful training and leading on the part of officers and by efficiently strict discipline and co-operation on the part of all that the demands of modern war can be met. I shall follow with interest the progress and work of my Canadians.

The King To His People: Being Speeches and Messages of His Majesty King George the Fifth delivered between July 1911 and May 1935.

♛ ♛ ♛

The Canadians were the first on whom [the Prince of Wales] called [on his visit to Dominion forces at the Front in 1918]. He was euphoric about his reception. "They are great lads these old 'Knucks'", he told Joey Legh, "real, husky stout-hearted fellows for whom I've a great admiration". He was overwhelmed by their cheerfulness and friendly informality: "How I wish I had been across to Canada, and living amongst them makes me just long to go there". His only complaint was that they tended to assume that they had done all the serious fighting and to speak with some disdain of the 'Imperial' or British troops.

Philip Ziegler, King Edward VIII.

♛ ♛ ♛

The Right Honourable Ernest Lapointe, Minister of Justice and the Prime Minister's Quebec Lieutenant, asks the House of Commons to support the Canadian declaration of war, 1939.

Mr Speaker, from the numerous documents which have been circulated and laid on the table there is one missing to which I desire to call the attention of the house, and it is an important one. I refer to the message which His Majesty the King broadcast last Sunday the third of September. With the permission of the house I should like to put in Hansard two or three sentences only of His Majesty's message over the radio. His Majesty said:

"In this grave hour, perhaps the most fateful in our history, I send to every household of my peoples, both at home and overseas, the message, spoken with the same depth of feeling for each of you as if I were able to cross your threshold and speak to you myself."

And further, speaking of the principle of the use of force and might against right:

"Such a principle, stripped of all disguise, is surely the mere primitive doctrine that might is right. If this principle were established throughout the world, the freedom of our own country and of the whole

British Commonwealth of Nations would be in danger . . .

"This is the ultimate issue which confronts us. For the sake of all that we ourselves hold dear, and of the world order and peace, it is unthinkable that we should refuse to meet the challenge.

"It is to this high purpose that I now call my people at home and my people across the seas who will make our cause their own."

Our King, Mr Speaker, is at war, and this parliament is sitting to decide whether we shall make his cause our own . . ."

I desire to conclude my remarks by referring to what was said by our gracious Queen at Halifax when she was leaving Canada to return to the homeland. Her words in French went to the heart of every man, woman and child in my province. She said, "Que Dieu bénisse le Canada". God bless Canada. Yes God bless Canada. God save Canada. God save Canada's honour, Canada's soul, Canada's dignity, Canada's conscience . . . Yes, God bless Canada. God bless our Queen. God bless our King.

Hansard, September 1939.

♛ ♛ ♛

The declaration of war for Canada by the King in 1939.

We drove up to the front of the little George IV house [Royal Lodge, Windsor Great Park]. I was received by a footman and was shown past furniture covered by dust-sheets into the dining-room. I noticed the gas masks of the King and Queen lying on a chair. In two or three minutes the door opened and in came the King, unattended and wearing the service uniform of a field marshal. He shook hands very cordially. I apologised for my intrusion in his country retreat and showed him the submission [for his approval of a proclamation declaring war between Canada and the German Reich], which he read. He then inscribed the word 'Approved' and his signature 'George R.I.' under it. The momentous words in the document ran as follows:

"It is expedient that a Proclamation should be issued in the name of His Majesty, in Canada, declaring that a state of war with the German Reich has existed in Canada as of and from September tenth.

The Prime Minister of Canada, accordingly, humbly submits to His Majesty the petition of The King's Privy Council for Canada that His Majesty may approve the issuing of such a Proclamation in His name."

We then had a short talk about the War. We mutually deplored the unhappy fate that had turned a madman loose on Europe and discussed for a few minutes the possibility of help from the United States. I then took my leave and drove away with Hart [Massey], who had watched us talking and had almost overheard us, sitting in the car just outside the window.

Vincent Massey, What's Past Is Prologue.

♛ ♛ ♛

In 1939 it was planned that the King and Queen would pay an extensive visit to Canada. The international scene was anything but favourable and there were war-clouds on the horizon. There was a strong division in the Cabinet as to whether Their Majesties should run the risk of a trans-Atlantic journey in the face of the international menace. They were, however, determined to go, and sound counsel encouraged them in their desire to accomplish a visit to which they had long looked forward, and which Canada was eagerly awaiting. The decision was both courageous and wise, and the tour was crowned with unbelievable success. An English friend of mine, during the war, gave a lift in his car to a Canadian soldier. He asked his passenger what had made him come so far to fight. This was the reply: "I saw the Queen when she was in Canada and I said if there is ever a war, I'm going to fight for that little lady".

Vincent Massey, What's Past Is Prologue.

♛ ♛ ♛

King George VI's first Christmas broadcast to the Commonwealth during World War II.

A new year is at hand. We cannot tell what it will bring. If it brings peace, how thankful we shall all be. If it brings us continued struggle we shall remain undaunted.

In the meantime, I feel that we may all find a message of encouragement in the lines which, in my closing words, I would like to say to you: – "I said to the man who stood at the Gate of the Year, 'Give me a light that I may tread safely into the unknown'. And he replied, 'Go out into the darkness, and put your hand into the Hand of God. That shall be to you better than light, and safer than a known way'".
May that Almighty Hand guide and uphold us all.

John W. Wheeler-Bennett, King George VI,
His Life and Reign.

♛ ♛ ♛

The [Beaver] club [in London for Canadian servicemen and women] was open for just over six years, from February 1940 when the King and Queen opened it, showing the most intense interest in the institution, visiting every department – not excluding the barber shop, in which customers of the moment were deeply embarrassed at being found in the barber's hands.

Vincent Massey, What's Past Is Prologue.

♛ ♛ ♛

On 8 June 1940 The Royal Canadian Horse Artillery, before a futile excursion to collapsing France, were inspected by the King and Queen at Leipzic Barracks in the United Kingdom.

That royal review is well remembered by then Gunner H.H. (Shorty) Rathbone, "C/54" Battery's tallest right marker on parades, and by Ken Grace who wrote that: "This lad of 6' 6" was so tired of being asked his height that he had fallen into the habit of replying 5' 18" to the inevitable question. Naturally, the Queen asked and, overcome by her regal presence, our stalwart blurted out: '5-foot 18, Ma'am'. Well! There was near apoplexy in the official party and near hysterical mirth in the ranks".

Major G.D. Mitchell, RCHA – Right Of The Line.

♛ ♛ ♛

Many Canadian servicemen and servicewomen had contacts with the King and Queen and other members of the Royal Family during the grim years of war.

In the early autumn of 1940, with Hitler's aerial navy overhead shooting up the skies above England's green and pleasant land and Hitler's invasion fleet gathering on the coast of France, a 48th Highlander friend and I happened to be in Windsor. We were making our way down the winding High Street along the castle wall to the railway station when a black Daimler moved slowly up the slope toward us. Neither of us really noticed the vehicle, until all of a sudden we saw an arm in Air Force blue come to the salute against the RAF wedge cap of the figure in the rear seat. A familiar face smiled through the window at us. It was my friend who came to life first. "My God", he blurted out, "it's the King!"

Our heads swivelled to the left in unison and both our right hands snapped tardily to the salute as the King's car passed. *The King had saluted us*. We had merely returned his salute. Like stupid tourists we stood gawking, unbelieving. The car disappeared through the castle gate. Immediately the Royal Standard broke from the castle masthead – a signal to the whole world, the enemy included, that the King was in his castle.

There was a lump in each of our throats. Our eyes were misty. My friend gasped. "Imagine that, *he* saluted *us*!" It is difficult, nearly three and a half decades later, even to understand the emotions of other far-off days, let alone explain them to another generation. But that day, had a regiment of German parachutists landed near by, each of us would have attacked the whole ruddy lot with our bare hands.

It's amazing what the *right* kind of salute can do to change a man's attitudes toward life – and death.

Strome Galloway, Monarchy Canada.

♛ ♛ ♛

On 17 October 1940 the King and Queen visited Canada House.

The King and Queen paid us a visit on Wednesday to see how the machinery works at Canada House. The High Commissioner had told the staff the night before that it was to be a "working" inspection, without ceremony, and that we weren't to make any special preparations. Everyone was to be at his job, in the normal way. One of our older English clerks took these instructions literally, and was so determined to carry them out, even at the risk of appearing to be discourteous to his sovereign, that when Their Majesties entered his sanctum, he refused to take any notice of them and kept on pushing his pen industriously and, he hoped, impressively. He had to be practically roared at before he would stand up to be introduced to the King and the Queen. However, he made magnificent amends by a bow which brought his forehead within a few inches of the floor, after which he hastened back to work again, to show how concerned he was about winning the war.

Lester Pearson, Mike: Vol. 1.

♛ ♛ ♛

In 1943 Lieutenant-Colonel Walter Bapty, M.D., a native of London, Ontario, who had joined the Canadian Scouts with John McCrae of Flanders Fields fame at age fifteen, was attached for a few days to No. XI Depot Training Establishment RAMC, Beckett's Park, Leeds, commanded by Lt-Col R.E. Watt. As a result he found himself a guest of the King's Aunt at Harewood. He was much amused when the rumour got round that he had been heard on the telephone inviting himself to visit Her Royal Highness.

31 Jan [19]43. Lunch today with our Col-in-Chief HRH The Princess Royal at Harewood House, & it was most interesting. Yesterday I phoned there & asked if I might call & pay my respects & shortly after rec'd the invitation to lunch. The Depot put a car at my disposal with an A.T. driver. She did not know the way but we landed OK just before one, the zero hour. The House is divided in two, the west half being given over as a convalescent hospital for officers. A young civilian answered the ring & escorted me to a living room, then to the library where the Earl of Harewood and Miss Kenyon-Slavey were seated. Later HRH entered dressed plain and quietly in a dark brown wool dress, brown sweater, brown skirt with a narrow white stripe. Conversation was general. When we discussed the Alaskan highway she produced an atlas with a poor map of Canada. The dining room lined with books overlooks the Italian garden & farther off the lake & hill & meadows. Canada geese (wild) were on the lake & on the slopes above could be seen swans & near a wood some black cattle (polled) Angus. The table was mahogany, no cloth, lunch was buffet, the four of us only & no help. Food consisted of a small joint of pork, apple sauce, gravy, French fried potatoes, Brussels sprouts, some plain salad & later some cream pudding & cheese & black coffee, all very good but simple. After each course we helped ourselves, piling our own dirty dishes & placing knife fork etc. in a tray. To drink I had asked for sherry while the Earl drank a plain white wine. The sherry

was good. The Earl and I talked most of the meal on farming generally, of cattle crops etc. He had to leave rather abruptly in order to preside at a Salvation Army function. Much of his time he says is taken up with Masonic work. Later I learned he is head of the Masons in England.

In leaving the dining room I looked for the door. It was as though camoflaged, covered with the fold backs of leather bound books. I was unable to ascertain if the other books likewise were false. On entering the corridor HRH remarked "I presume you would like to come to my sitting room". I followed to a room about the same size & adjoining the dining room. It was not warm, indeed the whole house was cool, but not cold. It was a friendly room, overcrowded with furniture & things. I endeavoured to tell HRH of the 2nd Bn [the 2nd Bn, Canadian Scottish Regiment (Princess Mary's) was commanded by Lt-Col Bapty 1935-39 and 1940-42] of their work, & movements & of where they now were. I told of MacGregor & of the Pipe Band, or my being taken away & of my present work [CO, RCAMC Training Centre Camp Borden A 22]. She told me of her inspection of the 1st Bn & of how favourably she was impressed, & of their demonstration of battle drill. She liked Parker but had been sorry to see Kingham leave.

At 2.30 she said "I suppose you would be interested in our hospital here". She led the way out to the general hall & spoke to an officer patient who notified the CO Col Lewis, DSO, RAMC. She bade me goodbye. I asked if I might convey her good wishes to the 2d Bn & to this she readily consented. She was very friendly but at the same time very business like & decisive. I liked her and hope I may have the privilege of seeing her again some time.

HRH looks well for a woman of 45. Her hair is dark brown. She had the eyes of the Royal Family, clear blue. She uses no visible make up. Her colour is good, she appears to be in good health. She seems to take a normal quantity of food, though they all ate rather quickly.

At the table at each place was a small individual cruet with salt pepper & mustard, & to the right a small covered dish containing a large block of the most excellent butter. The sherry was in a decanter & the glass for it of generous size.

The Earl, I should say, is in his sixties. He is a good conversationalist & of pleasing manner, quite of the Guards type. He would make an excellent Gov.-Gen.

Laura (Mrs David) Williams, Duncan,
British Columbia.

♛ ♛ ♛

We were up in Norfolk in eastern England. 'Baker' company was holed up in a castle called Hillington Hall. While we were there, we were invited out a number of times to dinner at the homes of several lords and ladies.

At one of these teas there was a lady-in-waiting to the Queen. She was Irish. The Padre, who was Irish himself, struck up a conversation with her. During the course of their talk, the thought came up that it would be a grand idea if the Irish Regiment guarded the King and Queen, who were coming to Sandringham for a holiday. Dave thought it was a fantastic idea. The idea went to warhouse. The reply was that, it was the craziest idea anyone had thought of. Who in their right mind would put wild Canadians in charge of such a duty! Dave wouldn't take that for an answer. He went right back and persisted. Finally, he won out and it was the first time in history that any Canadian Regiment had ever guarded the King and Queen. If it hadn't been for Dave, it would never have happened. The Colonel was dumfounded when word came back to select one major, three captains and a hundred men to be taken off everything so that they could be trained for this guard duty.

Barry D. Rowland, The Padre.

♛ ♛ ♛

August 8, 1943. Today I met the King, Queen and Princesses. It all happened like this. The Royal Family was inspecting a guard of honour and as usual as the official photographer, I was on hand. Unfortunately the morning was dark and very dull with the odd shower thrown in for good measure. The Royal Party arrived looking stunning. The King was met by the officer of the guard and the usual welcome was extended. Next the Royal Party proceeded to inspect the troops. First went the King followed by the Queen and Princesses. It was a grand sight. Unfortunately the sun refused to shine; however, I followed them with my camera and while I know that the shots will be poor, still I will have them. They soon came to the end of their inspection. The King spotted my collar and camera and walked right over to me. He asked my name and shook my hand. In the meantime Paul grabbed my camera and started shooting pictures of the greeting. The King asked me how long I had been in the service, where my church was in Toronto, how I liked my job and the kind of responses I got from the men. He then said that he was very pleased that I was preaching to his people that night. I told him that it was my honour. The Queen came forward and the King moved off. She gave me that million dollar smile of hers and shook my hand. "You have a wonderful lot of troops", she said. I replied, "I'm very proud of them". "I'm sure you are", she said. She too asked me how long I had been with them. When I told her she commented that it is not often a chaplain can stay with one unit for that length of time. She also reminded me of the evening service and hoped that it would be dry as it was an open air affair.

The Princesses were standing by during all of this taking everything in. I think they must get tired of all the formality. After the proceedings were over we had a group picture taken with all the officers sitting with their Majesties for the occasion. From there we walked with them to church. I had the honour of walking with the King's secretary and agent and in front of us was the Queen with the children. I found that I was given the very front seat, a distance of about ten feet from the Royal Family.

The service was very simple and plain and as I watched the Royal pew I noticed the Royal Family entering right into the service. Margaret Rose, however, didn't seem so interested in the service as she was looking around to see who was there. Now and then the Princesses smiled my way. I thought that they were just like any other children. I fancy they saw a few things that brought a smile to their lips.

After the service the Royal Family retired and then the congregation left. I went for dinner to the chaplain's rectory and rehashed the doings of the day. T'was a great morning and one that will live long in the memory of all whose good fortune it was to be in attendance. I felt that I more than shared in the honours. In the evening I arrived at the Royal Gardens with the King's chaplain. It was raining like Hades. There was a good number of people present including all the King's staff. I did my best and gave it all I had. After the service the King's recorder came and asked me for some part of the service that he had missed. Apparently I went too fast for his shorthand. I understand that a record of all that went on is presented. Afterwards I was taken for dinner to York cottage where all the Royal Family were born. We had a duck dinner. Not hard to take. When I came home around midnight, I was indeed ready for bed. The day and the opportunities were beyond my imagination and I never dreamed it would be my good fortune to meet the King and Queen, worship with them and preach on their estate. It was a great day for the Irish!

Barry D. Rowland, The Padre.

♛ ♛ ♛

It was a pleasant Sunday afternoon in the summer of 1943 when two friends and I decided to tour Windsor Castle. We were part of a Signal Corps (R.C.C.S.) unit stationed near Farnborough and we often took advantage of such tours available to us on weekends.

We were all impressed with the Castle and its well manicured grounds but we felt particular pride as Canadians in the very tall Douglas Fir flag pole that was a gift to the Crown by British Columbia.

Eventually the guide led us to the Victory Garden of vegetables that had been planted and cared for by HRH The Princess Elizabeth and HRH The Princess Margaret.

The garden was of particular interest to me as I had worked before enlisting for three summers on a farm in the Niagara Peninsula where our major crop was tomatoes. Sure enough the Princesses had a loving crop of this fruit and I was determined to taste a royal tomato.

The only thing standing between my desire and accomplishing this feat was the watchful eye of a guard who had informed us in no uncertain terms that the royal garden was *out of bounds*.

I was however able to prevail on my buddies to create a heated argument by the flagpole and in this moment of distraction I scooped the largest tomato I could see into my battledress tunic. The tunic was well designed to conceal such a piece of contraband but I patiently waited till I got back to camp to slice carefully and eat my prize.

The next morning I was first in line of the sick parade with a king-size bellyache as the tomato was at least two weeks from being ripe enough for human consumption.

All these years I have pondered unsuccessfully how best to return a tomato to the Royal Family without offending them or landing up in gaol.

A few years ago when the Royal Yacht was berthed in the Saint John, New Brunswick, harbour, it had been my intention to return a ripe tomato in style by landing on the deck by parachute but I was unable to get clearance from Transport Canada to fly over the harbour while the vessel was in port.

Warren Searle, Rothesay, New Brunswick.

♛ ♛ ♛

July 13, 1945. We went to the Palace by taxi. All London seemed to be crowded around the gates as we drove in. On arriving at the main steps of the Palace door, a very smart policeman guided us into an elegant room. Here our names were checked and we were ushered into our proper place in the line. We waited in this room for about 45 minutes and right on the dot of 11:00 a.m. our line started to move.

While the line was moving, a band played very softly as one by one, we went forward to receive our medals from the King. Eventually my name was called. I went forward, turned left facing the King, bowed, took one step forward and there I was right in front of him. His first words to me after pinning on the Cross were, "Where have I met you before?" I replied, "Sandringham, three years ago". "Oh", he said "how did the pictures turn out?" "You were excellent Your Majesty" I replied. He asked me a few questions about the Regiment, when I expected to go home, etc. I was amazed he remembered me. I had the distinction out of everyone in attendance, to have had the longest chat with him. When I got outside, many people, whom I didn't even know, were asking me why he talked to me so long and what he had to say. My uncle and aunt were thrilled with all they saw. There were a good number of pictures taken, so I may be sending some home very soon.

Barry D. Rowland, The Padre.

♛ ♛ ♛

There is one salute that must have confounded the Queen's enemies. It was 2 June 1953 in the Canadian lines opposite Hill 227, to the northward of Panmunjom in Korea. In the celebration marking the coronation of Queen Elizabeth II, "a bounteous rum issue provided the wherewithal for a toast to Her Majesty" by the 3rd Battalion, the Royal Canadian Regiment. But, not to be outdone by the "footsloggers", the divisional artillery and tanks of Lord Strathcona's Horse (Royal Canadians), supporting the RCRs, fired salutes. Some of these salvoes revealed themselves to be red, white and blue smoke enveloping "two humps known to be occupied by the enemy".

E.C. Russell, Customs and Traditions of the Canadian Armed Forces.

♛ ♛ ♛

Speech by Elizabeth II to the Royal 22e Régiment, Quebec City, 23 June 1959.

Commanding Officers, Officers, Non-Commissioned Officers and Privates: I am pleased to be in Quebec City with my French Canadian regiment; I am proud of the regiment and take pleasure in presenting it with new colours.

I am aware of your history which dates back to the beginning of the First World War. French Canadians decided at that time to form a regiment recalling their origins. The regimental insignia bears the motto *Je me souviens* (I remember). It is a moving tribute to the country of your forebears.

On the colours that I have just presented to you are inscribed the names of French towns in whose liberation you participated. What emotion you must have felt in liberating people of your own blood, and what joy they must have felt in welcoming the descendants of the French men and women who three centuries before had set sail for Canada.

You have had a short but glorious history. During the two world wars and the operations in Korea the regiment forged a noble tradition of honour, courage and sacrifice.

I have been able to see today that in peacetime you maintain the same laudable tradition of discipline and dress, for which I warmly congratulate you.

I know that my father, King George VI, had the highest regard for his French-Canadian regiment. He clearly proved this by becoming its colonel-in-chief in 1938, and I took pleasure in succeeding him in this position.

I thank you with all my heart for the faithful dedication that you have always shown me in the past and on which I know I can always rely.

The alliance that exists between you and the Royal Welsh Fusiliers, another brave regiment of which I am colonel-in-chief, gives me great joy.

I entrust these new colours to you in complete confidence. Your past makes me certain that you will defend them as your predecessors defended the old colours – fearlessly and faultlessly.

E.C. Russell, Customs and Traditions of the Canadian Armed Forces.

♛ ♛ ♛

Speech to sailors by Elizabeth II after presenting the Queen's Colour of the Royal Canadian Navy, Halifax, 1 August 1959.

This is a solemn moment in the history of the Navy. You are bidding farewell to one Colour and are about to pay honour to another . . .

I have no doubt that my Colour is in very good hands . . . During the Second World War, and particularly during the Battle of the Atlantic, you most admirably fulfilled your responsibilities to the Crown, to your country, and to the free world.

I now commend to your keeping this Colour. I know that you will guard it faithfully and the ideals for which it stands, not only in war but during the peace, which we all hope so sincerely will ever continue. Remember always that, although it comes from me, it symbolises not only loyalty to your Queen but also to your country and service. As long as these loyalties are in your hearts, you will add lustre to the already great name of the Royal Canadian Navy.

E.C. Russell, Customs and Traditions of the Canadian Armed Forces.

♛ ♛ ♛

HMCS Annapolis, commissioned, in 1964

This ship [HMCS *Annapolis*] derives its name from the Annapolis River in Nova Scotia, which is symbolized [on the ship's badge] by the white and blue wavy diagonal. The crowned cypher of the letters AR has a treble significance in that its suggests Annapolis Royal in Nova Scotia from which settlement the river got its name; Annapolis, Maryland the site of the United States Naval Academy; and Queen Anne, in whose honour these places were named.

Badges Of The Canadian Forces/Insignes Des Forces Canadiennes.

♛ ♛ ♛

The customs of the Loyal Toast for the Forces

The Loyal Toast in Canadian Forces messes today follows the ritual of passing the port. The table cleared, a decanter of port wine is placed before Mr President and Mr Vice . . .

When the president is satisfied that all glasses have been charged with wine (or may be water, though the sailor's superstition dies hard that the personage toasted in water will depart this life by drowning), he stoppers the decanter, raps the table for silence and says, "Mr Vice, the Queen", in English or French. Mr Vice alone rises and proposes the toast "Gentlemen (or Ladies and Gentlemen), The Queen of Canada", in the other official language. If a band is present, the first six bars of "God Save the Queen" are played immediately upon Mr Vice proposing the toast, for which, of course, all members stand. All present at table then raise their glasses and reply, "the Queen".

Here, again, unit tradition is very much alive. In artillery messes it is considered improper to add the fervent "God bless her", which is the normal response in other messes, for example, officers of field rank and above in the Queen's Own Rifles of Canada.

The custom of drinking a toast to the health of the sovereign is universal in the Canadian Forces, but, as can be seen, the procedure is not uniform in all units, ships, stations and bases, and in these matters it is incumbent upon hosts to inform and assist their guests at dinner.

While the Loyal Toast is in most messes drunk standing, such is not the case in HMC ships, where the health of Her Majesty the Queen is honoured while seated. The origin of the privilege enjoyed by naval officers has been attributed to several sovereigns. But the story generally accepted is the one about King Charles II returning to England in 1660 after the Cromwellian interregnum, who, replying to the Loyal Toast, rose and struck his head on a low deckhead beam, typical of ships of the time, and declared that, henceforth, wardroom officers should drink the King's health safely seated. Some idea of the antiquity of this custom may be seen in a print published in 1793 showing King George III, who reigned from 1760 to 1820, with a group of officers in the great cabin of a ship-of-the-line, glasses in hand for toasting the royal guest, and seated.

In this connection, the officers of CFB Halifax to this day adhere to the old Queen's Regulations for the Royal Canadian Navy (QRCN) which ordered that the health of Her Majesty the Queen shall be honoured while seated in all naval messes whether on shore or afloat, even when "God Save the Queen" is played, on all occasions except when Her Majesty or a member of the Royal Family is present (when the personage's pleasure as to procedure is previously sought), or when official foreign guests are present.

E.C. Russell, Customs and Traditions
of the Canadian Armed Forces.

12

FOUNTAIN OF HONOUR

Regrettably the word "patronage", because of its political implications, has acquired an unsavoury aura in modern Canada. There is another meaning to patronage, that is the encouragement of excellence in the diverse cultural, humanitarian, sporting, commercial, industrial, spiritual and even political aspects of society.

The Sovereign, the Royal Family and the Sovereign's representatives in Canada have played a fundamental role in giving birth to, fostering and setting standards in all parts of society. In some cases the support has taken the form of the indirect but significant act of giving a royal name or accolade to recognise the achievements of an individual or institution, thus encouraging similar efforts on the part of others. In other cases it has been the Monarchy which has actively created or pursued a line of excellence.

It has been said that were it not for the Church and the Monarchy there would be nothing to see in Europe. That may be an extreme perspective, but there is much truth in it. Similarly, without the Monarchy, Canadian society would be much the poorer.

Dedication by the Quebecer Joseph Bouchette of his great topographical work, the first major one on Canada, to the King.

TO
HIS MOST EXCELLENT MAJESTY,
WILLIAM IV,
OF THE UNITED KINGDOM OF GREAT BRITAIN AND IRELAND
KING, DEFENDER OF THE FAITH
ETC. ETC. ETC. ETC.

Sire,

In approaching your Majesty, with feelings of the most profound veneration and respect, to depose, for the second time, the result of my humble topographical and statistical colonial labours, at the foot of the throne; I feel deeply penetrated by a sense of gratitude for your Majesty's condescension in graciously permitting that my work should appear under your Majesty's exalted patronage and royal auspices.

This distinguished honour, whilst it sheds lustre upon my humble, but zealous endeavours, to develop the many natural resources and improvable advantages of your Majesty's flourishing trans-Atlantic dominions, must conspicuously mark your Majesty's paternal solicitude for their loyal inhabitants, and add a further incentive to the approved devotion and attachment that have ever characterized your Majesty's loyal subjects in that distant part of the empire, where the recollection of your Majesty's visit, in early life, is still alive in the breasts of the people, and has doubly become the theme of congratulation since your Majesty's happy accession to the throne of these realms.

With sentiments of the deepest respect, attachment, and gratitude,

I am,

Sire,

Your Majesty's most loyal, and most devoted,
obedient subject and servant,
Joseph Bouchette.

Joseph Bouchette, The British Dominions In North America; Or A Topographical And Statistical Description Of The Provinces Of Lower And Upper Canada, New Brunswick, Nova Scotia, The Islands of Newfoundland, Prince Edward, And Cape Breton.

♛ ♛ ♛

Nelson Cooke was a very well-known Toronto painter ... [and] a local committee commissioned from him a portrait of Sir Francis Bond Head, the stubborn and autocratic Tory governor. Cooke's canvas was then sent to England to be used for the engraving of a portrait print; local sponsors expressed great pleasure at this turn of events since they were sure London connoisseurs would be delighted to see such an excellent Canadian painting. Although not in good condition, the canvas, now in the National Gallery of Canada, appears always to have been a lifeless thing. Head's friends, in an extra burst of zeal, requested permission to dedicate the new print to the youthful Victoria. Much aware of her local governor's unpopularity, the Queen was pleased *not* to give her consent. First proof copies of the print arrived in Toronto during December 1837; less than a week later William Lyon Mackenzie marched on the city in his short-lived rebellion.

J. Russell Harper, Painting in Canada – A History.

♛ ♛ ♛

Most valuable of all [recognition of Sir Alan MacNab's military role in dealing with the Rebellion of 1837] was the Knighthood recommended by Head and bestowed by Queen Victoria in March 1838. It marked the Sovereign's high approbation of his and the militia's conduct, which MacNab in his romantic way cherished. It was the sort of obvious distinction he always coveted. He was now Sir Allan, or alternatively 'the gallant knight'. For the rest of his life the designations reminded contemporaries of the important role he had played in the events of 1837-8. He became the personification of the Upper Canadian militia, and whether it involved organising annual dinners for the men who had cut out the *Caroline*, restoring Brock's monument, or advising on military organisation, he relished the part.

Donald R. Beer, Sir Allan Napier MacNab,
Dictionary of Hamilton Biography.

♛ ♛ ♛

Admiral Sir Edward Augustus Inglefield was descended from a naval officer who had served in Halifax early in the nineteenth century. He himself commanded Lady Franklin's steam yacht, the *Isabel*, in a search for her husband. His diversion during the Arctic hunting for traces of the *Erebus* and *Terror* was a music box which Lady Franklin gave him, and as a reciprocal gesture he presented her with his own sketch of the *Isabel*. Alfred Lord Tennyson, after hearing his eloquent speeches on his return to England, admitted that he felt there was little left in life but to have an Arctic inlet or river named after him. On the voyage, Inglefield carefully painted many delicately toned water-colours, which seem almost inappropriate for the harsh north.

When Inglefield was received by Queen Victoria at Windsor Castle in November, 1853, a maid of honour noted how the Queen looked at his paintings:

"Captain Inglefield came here this afternoon, and brought all his drawings and sketches of the Arctic scenery; quite beautiful and wonderfully clever; enormous for sketches, some of them 3 feet long and 18 or 20 inches wide, and though slight, not too rough, and with the most pleasing air and truthfulness about them. They were all arranged in the corridor, for the Queen to see after lunch, and we took the liberty of examining them till she came. He was there himself and explained them to her, an intelligent, active looking youngish man, with very dark hair and eyes; he is one of the very few who are still sanguine about poor Franklin. It was awful to see how slight and small the ship (not a very large one in reality), looked among the gigantic icebergs and in the 'pack'."

Inglefield lived in Halifax during 1878 and 1879 as Vice-Admiral commanding the North American and West Indian Fleet of the British Navy. He visited Rideau Hall, Ottawa, where Princess Louise drew his portrait, and when he exhibited his own water-colours at the Nova Scotia Provincial Exhibition of 1879 was awarded a first prize.

J. Russell Harper, Painting in Canada – A History.

♛ ♛ ♛

From Russia I returned to London for the opera season of 1874, singing in my previous operas, the *Sonambula*, *Lucia*, *Linda di Chamonix*, *Marta*, etc., etc., and also singing in many concerts both public and private.

It was during this season that I was honoured with a command to sing at Windsor, where for the first time I saw Queen Victoria, and here began that warm appreciation and faithful interest in me on the part of Her Majesty – I might almost venture to say *friendship* – which ended only with her life . . .

On that first occasion I sang, quite privately for Her Majesty, "Caro nome", "Robin Adair", the "Ave Maria" of Gounod, and "Home Sweet Home", all of which the Queen was pleased to say she had much enjoyed. She praised my voice and my singing, and with a discrimination that told me at once how thoroughly she understood music and the art of singing. Indeed, as I continually noticed in after-years, it was all but impossible to find any subject on which Her Majesty was not well informed, and generally far better informed than any one else who might happen to be present.

That she loved music it is scarcely necessary for me to say. Almost every school of music appeared to appeal to Queen Victoria. Sometimes she would ask me to sing two or three or more little French songs, one after another. Then she would suggest something by Brahms, or perhaps Grieg, or possibly Handel or Mendelssohn; and often I have concluded with some simple song that I knew she was fond of. Scotch songs, in particular, appealed to her very strongly. She never grew tired, for instance, of "The Bluebells of Scotland", which she generally spoke of as "the Hieland Laddie song". Other Scotch songs of which she was fond were "Annie Laurie" and "Within a Mile of Edinboro' Town". On occasions she would ask me to sing for an hour or more nothing but Mendelssohn. He and Lablache had been her music masters in the early years of her married life, and Prince Albert had always entertained a very high opinion of Mendelssohn in particular. I am inclined to think, though I may of course be mistaken, that my singing of Mendelssohn sometimes recalled to the Queen's memory pleasant recollections of the years that had fled. Number after number of Mendelssohn's oratorios would she listen to with rapt attention, and often when I stopped singing she would remain for some moments in a sort of reverie. Sometimes she failed to remember the words of some song she particularly wished me to sing. On those occasions – rather rare occasions, I am bound to admit – she would herself hum over the air in order to recall the piece to my memory.

Another of Queen Victoria's favourite composers was Gounod. His opera *Faust* was composed only just before the death of Prince Albert, and as, after the Prince Consort's death, she made up her mind never to attend another public performance either at the opera or at a theatre, she did not see it produced. Yet she never wearied of hearing me sing bits out of the opera. Then, when Sir Arthur Sullivan wrote for me his glorious *Golden Legend*, I induced the Queen to listen to certain portions of it that I thought would prove irresistible. In the end she became intensely eager to attend a performance of Sir Arthur Sullivan's masterpiece, and though I did not venture actually to suggest it, I did endeavour indirectly to foster her desire to be present at one performance. Finally the *Golden Legend* was produced at Leeds. For some months after that the Queen did not again broach the subject of attending a public performance. Then one morning to my surprise and great delight, she sent word to me to say that she had definitely decided to witness the performance of the *Golden Legend* just advertised to take place at the Albert Hall. The day arrived, and when I came forward to sing my first solo and saw the Queen occupying the Royal box, attended by several members of the Royal Family, I think I felt more delighted than I have ever felt in my life before.

One of her ladies-in-waiting was the Dowager Lady Erroll, whose sister Mrs Rich was an intimate friend of mine in Malta. These sisters were the nieces of the Duchess of Inverness, to whom this title had been given after the death of her husband the Duke of Sussex, and the Queen, on being told of our intimate acquaintance, had invited Mrs Rich to be present. Her Majesty had also heard from Mrs Rich that I was a Roman Catholic, and with that tact and thoughtfulness which, as I very soon came to discover, was, in the Queen, ever present, Her Majesty selected a most beautiful pearl cross and necklace, which were sent to me the next day with the following letter from Sir Thomas Biddulph, by the Queen's command:

Windsor Castle,
July 8, 1874.

Sir T.M. Biddulph presents his compliments to Madame Albani. He is desired by the Queen to ask her to accept the accompanying necklace and cross as a souvenir of her visit to Windsor last week.

This cross I have worn almost without intermission ever since.

Amongst other presents from Queen Victoria were two portraits of herself; one was the first one taken when she came to the throne, the other taken at the time of her jubilee. She also gave me a small portrait in a silver and enamel case, saying at the time, "I hear that you always carry my photograph with you in your travels. This one will be a more convenient one". I need hardly say that this one has been with me ever since.

Emma Lajeunesse, Madame Albani,
Forty Years of Song.

♛ ♛ ♛

The Marquis of Lorne and the Royal Canadian Academy

Lorne wanted both a grander academy of meritorious painters, sculptors, and architects than the parochial Ontario Society of Artists and a Royal Society for writers and intellectuals. His predecessor, Lord Dufferin, had patronised the Ontario Society of Artists and even joined the professionals in their club rooms on sketching evenings. L.R. O'Brien, the society's vice-president, requested continuing viceregal patronage when calling on the new governor in February 1879. Lorne, in accepting, proposed the establishment of a Royal Canadian Academy of Arts similar to England's august academy, and mentioned this pet scheme again when opening the annual Art Association of Montreal exhibition. At a second meeting with O'Brien he proposed that the Canadian Academy should institute a National Gallery which would be initiated by diploma-paintings; the Academy would also hold annual exhibitions alternately in Ottawa, Halifax, Saint John, Montreal and Toronto, and would establish art schools for the advancement of painting and the improvement of design.

The new academy was born in a "marvellous amount of bitterness and bad language; half the artists are ready just now to choke the other half with their paint brushes". Suave, diplomatic O'Brien calmed ruffled tempers and was named the society's first president as his reward. Fourteen of the Ontario Society of Artists and four Montrealers were the charter members. The next year, by Queen Victoria's command, "Royal" was prefixed officially to "Canadian Academy of Arts".

The first exhibition was held in Ottawa just thirteen months after Lorne's original proposal. A crush of six hundred guests at the opening included cabinet ministers, senators, members of Parliament, and leading citizens. A military band in the corridors added a touch of pomp. The academicians themselves were overlooked completely, but were probably an unobtrusive group since a decade later some reporter described them as a "scrubby" lot except for debonair Dickson Patterson, the Academy Beau Brummel. There was a confusion of 594 paintings and sketches chosen by a Committee of Academicians. Lorne, paying more than lip service to his new toy, purchased for Queen Victoria paintings by Homer Watson, A. Godson, John A. Fraser, and Lucius O'Brien, as president, received the special honour of a sale of three works to the Queen. Not only was this a gesture to his position in the organisation, but it repaid him for his diplomatic manoeuvring during the organisation of the Academy.

J. Russell Harper, Painting in Canada – A History.

♛ ♛ ♛

[Homer] Watson's studio was from the first in Doon, [Ontario] and there he made his permanent home. Other early paintings done there were based on his American tour, but some were frankly and unashamedly wildly romantic, even to picturesque mills, rushing streams and menacing cliffs replete with Victorian sentiment. His elaborate *The Pioneer Mill* was bought during the first Royal Canadian Academy *Avernissage* by the Marquis of Lorne for the Windsor Castle collection, and Queen Victoria was so pleased that she ordered further canvases.

J. Russell Harper, Painting in Canada – A History.

♛ ♛ ♛

When the Prime Minister of Canada, Sir John Thompson, died at Windsor Castle in December 1894, Queen Victoria herself placed a personal tribute on his coffin as it lay in state at the castle. Senator Sanford suggested to Toronto artist F. M. Bell–Smith that he do a painting to commemorate the Queen's gracious act. The Queen agreed and Bell–Smith was granted a private sitting.

Friday [5 July 1895] came and 3 o'clock found me with everything arranged, and waiting in the White drawing room of Windsor Castle. . .

In about a quarter of an hour the door was thrown open and the . . . 'usher' or 'page' announced 'the Queen'. As he did so I heard the sound of a voice speaking in so high a key that I thought, 'Who can presume to talk so loud just outside the private rooms of the Queen?' Then came the thought, 'it must surely be the Queen herself!' and so it proved. From where I stood in the centre of the spacious drawing-room, I could see to the end or turn of a passage, and in a moment or two there appeared a group. A little old lady, very short, and very stout with one hand resting lightly on the arm of a tall erect Indian attendant, and using with the other a black walking stick with richly carved gold handle was advancing with a quick short step which was so brisk as to suggest the idea that the stick and attendants' arm were not very necessary. At her side walked the Princess Louise, while a lady-in-waiting and another attendant followed. As the Queen entered I bowed very low and slowly, and I distinctly recall the impression that the Queen was so very short that I could not bow low enough, for the lower my head got the lower the Queen seemed to be, till at last I felt in imminent danger of toppling over and falling ignominiously at her feet. I quickly recovered myself, however, and slowly resumed my full six feet of stature. The Queen bowed as she entered and said in a voice that will always remain in my memory, 'I am sorry to have kept you waiting!'

As soon as she was seated the Queen turned to me and said, 'Now, you will place me in just the position you desire', which I proceeded to do, not I fear without some feeling of nervousness. I then took my place at my easel – standing, of course, for I knew well that no one ever sits in the presence of the Queen unless told by her to do so. But with that quick perception and thoughtful consideration for which she was so remarkable, she saw that the point of view would not be good, and addressing her daughter she bade her hand me a chair. I have spoken of that voice. It was a voice to be remembered whenever heard – strong, clear as a bell – of extraordinary musical quality, and without the slightest trace of tremor or the hoarseness of age. All of which was wonderful when it is remembered that she was then turned 76. I have said she was short, but I was not prepared to find her less than 5 feet in height. She was immensely stout, of unwieldy proportions and yet in spite of this she had a carriage – a dignity of manner, a poise of the head, and general grace of mien that marked her Queen and Empress. Her hair was silver white with just a suspicion of a golden shade which suggested that it might have been originally red in tone. Her complexion was fresh though not florid, her lips well coloured, and very few wrinkles. Her eyes a light blue with very light eye lashes. When she spoke or smiled the heavily marked jowl which is so noticeable on all her photographs and which gives such a heavy and wholly unfavourable and unnatural expression to her face, seems to quite disappear and the mouth takes a really beautiful form. I regretted at the time that the occasion for the picture I was to paint prevented me from using this quite natural and pleasing feature in any other than a very sober not to say sad expression.

I have had many sitters in my time – Parisian models, and personages of greater or less distinction, some of whom sat like graven images, but not one that I could remember retained the pose allotted better than did the Queen of Great Britain and Ireland and Empress of all the Indies.

Not the least embarrassing circumstance of this sitting which lasted for an hour or more, was the fact that HRH The Princess Louise – herself an artist and sculptor of some distinction stood at my side, and not only watched every touch of my brush with the keenest interest, but volunteered many remarks, criticisms, and advice, and once, taking the brush from my hand, illustrated her words with a firm well directed touch.

The conversation mostly conducted in German, related chiefly to the doings of some of the royal great grandchildren in whom the Queen seemed to take the liveliest interest.

"At last the Queen remarked, 'Ich bin sehr schlavrig' and the sitting was brought to a close.

Before leaving Her Majesty saw the sketch, which she approved, and was particular to ask me if I had seen all that was needed and mentioned several matters to be sure that nothing had been omitted.

F.M. Bell-Smith, How I Painted Queen Victoria.

♛ ♛ ♛

Now Know Ye that by and with the advice of Our Privy Council for Canada, We, by these Presents, do institute, erect, constitute and create a society of honour to be known by and have for ever hereafter the name, style and designation of the "Order of Canada".

Letters Patent from Queen Elizabeth II,
Canada Gazette, 1 July 1967.

13

OH, LISTEN DEAR—
THEY'RE PLAYING
OUR TUNE
Vicky

HAPPY AND GLORIOUS

"God Save The Queen" is the Royal Anthem of Canada and the National Anthem of the United Kingdom, which makes no distinction between a royal and a national anthem. Because of the latter, its use is sometimes criticised in Canada as being too "British". In fact the anthem, in its principal verses, makes no reference to any nation or state, British or otherwise.

What is "God Save The Queen?" It is essentially a prayer and it is about a personal relationship between the singer; God, to whom it is sung; and the Queen, for whom it is sung. Because of this it is able to transcend national boundaries and it is so well liked translations have been used as royal anthems in Germany, Liechtenstein and Norway for their monarchies. While it is not absolutely certain it is very likely also that the anthem is French not English in origin. The words to an anthem for Louis XIV exist, and they scan precisely the same way as "God Save The Queen". The music, by Lully, has been lost but as this anthem predates the earliest known English rendition, "God Save The Queen" is probably an English adaptation of the original French, composed in honour of the king who first made a Canada a royal province.

For all these reasons Canadians can claim as much right to the anthem as any other people, and throughout their history have done just that.

On a visit to Detroit, the first Lieutenant-governor of Upper Canada camped near the site of modern-day London, Ontario.

The party, on the 25th February, started out from Detroit on their return to Niagara by pretty much the same route as they had travelled when going to the west. On the 28th they stopped at an old Mississagua hut, on the south side of the Thames, when, as Major Littlehales relates, "After taking some refreshment of salt pork and venison, they, as usual, sang 'God Save the King', and went to rest".

D.B. Read, The Life And Times of Gen. John Graves Simcoe.

A French Canadian perspective

The members of the Quebec bar of forty-five years ago were as close as brothers. The dinner that they ate together on the last day of each term of the court of king's bench added much to preserving a spirit of perfect harmony. Nothing could be livelier that these dinners *en famille*, as we used to call them, which were also attended by the sheriff and the clerks of the court...

By dessert a veritable running fire of wit, comic songs, and high spirits marked the proceedings. The dinner always lasted well into the night, and it was when we had reached the highest pitch of hilarity that [Judge Joseph-Rémy] Vallière [de Saint-Réal] used to sing the familiar ditty, "Londrès qu'on m'a tant vantée", in order to bait Fletcher. It was usually our English-Canadian friends who egged Vallière on, having a good enough sense of humour to be tickled by this facetious song. I never knew anyone more prejudiced against French Canadians than Fletcher, although I should add that he disliked everything that wasn't English to the core.

Mr Fletcher was a London attorney-at-law who had come to practice in Quebec and died a judge. He was certainly a man of the most distinguished talents and vast erudition, but, *Bon Dieu*! what a disagreeable voice he had when pleading! It would have grated on someone tone deaf. Imagine with what sort of music he regaled us when he took it into his head to sing!

Fletcher was stung almost to fury when Vallière sang the aforementioned satiric verses. His large, protruding eyes threatened to burst out of their sockets, and he revenged himself, or so he believed, by intoning "God Save the King". Lully would never have recognised his composition, and Louis XIV would have fled the room. The lyrics were written in the king's honour and sung by the pupils of Saint-Cyr when he visited the convent with Madame de Maintenon.

The lyrics, which the English translated practically word for word, were written by Madame Brinon. Here they are:

Grande Dieu! Sauvez le Roy, (*bis*)
Vengez le Roy!
Que toujours glorieux,
Louis victorieux,
Voye ses ennemis
Toujours soumis!
Grand Dieu! Sauvez le Roy!
Grand Dieu! Vengez le Roy!
Sauvez le Roy!

The learned Fletcher probably had no idea of the origin of the national anthem, which the English had the good taste to adopt and the French the bad taste not to appreciate. Had he realised that England owed this fine song to a Frenchman and that it had been composed for a French monarch, he would have sung "Rule Britannia" at the risk of forcing even the most tin-eared individuals to leave the room.

Man of Sentiment, The Memoirs of Philippe-Joseph Aubert de Gaspé 1786-1871.

♛ ♛ ♛

Even the Rebels of 1837 sang their grievances to the tune of 'God Save the Queen'.

Lord! o'er our own Loved Land
Spread Thy protecting Hand!
Help 'ere we fall!
Free us from monarchy –
Free us from hierarchy.
Sabres for Squire-archy –
Lord free us all!

♛ ♛ ♛

During the 1860 tour by the Prince of Wales [Edward VII], there were many local adaptations of the Royal Anthem for the occasion.

Hail! Prince of Brunswick's line,
New Brunswick shall be thine:
Firm has she been
Still loyal, true, and brave,
Here England's flag shall wave,
And Britons pray to save
A nation's heir.

Two indigenous verses appeared in two cities welcoming the Prince of Wales in 1860. In Halifax he was greeted with

Welcome! our Royal Guest:
Welcome! from every breast,
From every tongue;
From hearts both warm and true,
Hearts that beat high for you,
Loudly our welcome due
To thee be sung!

Prince of a lofty line,
The virtues all be thine,
Which grace our Queen!
To her we pay through thee,
Love, faith, and loyalty -
Homage which fits the free;
God save the Queen!

And in Toronto with

Victoria's heir we meet,
With loyal welcome greet,
To love our Queen.
Trained by her Royal care,
May he her virtues share,
And with us long join in prayer -
God save the Queen.

Robert Cellem, Visit of His Royal Highness The Prince of Wales To The British North American Provinces And United States In The Year 1860.

♛ ♛ ♛

Even in Goldwin Smith's day the diversity of Canadian life offered a welcome contrast to other areas of the continent, as he would have discovered soon enough had he ever ventured from his Toronto retreat to explore his chosen land whose prospects he so perversely underrated. We are told how in 1879 the city of Quebec, preparing for the official reception of a new Governor General, commissioned a composer to write a cantata of welcome:

He was told to spare neither means nor effort for this grand occasion. Full of enthusiasm he set about writing the music and assembled nearly 300 musicians ... The climax of the cantata, to words by the poet Napoléon Legendre, was a simultaneous rendition of 'God Save the Queen', 'Vive la Canadienne' and 'Comin' Thro' the Rye' – a feat of contrapuntal composition which created a sensation.

Vincent Massey, Confederation on the March.

♛ ♛ ♛

Some of us went into the gallery [of the House of Commons] at 5 a.m. after a dance, to see the end of a long and stormy sitting. The House was very uproarious. Some members had brought in a cricket-ball, and they were throwing each other catches across the House. To the credit of Canadian M.P.s, I must say that we never saw a single catch missed. When Sir John rose to close the debate, there were loud cries of, "You have talked enough, John A. Give us a song instead". "All right", cried Sir John, "I will give you 'God save the Queen'". And he forthwith started it in a lusty voice, all the members joining in.

Lord Frederic Hamilton, The Days Before Yesterday.

♛ ♛ ♛

The first time I went to South Africa for a concert tour was during the reign of the Boers. At Johannesburg I was told that "God Save the Queen" had been prohibited by Kruger. My first concert was a great success, so at the end I started the tabooed hymn, which was taken up by the audience amidst wild enthusiasm. The police did not interfere, but I think that, if they had, the Boer War would have begun prematurely!

Emma Lajeunesse, Madame Albani,
Forty Years of Song.

♛ ♛ ♛

Sir William Van Horne, builder of the Canadian Pacific Railway is mistaken for King Edward VII.

At this period of his life Van Horne bore some slight resemblance to the late King Edward [VII] – sufficient to cause an occasional mistake. One evening in Paris he took his son and Lord Elphinstone to dinner at Henri's, where, with Lord Elphinstone in attendance, His Majesty frequently dined, incognito. On the arrival of the party, the head waiter came forward with much *empressement* to receive them, and the orchestra, to Van Horne's great embarrassment, played "God Save the King".

Walter Vaughan, Sir William Van Horne.

♛ ♛ ♛

It is stated that a man named Creighton murdered his wife at Owen Sound, Ontario, because she refused to sing [God Save the King] on Empire Day.

Percy A. Scholes, God Save the Queen! quoting from
Musical News, 13 June 1908.

♛ ♛ ♛

At Ottawa the school-children, who had assembled to the number of 1,500, hit upon an ingenious plan to gratify their ambition and have a good long stare at Prince Arthur. As the royal party approached they struck up the National Anthem, and they sang it through from beginning to end. The Prince naturally stood uncovered until the end of the last line, when the youngsters cheered with delight and the Prince, much amused, went smiling on his way.'

Major-General Sir George Aston, His Royal Highness The Duke of Connaught and Strathearn, A Life and Intimate Study.

♛ ♛ ♛

On the 1927 royal tour, the Prince of Wales' Assistant Private Secretary was struck by the way in which Canadians sang the Royal Anthem.

The "impressive loyalty" of Canada *is* most impressive, and moves me very much. They sing 'God Save the King' as if it really was a prayer, and with their whole hearts in it. Their devotion to the British throne is entirely genuine, and almost an article of faith. It makes one feel – particularly when at some western station you see a crowd of people who've ridden in forty or fifty miles just to get a glimpse of the two brothers [the Prince of Wales and Prince George later Duke of Kent] – that there must be something worth working for in an institution which stirs a fine people so deeply. For they *are* a very fine people, underneath the crudity and lack of culture which is natural to any young nation that has been too busy wrestling with the forces of nature to think of polishing itself.

In Royal Service: The Letters and Journals of Sir Alan Lascelles 1920–1936.

♛ ♛ ♛

Accounts differ but when William Butler Yeats (1865-1939) gave a poetry recital in Massey Hall in 1932, he outraged the audience by walking out during the ceremonial playing of "God Save the King". Questioned about his action, the tone-deaf Irish nationalist is said to have replied: "Is *that* what they were playing?"

John Robert Columbo, Canadian Literary Landmarks.

♛ ♛ ♛

Perhaps best known of the additional Canadian verses to God Save the Queen is

Our loved Dominion bless
With peace and happiness
From shore to shore;
And let our country* be
Loyal, united, free,

True to herself and thee
For evermore

♛ ♛ ♛

The Princess [Royal] has also worked hard for the Olympic movement, attending meetings of the IOC all over the world. Despite her international commitments she has exhibited her own patriotism, remarking that English sportsmen would benefit from a national song to inspire them in a way the National Anthem cannot. "God save the Queen" is an anthem that does not belong to England alone, so why should it be played to represent that country's teams when they are competing against other countries of the U.K. or the Commonwealth ?

Berkswell's Royal Year, vol. 17, 1990.

EPILOGUE

The Prince of Wales (Prince Charles) received an honorary doctorate from Queen's University, Kingston, Ontario on 28 October 1991. Afterwards HRH addressed Convocation but his speech was directed to all the people of Canada, who were facing the possible breakup, as a result of domestic squabbles, of the Canadian federation that the Royal Family had been a force in bringing about. As Heir to the Canadian Throne the Prince looked back in history and forward to the future.

Within the Canadian federal home there are many rooms, each with its own particular memories. That home has housed the native aboriginal peoples, the two founding immigrant European communities, each with its language and culture, and generations of other immigrants which Canada has never ceased to welcome from all the corners of the world.

All have survived under one roof, thanks to a steadfast commitment to peace, the rule of law and good government; to the traditions of parliamentary democracy and a constitutional monarchy all of which, I believe, have served the country well...

Other countries ... look at the Canadian example with envy and admiration. There is a certain genius in the Canadian political culture which helps to explain the extraordinary resilience it has shown in dealing so constructively and for so long with the stress and strains of cultural and regional pluralism...

Other strengths, too, are associated with Canada's political culture: practicality, common sense, realism, tolerance, and a concern always to try to move forward by consensus...

The world, in brief, needs Canada...a federation which remains the envy of much of the world and holds out the prospect...of a great future built upon a most distinguished past.

ACKNOWLEDGEMENTS

The editors and publisher gratefully acknowledge permission to include copyright material in this volume as follows (unless otherwise indicated, permission to reprint is given by the publisher). Care has been taken to trace the ownership of copyright material used in the text. The editors and publisher welcome any information enabling them to rectify any reference or credit in subsequent editions.

Achard, Eugène, *Georges VI, Roi Du Canada*. Montréal: Libraire Générale Canadienne, 1942.

Affectionately Yours: The Letters of Sir John A. Macdonald and His Family. Toronto: Macmillan, 1969.

Aird, John Black. *Loyalty in a Changing World*. Toronto: Office of the Premier, 1985.

Armstrong, G. H. *The Origin And Meaning of Place Names In Canada*. Toronto: Macmillan, 1972.

Badges Of The Canadian Forces / Insignes Des Forces Canadiennes. Ottawa: Supply and Services Canada, 1977.

Beer, Donald R., "Sir Allan Napier MacNab", *Dictionary of Hamilton Biography*. 1984.

Bell Smith, F. M. *How I painted Queen Victoria*. Edited by Roger Boulet. Victoria, B.C.: Art Gallery of Greater Victoria, 1977.

Bird, Florence. *Anne Francis: An Autobiography.* Toronto: Clarke, Irwin, 1974.

Bond, Richmond P. *Queen Anne's American Kings*. Oxford: Clarendon, 1952.

Butler, Peter. *More Wit of Prince Philip*. London: Leslie Frewin, 1973.

Butler, Peter. *The Wit of Prince Philip*. London: Leslie Frewin, 1965.

Byng of Vimy, (Evelyn) Viscountess. *Up The Stream Of Time*. Toronto: Macmillan, 1945.

Carey, M.C. and Dorothy Margaret Stuart. *The King's Service*. London: Harrap , 1935.

Carney, Pat. *Tiara and Atigi: Northwest Territories 1970 Centennial - The Royal Tour*. Government of the Northwest Territories, 1971.

Columbo, John Robert. *Canadian Literary Landmarks.* Toronto: Hounslow Press, 1984.

Cowan, John. *Canada's Governors General: Lord Monck To General Vanier*. Toronto: York Publishing Company, 1965.

Cuthbertson, Brian C. *The Loyalist Governor: Biography of Sir John Westworth.* Halifax: Nimbus, 1983.

Dempsey, Lotta. *No Life for a Lady*. Toronto: Musson, 1976.

Diefenbaker, John G. *One Canada.* Vol. One. Toronto: Macmillan of Canada, 1975.

Eccles, W. J. *Canada Under Louis XIV 1663-1701*. Toronto: McClelland and Stewart, 1964.

Edward, Anne. *Matriarch: Queen Mary and the House of Windsor.* New York: William Morrow, 1984.

English, L.E.F. *Historic Newfoundland And Labrador*. St John's: Department of Development and Tourism, Province of Newfoundland and Labrador, 19th Edition, 1988.

Farthing, John. *Freedom Wears A Crown*. [n.p.]: Kingswood House, 1957.

Fleming, Donald M. *So Very Near: The Political Memoirs Of The Honourable Donald M. Fleming*. Toronto: McClelland and Stewart, 1985.

Fowke, Edith and Alan Mills. *Canada's Story In Song*. Toronto: Gage 1964.

Gillen, Mollie. *The Masseys: Founding Family.* Toronto: Ryerson, 1965

Hall, Trevor. *Royal Canada.* [n.p.]: B. Mitchell, 1989.

Hamilton, Lord Frederic. *The Days Before Yesterday*. London: Hodder and Stoughton, 1972.

Harewood, 7th Earl of. *The Tongs And The Bones: The Memoirs of Lord Harewood*. London: Weidenfeld and Nicolson, 1981.

Harper, J. Russell. *Painting in Canada - A History*. Toronto: University of Toronto

Press, 1966.
Hibbert, Christopher. *Edward VII.* London: Allen Lane, 1976. Reprinted by permission of David Higham Associates.
Hitsman, J. Mackay. *The Incredible War of 1812.* Toronto: University of Toronto Press, 1965.
Jeffreys, C. W. and A.J. Casson. *The Visits Of Royalty To Canada.* Toronto: North American Life Assurance Company, 1939
Jones, Elizabeth. *Gentlemen and Jesuits: Quests For Glory And Adventure In The Early Days Of New France.* Toronto: University of Toronto Press, 1986.
Judd, Dennis. *Prince Philip.* London: Michael Joseph, 1980. Reprinted by permission of David Higham Associates.
Kerr, Mark. *Prince Louis of Battenberg, Admiral of The Fleet.* London: Longmans, Green, 1934.
Kos-Rabcewicz-Zubkowski, Ludwik and William Edward Greening. *Sir Casimir Stanislaus Gzowski: a biography.* Toronto: Burns and MacEachern, 1959.
Krotz, Larry, *Royal Visits, a Manitoba album / Visites Royales, un album-souvenir du Manitoba.* Winnipeg: Turnstone Press and Province of Manitoba, 1984.
Lanctôt, Gustave. *The Royal Tour of King George VI and Queen Elizabeth in Canada and the United States of America, 1939.* Toronto: E.P. Taylor Foundation, 1964.
Leacock, Stephen. *Leacock's Montreal* edited by John Culliton. Toronto: McClelland and Stewart, 1963.
Leacock, Stephen. *Canada: The Foundations of its Future.* [n. p.]: House of Seagram, 1946.
Longford, Lady. *The Oxford Book of Royal Anecdotes.* Oxford: Oxford University Press, 1989.
Macdonald, R. H. *Grant MacEwan: No Ordinary Man.* Saskatoon: Western Producer Prairie Books, 1979. Reprinted by permission of the author.
Massey, Vincent. *What's Past Is Prologue.* Toronto: Macmillan, 1963.
Massey. Vincent *Confederation on the March: Views On Major Canadian Issues During The Sixties.* Toronto: Macmillan, 1965.
McLaughlin, Florence. *First Lady of Upper Canada.* Burns and MacEachren, 1968.
MCreath, Peter L. and John G. Leefe. *A History of Early Nova Scotia.* Tantallon, Nova Scotia: Four East Publications, 1982.
Mitchell, Major G.D. *Right Of The Line: An Anecdotal History of the Royal Canadian Horse Artillery From 1871.* Ottawa: [n.p.], 1986.
Monck, Frances Elizabeth Owen. *My Canadian Leaves.* Toronto: University of Toronto Press, 1963.
Morison, Samuel Eliot. *The European Discovery of America - The Northern Voyages A.D. 500-1600.* Oxford: Oxford University Press, 1971.
O'Neill, Paul. *A Seaport Legacy - The Story of St John's, Newfoundland.* Erin, Ontario: Press Porcépic, 1976.
Pacey, Elizabeth. *Historic Halifax.* Toronto: Hounslow Press, 1988.
Pearson, Lester B. *Words & Occasions.* Toronto: University of Toronto Press, 1970.
Pearson, Lester. *Mike:* Vol 1. Toronto: University of Toronto Press, 1972.
Reaney, James. *Poems.* Toronto: New Press, 1972.
Regina *Leader Post.*
Rowland, Barry D. *The Padre.* Scarborough: Amethyst, 1982.
Russell, E. C. *Customs and Traditions of the Canadian Armed Forces.* Toronto: Deneau, 1980.
Scott, Duncan Campbell "Farewell To Their Majesties", a poem broadcast by the C.B.C. on the occassion of the departure of King George VI and Queen Elizabeth from Canada, 15 June 1939, and quoted from *The circle of affection, and other pieces in prose and verse.* Toronto: McClelland and Stewart, 1947.
Senior, Elinor, "Robert Bouchette ardent Patriote et fervent Royaliste", edited from the Mémoires of Robert Shore Milnes Bouchette. *Monarchy Canada.* August, 1980.

Smith, Donald B. *Sacred Feathers.* Toronto: University of Toronto Press, 1987.
Smith, Mary Larratt. *Young Mr Smith in Upper Canada.* Toronto: University of Toronto Press, 1980.
Speaight, Robert. *Vanier: Soldier, Diplomat and Governor General.* Toronto: Collins, 1970
St Aubyn, Giles. *William of Gloucester: Pioneer Prince.* London: Frederick Muller, 1977.
Stacey, C.P. "Mackenzie King and The Monarchy" in *Monarchy Canada*, May 1978.
Stamp, Robert. *Royal Rebels: Princess Louise & the Marquis of Lorne.* Toronto: Dundurn Press, 1988.
The Arms, Flags and Emblems of Canada. Ottawa: Deneau and Greenberg in co-operation with the Secretary of State, 1978.
Thomson, Dale C. *Louis St Laurent: Canadian.* Toronto: Macmillan, 1967.
Upton, L.F.S. *The Loyal Whig: William Smith of New York & Quebec.* Toronto: University of Toronto Press, 1969.
Vorres, Ian. *The Last Grand Duchess: Her Imperial Highness Grand Duchess Olga Alexandrovna 1 June 1882 - 24 November 1960.* London: Hutchinson, 1964. Printed by permission of the author.
Wake, Jehanne. *Princess Louise: Queen Victoria's Unconventional Daughter.* Toronto: Collins, 1988.
Wheeler-Bennett, John W. *King George VI.* London: Macmillan, 1958.
Willis-O'Connnor, H. and Madge Macbeth. *Inside Government House.* Toronto: Ryerson, 1954.
Windsor, H.R.H. The Duke of. *A King's Story.* New York: G.P. Putnam's Sons, 1947-1951.
Ziegler, Philip. *King Edward VIII: The Official Biography.* London: Collins, 1990.

The authors would like to thank the many people from across the country who provided stories for this book, and especially Vicky Gabereau (on whose stimulating CBC radio show the idea for this book was born), Patricia Smith and Tom Suddon who directed us to several others. They would also like to thank Claudia Willetts, who prepared the index, helped prepare the manuscript and assisted in many other ways, and Richard Fiennes-Clinton who assisted with typing and proofreading the genealogical chart.

INDEX

Page references in italics refer to personal sources of anecdotes

CANADA'S KINGS AND QUEENS

Royal Line Since Confederation

Albert, Prince Consort. Prevented war with U.S. over Trent affair 1861. His Great Exhibition of 1851 inspired Crystal Palaces in major Canadian cities. Prince Albert, Saskatchewan named for him

EDWARD VII 'The Peacemaker' (1901-1910) His 1860 tour as Prince of Wales helped prepare ground for Confederation. Bestowed 'Royal' on RCMP 1904. Gave Manitoba, PEI, BC, Saskatchewan and Alberta coats of arms

Arthur, Duke of Connaught. Governor-General of Canada 1911-1916

Louise. Alberta named for her (from her middle name). Lived in Canada 1878-9, 1880, 1882, 1883. Patron of Canadian arts. m. John Campbell, Marquis of Lorne, Governor General of Canada 1878-83, founder of Royal Canadian Academy, National Gallery and Royal Society of Canada

Alice. m. Ludwig IV, Grand Duke of Hesse and by Rhine

Leopold, Duke of Alban Sought to become Gover General of Canada 188

Alice. m. Alexander, Earl of Athlone (brother c Queen Mary and great grandson of George III), Governor General of Canada 1940-46

GEORGE V (1910-1936) Presided at Quebec Tercentenary 1908. Appointed Canada's first foreign representatives 1920, 1926. Assumed separate Royal Arms for Canada 1921

Arthur. Made Canadian tours in 1906 and 1918

Patricia. Col-in-Chief, Princess Patricia's Canadian Light Infantry. Made Ric-A-Dam-Doo for PPCLI 1914

Victoria. m. Prince Louis of Battenberg, Marquess of Milford Haven. He opened the CNE 1905

EDWARD VIII (1936) Unveiled Vimy Memorial in France to Canadian War dead 1936. Bought EP Ranch at High River, Alberta 1919. As Prince of Wales was made Canadian Privy Councillor 1927. Abdicated 1936. d. 1972

GEORGE VI 'The Good' (1936-1952) First Monarch to meet his Canadian Parliament in Person and give Royal Assent and to tour Canada as King 1939

m.

Elizabeth. Patron of VON. Patron of Ontario Jockey Club

Alice. m. Prince Andrew of Greece

Louis, Earl Mountbatten Burma. Planned Diepp Raid led by Canadians 1942 and commandec Canadians in SEAC 1943-46. Opened CNE 1948, 1959

ELIZABETH II (1952-) Adopted separate title 'Queen of Canada' by Act of her Canadian Parliament 1953. Proclaimed National Flag 1965 and revised Constitution 1982

m.

Philip, Duke of Edinburgh. Canadian Privy Councillor 1957. Founded Duke of Edinburgh's Award in Canada 1963. Noted conservationist, credited with saving wood bison from extinction in Canada